Bernard Wills

Whose Beliefs Count?

MINKOWSKI
Institute Press

Bernard Wills
Humanities Program
Grenfell Campus
Memorial University of Newfoundland
Corner Brook, NL Canada A2H 6P9

Cover: Praying Hands by Albrecht Dürer.
Image taken from `https://commons.wikimedia.org/wiki/File:`
`Albrecht_D\unhbox\voidb@x\bgroup\let\unhbox\voidb@x\`
`setbox\@tempboxa\hbox{u\global\mathchardef\accent@`
`spacefactor\spacefactor}\accent4u\egroup\spacefactor\`
`accent@spacefactorrer_-_Praying_Hands,_1508_-_Google_`
`Art_Project.jpg`

ISBN: 978-1-927763-78-0 (softcover)
ISBN: 978-1-927763-79-7 (ebook)

Minkowski Institute Press
Montreal, Quebec, Canada
http://minkowskiinstitute.org/mip/

For information on all Minkowski Institute Press publications visit our
website at http://minkowskiinstitute.org/mip/books/

CONTENTS

4

PART 1

1 INTRODUCTION

800 years ago this question had a clear answer. On all matters of ultimate concern theologians spoke. Perhaps though I should say 'the theological tradition' spoke. Not of course that modes of dissent were absent in the high middle ages or that all questions were settled. What I mean is that there was a tradition of default answers. Basic issues in ontology, metaphysics, science, ethics and theology were addressed by a tradition of discourse going back to Aristotle. In the so called 'Gothic' period this tradition had reached a kind of maturity with elaborate systemizations in the work of Aquinas, Bonaventure and others. How this hegemony broke up is a long story we need not tell here. Let us flash forward to perhaps 100 years ago. In the early part of the last century the scientific revolution had reached a maturity comparable to that achieved by the theological tradition in medieval Europe. Its three great theoretical constructs, evolutionary biology, relativistic physics and quantum mechanics were rounding into form. A tradition of default answers now existed on fundamental questions of the universe and our place in it and these were those of the modern sciences. There are still people in the Catholic church and elsewhere who accept broad elements of the medieval synthesis. Many people vehemently assert the permanent validity of the scientific revolution which they defend using a philosophical theory we might call 'naturalism'. The latter however (just like the former did in the past) now do so defensively. There is a subtle point in the history of the mind where a default position suddenly becomes a contested position and those with epistemic privilege are suddenly put on the defensive. They are put in the awkward position of having to justify a privilege which was once simply assumed. They now have to put out fires. This happened to the scholastic synthesis in the period up to and including the protestant reformation. This happened to the reformation itself in the 19th Century with the rise of Darwinian biology and modern Geology. Now the scientific revolution itself has to put out fires. In America a revanchist 'National Protestantism' (Evangelical Protestantism leavened with Gnostic elements) rejects Darwin though it loves most other expressions of technocracy. Neo-Marxists and other progressives question the way science can be used as an ideological tool to support Capitalism and various strains of post-modernism question its (and every other) claim to universal a-historical validity. We exist in the

kind of ferment that existed in the Victorian period and earlier in the early modern period. Suddenly epistemic privilege is contested and there is no default answer as to who should be granted it.

The essays contained in the book reflect this ferment though the author is not so ambitious as to think he has resolved it. Let me be clear on a few matters however. When hegemonies are reduced to options (that must compete with other options) the beneficiaries of those hegemonies do not react kindly. They develop counter discourses which are often polemical and shrill especially if the 'challenges' take on extreme and potentially dangerous forms such as Anabaptists, Social Darwinists or anti-vaxxers. This can be seen with respect to one ailing hegemony, that of white Anglo-Saxon Protestants. This has taken two prominent forms one religious, one secular. National Protestantism in the United States and to a somewhat lesser extent in Canada is one such reaction. It is a gnostic/apocalyptic form of spirituality that has aligned itself with 'white identity' and seeks an eschatological conflict with 'progressives' and Islam (absurdly, it draws no apparent distinction between the two). Almost all conservative Christianity in North America is to some degree implicated in this cult including most evangelical protestants. Conversely, naturalism (still the default philosophy of all kinds of ordinary, honest people) has also taken on a cult like identity through the rise of 'new atheism' and its epigones. This is a secularized version of National Protestantism which worries above all about the contamination of the secular institutions of the west by 'Muslims' and various 'others'. While not initially racialist in tone it is increasingly becoming so with advocates like Sam Harris now taking up *The Bell Curve*.[1] Clearly 'whites' are the bearers of the enlightenment and the defense of its supposed values involves a reflexive opposition to multi-culturalism, immigration and increasingly feminism. I think this move was implicit in the public ideology of 'Anglo-Saxon Atheism' all along as it was from the start a defense of hard core realism in philosophy and when the elite defend 'the facts and just the facts' they do not mean your facts but their facts especially if you are a woman or a person of color or a Muslim. Western notions of objectivity and reason are defended first and foremost as parochial possessions of an identifiable group of people who are under threat from other people, the 'others' such as Muslims and their traitorous fellow travelers the 'regressive leftists' among whom 'cultural Marxists' figure most prominently.[2] Of the latter all I can say is that it is indeed a

---

[1] The logic of this move is laid out by Luke Savage writing in The Jacobin (https://www.jacobinmag.com/2014/12/new-atheism-old-empire/) Savage writes: "Beneath its superficial rationalism, then, the New Atheism amounts to little more than an intellectual defense of empire and a smokescreen for the injustices of global capitalism. It is a parochial universalism whose potency lies in its capacity to appear simultaneously iconoclastic, dissenting, and disinterested, while channeling vulgar prejudices, promoting imperial projects, and dressing up banal truisms as deep insights" .

[2] Neo-conservatism is the actual ideological expression of new atheism (see Flim and Fluss https://jacobinmag.com/2018/10/steven-pinker-enlightenment-now-review). As well as misunderstanding the enlightenment (see Wills "Pinker's Enlightenment" in

remarkable kind of 'rationalism' that attacks the academy itself and insists on a blunt, dogmatic realism in epistemology in despite of so much that philosophers, social scientists and other scholars are currently doing. Culture wars, however, make strange bedfellows.

Stepping back from this however let me make an observation. The best title for a novel I know is J.H. Newman's *Loss and Gain* and it clearly applies here. There is much worthy of attention in the achievements of the medieval world, the reformation and the European enlightenment. To say that none of these any longer constitutes a hegemony is not to dismiss them from consideration or to deny that any of them are voices in the current discussion. Dante, Luther and Darwin are not going anywhere and it would be a profound loss if they did. I however am an optimist to this extent: I do not believe the achievements of these past phases of European civilization rest on the privileges of a class or elite grouping that purportedly represents them whether that is the hierarchy of the Catholic church, The Southern Baptist Convention, or MIT grads. Nor, as I shall explain below, does it preclude 'data' from previously despised sources which may include even the folk conceptions of European descendants themselves. This is a two-fold process in that legitimate challenges to hegemony will initially be mixed up with bizarre and dangerous ones. With Luther will come Munster. With Darwin will come *Mein Kampf.* With the end of Anglo-Saxon Protestant technocracy will come new age books and quack medicines. These excesses will force people to retrench for reasons that are entirely forgivable if ultimately unsustainable.

In my two previous books *Why Believe* and *Believing Weird Things* I examined some of the ways in which things like naturalism and fundamentalism can be constructed to suppress not only religious and cultural minorities but the humanities themselves. A defensive reaction to a supposed rise of irrationality (it may be quite rational to be irrational these days given the world 'reason' has created) insists on 'science' and 'reason' (both profoundly misconstrued) as the only valid mode of discourse and the only hedge against superstition and folly. This, of course, conflicts with the discourse of 'National Protestantism' though on far fewer points than one might casually think. It also conflicts with the many narratives of liberation being told by oppressed peoples in a post-colonial context. This is why 'new atheists' increasingly turn their ire towards 'regressive leftists' as well as fundamentalist protestants. To my mind, it is, alas, impossible to square a triumphalist account of western science and its purported superiority with these emerging narratives. Actual scientists for instance,

---

Why Believe: Essays on Religion Rationality and Belief) Pinker joins people like Harris and Jordan Peterson in constant swipes at the left for not embracing their neo-liberal and increasingly racialist politics. Yet this 'rationalism' is an exercise in profound naiveté. As Flim and Fluss put it "Pinker wants to see the world as it really is, apart from any meta-narratives or grand ideologies. But from the beginning, this is a doomed project. Humans are not optical scanners that passively take in isolated data points; we necessarily narrate our perceptions into some intelligible worldview. So the question is not whether to do metaphysics — to develop some narrative to explain the world — but only whether our metaphysics is any good, and can be sufficiently argued for."

6

who tend to get left out of this conversation, recognize the utility and importance of various forms of local knowledge. Apologists for 'Science' typically, and angrily, do not. I could illustrate this by referring to the work of feminist theorists of knowledge such as Lorraine Code and Helen Longino. I could also appeal to the work of Said and his successors to illustrate the pernicious imperialism embodied in the 'scientific' and 'objective' stance towards the non-western world.

I, however, will use a different example, one closer to my own interests and experience. In the institution in which I teach a significant portion of the students are of indigenous Miq'maw heritage. They are, by and large, NOT interested in hearing that their elders convey a secondary and qualitatively inferior kind of knowledge when compared to western scientists. Now, you could say that this is simple perversity on their part; they should 'man up' and accept the gospel of science! Things are not however so simple. It is idle to claim that the experience of colonial oppression is irrelevant because science is universal, objective and politically neutral. It is idle to claim that the elevation of scientific procedures to qualitative superiority has no social and political ramifications for those whose knowledge forms are thereby granted second class status. This is because the question of scientism is bound up with the question of authority. The fact that indigenous knowledge traditions are grounded in local knowledge, in traditional lore and in story means that on questions of importance to them indigenous peoples cannot speak. It means they have to listen to others who 'know better' because the propositions they utter have the form of science. Thus, whether INTENDED OR NOT the elevation of scientific knowledge to superior status over indigenous knowledge elevates white settlers to authority over indigenous people and justifies the theft of their land and even of their children. Worse, indigenous people can see for themselves (because they are not blind) that this privileging of settler knowledge over their own is NOT benign. It is viciously exploitative and intended to keep indigenous peoples in a place of dependence and inferiority.[3] Thus the facile assumption that 'scientism' is ideologically innocent and 'science' apolitical will not stand even cursory examination.

In this collection I want to explore a bit more deeply questions of speech, representation and alterity that follow on this consideration. These will be explored in the first section of the book. Several of the pieces here are grounded on my own experience teaching in an interdisciplinary humanities program at Grenfell Campus in Corner Brook. They are, if you

---

[3]See D. Simmonds on this point (addressing an anti-indigenous activist notorious in Canada): "My particular interest here is the way in which science has been reified by Widdowson and Howard and used to legitimate state decision-making on behalf of oppressed peoples. Science is counterposed to indigenous traditional knowledge, which by way of a children's parable (The Emperor's New Clothes) is denounced as mere superstition in the service of a corrupt "aboriginal industry." The state is called upon to harness scientific rationalism in the old colonial interest of "civilizing the savages." In the words of Widdowson and Howard, "It is not clear how the remnants of Neolithic culture that are inhibiting this development can be addressed without intensive government planning and intervention" (http://uppingtheanti.org/journal/article/11-residual-stalinism,252).

like, the fruit of my own pedagogical self-reflection. As adverted to above one of the issues facing this institution is the emerging self-consciousness of our many indigenous students and I, along with my colleagues, have been challenged to think about the place of indigeneity in post-secondary education. Once one begins this process a certain gestalt shift happens: questions that once seemed easy and obvious are suddenly troubling. At the same time exciting possibilities emerge for re-envisioning our own settler civilization which, to be blunt, is not sustainable in its current from. Here I need to thank my friend and colleague Dr. Maura Hanrahan. Had she and I not crossed paths in life I would still be in my dogmatic slumbers and unfit even for the limited reflections I have undertaken here. Of more immediate concern, perhaps, to a wider readership outside the university are the issues I address in the more directly political pieces here though they are concerned as well with the problem of mediating between multiple clashing perspectives. Here I must thank the students and ex-students of Grenfell for the issues I discuss here are the issues I discuss with them and I thank both for forcing me to think about these issues *and* for forcing me to think *harder* about them. The fact that so much of the material in this book has originated this (somewhat) *ad hoc* way means that *Whose Beliefs Count* like my previous book *Believing Weird Things* is somewhat eclectic in form and a bit more of a collection than a book. Certainly, I see no necessity for the reader to read it straight through rather than skip to the topics of particular interest to him or her.

The second section will deal broadly with the issue of science as an ideology vs. science as a practice. This is a theme I have touched on in a previously and I want to expand my consideration here. My exploration of the subject will explain why the ideology of 'scientism' is not an adequate account of 'reason' or even of science when considered as a humane practice. I do this because, as I have noted above, the supposed 'neutrality' of science does not secure for it political innocence and 'scientism' is clearly an ideological position not a 'rational' or 'scientific' one. Plus, 'scientism' makes itself look ridiculous when it undertakes the critical task of examining the content and nature of religions and other complex cultural sign systems precisely for its ignorance of the nature of critique and lack of hermeneutic culture. Accordingly, I will examine the limits of scientistic discourse and its relation to the domain of natural theology and other forms of 'weird' discourse. Both sections will, I hope, contribute to a more pluralistic account of public reason adequate to the political crises I touch on in part one.

I realize of course that my attempt to defend a broader hermeneutic account of rationality will seem a mere abstraction to certain of my readers. This is because they do not practice interpretation in the broad sense and think it arbitrary and whimsical if they think of it at all. To this day I have friends who think that literary critics, like modernist painters, are just 'faking it'. I still know people who think historians can 'just say anything' about the past unlike chemists who are bound by the 'facts'. I don't decry people who say openly what others tacitly assume.[4] Not many people believe in 'scientism' as a reflective position but many quietly assume that knowledge claims outside the sciences are not quite legit in the same way as scientific ones. They think this because they have some conception of 'scientific method' as the single legitimate form of pressing a rational claim. Of course, not all claims in science are pressed in the same manner. Nor are all claims pressed in the manner in which scientists press claims. Illustrating this fact is best done by demonstration of course (the validity and necessity of hermeneutic reason is discovered in reading a book of sufficient complexity) but I will at various junctures in this book address issues of interpretation and its application to artefacts such as sacred or poetic texts. As I pointed out in my previous book there is a pernicious politics of reading that underwrites phenomena like fundamentalism and islamophobia and the nature of responsible reading is always a timely question. Pursuing these three lines of inquiry I have no aim but to reproduce in the reader's mind the ferment that is in my own. I neither expect nor desire any 'conversion' as a result. Truth, if you like, is a moving target. Between reader and text (whether that text be Shakespeare or a river's eco-system) moves the interpreter (like Hermes between the living and the dead) and this spirit, we are told by another tradition, blows where it lists.

One last thing: the author would like to thank Dr. Adam Riggio for his comments on my previous work as well as Dr. Jason Holt, Dr. Richard Matthews, Dr. Steven Blackwood and the students of Grenfell Campus especially the excellent Charlotte May Hobden who ably lead our humanities and philosophy society. All of the above, in ways unbeknownst to them, have had a hand in shaping the discussions in this book. Lastly but most importantly I must thank Jean Haliburton Wills and our children for what has been an enriching, quirky adventure together!

---

[4]At the bottom of such worries lies a legitimate concern. History and literary criticism, like philosophy, allow multiple interpretations of the same phenomenon to stand which raises the issue of a fundamental relativism and perspectivalsim. Many scholars in the humanities will be familiar with the experience of reader's reports which flatly contradict each other leaving one to wonder if academic peer review is anything but capricious. Indeed, as any academic article whatsoever fails to do something every article can in principle be rejected though I suppose our journals cannot, like certain poems of Mallarme, just consist of blank pages. The mistake such people make is to think that the sciences do NOT raise these same issues.

2 FREE SPEECH FOR PROTESTANTS: THE MILTONIC EXCEPTION

My title, I confess, is quirky. My subject is whether free speech can exist or whether enabling one form of speech inevitably means suppressing another. Milton, a great defender of free speech, notoriously did not apply it to English Catholics[5]. (1974; 299) In this he expressed the fundamental principle shared by Catholics, Puritans, Anglicans and all others of his time: that free speech meant free speech for an 'in group' and enforced silence for an 'out-group' with each side disagreeing only about who should be in and who should be out. All agreed that, as the Roman theologians used to say, error has no rights. When I was young the 'sophisticated' position on this matter was expressed by people like Alan Borovoy: any and all restrictions on free speech were an invitation to tyranny as, the instant we opened Pandora's box, more and more interests would find more and more reasons to suppress more and more speech. We could not, like Milton did, make exceptions even of the speech of our professed enemies. For this reason, Borovoy and others defended even the rights of neo-Nazis (such as Ernst Zundel) to spread their views.[6] Most of the public, I suspect, still

---

[5]English Catholics were the 'fascists' of their day: i.e. their views represented a fundamental challenge to the established order in politics and religion. As a presumed threat to the very foundations of state and church they could not be granted the same liberties as others: even a man of genius like Alexander Pope could not attend university in England without subscribing to the 39 articles. In other words, they were presumed to be outside the circle of discourse as not recognizing its fundamental rules and conditions. Of course, Catholic emancipation was one of the happy results of the broadening of civil liberties in the 19th Century and as the author is of that confession he can only be grateful. At any rate, English Catholics in the 17th century spoke from a position of assumed error as a creationist today would be speaking from a position of assumed error. It may be the case that ALL societies contain such people and that free speech is a chimerical idea: this remains to be seen.

[6]Mr. Borovoy spelled out his views in When Freedoms Collide: The Case for our Civil Liberties which garnered him a Governor General's award in 1988. For an interesting contrast see Leo Strauss Persecution and the Art of Writing. Strauss tells us that the modern philosophers: "Believed that suppression of free inquiry, and publication of the results of free inquiry, was accidental, an outcome of the faulty construction of the body politic, and that the kingdom of general darkness could be replaced by the republic of universal light" (500). It seems to be his view, rather, that philosophers will always hold things at odds with the society in which they live and will, thus, always be under the requirement of pulling their punches if they want to live and eat.

hold something like this view. Indeed, everybody seems to accept that 'free speech' is a good thing in the abstract even if they have difficulty applying it to any speech but their own. Some academics, on the other hand, seem to have reverted to the early modern position (though few of them want to admit that this is what they have done). I do not say this as a criticism but merely state a fact. There are many good reasons to hold the position of Milton (who was no fool after all) and many good reasons to think Mr. Borovoy was wrong.[7] That said the Miltonic position seems to be gaining ground. It is now more common to hear what a few decades ago would have been unthinkable outside religiously conservative circles: that certain people should not speak because they speak error and error of a sufficiently fundamental kind cannot be tolerated. This is not crazy: it is the position held by most people throughout time. Every society whatsoever tolerates speech about some things and suppresses speech about others: Astrologers in ancient Rome could not speak about the death of the emperor though they could draw personal horoscopes. In 16th Century Spain the nature of free will could be debated by Jesuits and Dominicans but the doctrine of Transubstantiation could not. These societies used the institution of censorship to define what was up for discussion and what was not. Even today phlogiston is not up for discussion in Chemistry departments and intelligent design is not up for discussion in Biology departments. Censorship, whether formal or informal, seems always and everywhere the order of the day. In other words, free speech is for 'protestants' or whatever group stands in the lucky position of being 'protestants'.[8]

---

[7]There is one point I should mention here. Milton's statement that his views by no means apply to 'popery' has the air of a hasty apology, as if he were seized with a sudden anxiety that he had gone too far. Milton was not in fact the sectarian bigot he is sometimes assumed to be, counting a number of Italian cardinals among his friends (19). It is well to remember that Milton was a dissenter among the dissenters (like his successor Blake) and subscribed to no orthodoxy Puritan, Anglican or Catholic. Might Milton have privately, or as Strauss would have it 'esoterically', countenanced a far more radical society which allowed the printing of Catholic, Jewish or even atheistic books on the principle that truth will always win a fair fight? I leave the question to Miltonists. I note though, that after the Restoration Milton himself became an 'exception'.

[8] Ironically it is now historic Protestants who stand increasingly in the position of being 'Catholics'. Conservative evangelicals and fundamentalists now speak from a position of assumed error at least where elite institutions like the academy are concerned. This is because they accept a position, the authority of the Hebrew and Christian scriptures mediated by the historic Protestant confessions, that currently has no epistemic status. Catholics who stand in the tradition of Aquinas and the historic Church Councils are in a similar boat. Neither group can bring forward anything recognized as knowledge in the public sphere even if, as Catholic Thomists do, they are willing to speak the language of reason. I tend to think that this exclusion only twists adherents of these positions into stances more radical and dangerous than they would otherwise take. One problem here is the adversarial legal framework in which we handle complex ethical and social issues such as euthanasia or same-sex marriage. Regardless of the right or wrong of the decisions themselves one side wins and the other loses. In the early part of this century it was safe to assume that liberalism was the broad consensus position and that the 'losers' (like conservative Evangelical Christians) would go off in a corner and sulk. I doubted this at the time and now it is clear my hunch was correct: what the losers actually do is join fascist movements that are only a protest vote away from power. One should never ignore the law of unintended consequences to which even

I find it odd then that people who adhere to this eminently sensible view are so unwilling to defend it as such. They tell us "I believe in free speech....but...." or "I abhor censorship... but" when the protestation is completely unnecessary. They do not believe in free speech and nor should they. They are fine with censorship as well they should be. Yet something, I assume, nags their conscience. The libertarian position of Mr. Borovoy still holds a powerful moral appeal so that even those who self-evidently reject it still want to *appear* to be defending it. Indeed, his position still has powerful advocates. Let us turn to an august body, the Canadian Association of University Teachers. Listen to the president of CAUT Mr. James Compton writing in the Nov. 2017 CAUT Bulletin: "The right to academic freedom "without constriction by prescribed doctrine" in teaching and research is a bedrock principle... " . Mr. Compton notes that corporate interests are an obstacle to this principle and then continues "But sometimes calls to cancel controversial speaking events emanate from both students and faculty themselves. In addition, respectful workplace policies are sometimes used to circumscribe academic freedom through definitions banning speech that makes others uncomfortable." This, he informs us "... can have a chilling effect on the ability of professors to teach controversial subject matter." Thus while harassing and threatening speech should not be tolerated "... challenging political and social assumptions is at the core of academic life and sometimes that makes people uncomfortable."

If we were to unpack what Mr. Compton is saying, we will find that he is taking the traditional civil libertarian line exemplified by Mr. Borovoy. Free speech does not cover any and all speech acts and no exponent of free speech has ever said that it did: threats and insults can be sanctioned as any other anti-social behavior can be sanctioned. It does, however, embrace anything we may call the statement of facts, purported facts, opinions, judgments, theories and so on. Thus if I said "You Nazi scum!" this would not be protected speech though it might be *permitted* speech. If, however, I uttered the proposition "Nazis are scum" this is an assertion that could be debated and thus protected speech. In principle, anyone would be free to utter this or any other proposition so long as they stick to the form of a proposition for or against which evidence and arguments could be offered.[9] The university on such a model would be a place where any assertion could be uttered and any assertion questioned so long as it was not a threat or an insult directed at a specific person or group of people. The justification for this license varies but one way it can be stated is this: throughout history many opinions at first considered heretical or

---

the best human intentions are subject.

[9] Of course one can phrase an insult as a proposition. If I say "Nazis are Scum" I am most likely inviting comment on the morality or lack thereof of Nazis. If I say "God hates fags" I am not uttering a theological proposition to be debated by the relevant experts. I am simply making a gesture of profound disgust and disapproval. As we shall see below the fineness of these sorts of distinctions will make for some trouble as we shall have to ask whether some statements that are indisputably propositions are nonetheless insulting and threatening.

foolish or dangerous have been crucial to progress in the sciences, arts and politics. Censorship will of its very nature over-censor.[10] Along with many genuinely foolish or wrong statements many fruitful ones will be censored as well with significant loss to human progress. It is better, then, to tolerate all opinions than to empower censors with very fallible judgment to pick and choose (censors have virtually *never* applied this power wisely or productively and, in fact, reliably make fools of themselves). Thus to *protect* significant speech we allow all speech confident that the cream will rise slowly but surely to the top. Under this view error *does* have rights in this limited sense: that separating truth from error is a vexed process best left to the community of speakers as a whole rather than to the narrow judgment of individuals. The self-policing over time of the community of speakers will produce better results than rules and legislation which will time and again censor or outlaw the wrong things. I recall seeing a warning sticker for children on a copy of Kant's first critique. Do you or I or anyone want to see the person responsible for this determining the legitimate boundaries of speech? At any rate on this view the circle of speakers is assumed to be *open* as this is the best way to ensure the triumph of truth over falsity. This, if we want to contrast it to the Miltonic position, may be called the Libertarian position (to whose formation Milton, in fact, contributed mightily).

Not everybody sees things this way however. The Miltonic position has its proponents now (as always) and they may even be in the ascendant. There are those think that while we may tolerate much error we cannot tolerate all. A few years ago maverick British scientist Rupert Sheldrake was scheduled to speak at the University of British Columbia. Dr. Sheldrake has done research on parapsychology and extra sensory perception and on this basis the Psychology Department demanded that he be forbidden from speaking: belief in E.S.P was too fundamental an error to allow any proponent of it to speak in an institution of higher learning. This is old-fashioned censorship based on the venerable principle that error has no rights and it is vulnerable to the kind of critique laid out above. However, there are other proponents of Miltonism that are not so easily dismissed. One of them is Ms. Abigail Curlew writing in *Vice*. Ms. Curlew is, she assures us, a defender of free speech. However, it is clearly Miltonic free speech she defends rather than the libertarian version outlined above. The reason is that free speech (in the libertarian sense) is impossible as "our society suffers from extreme stratification along the lines of race, gender, sexuality, and class. Your identity shapes where you might be located within society's opportunity structure." This is hyperbole: Canadian society is far *less* stratified than many other past or current societies so it can hardly be said to be 'extreme'. Still, there are stratifications within it which should certainly be questioned. Curlew continues: "For transgender

---

[10] That dullards are so over-represented in the profession may give us pause about censors in general. Milton himself pointed out that the problem with censorship is that no one qualified to do it would want to. (222) The very profession seems contrived to attract fools and scoundrels.

folks, this positions us in a precarious reality. A great portion of Canadian society doesn't recognize trans folks as real persons. And when they recognize us, it is often filtered through crude stereotypes that emphasize perversion or mental illness. The point is, we must go to great lengths to justify and defend our very existence in everyday situations. This extends to the classroom where many undergraduate trans students, who already face risky social situations, may find themselves working under prejudiced instructors." For this reason: "The pressures of daily transphobia and cissexism push us back into the closets where we are unable to express our voices. The "freedom of speech" of those who hold bigoted views silence the freedom of speech of those they target."

Let us unpack these statements as we did with Mr. Compton. First note that most university CA's take a strong libertarian view of Academic freedom. At the same time most universities want to position themselves as welcoming to students who are trans, queer or belong to some other racial or sexual minority. Thus, Academia as a whole is internally divided on this question. What happens then when a professor makes a statement criticizing the demands of trans students, say, for the use of gender neutral pronouns? Is this proposition uttered from a position of assumed error and as such subject to censure like a 17th Century Catholic denying that the King is head of the English church? I am not sure: however, at very least such a statement is, whatever truth value we assign to it, perceived as demeaning and threatening by the trans community. Let me explain it this way: when I was an undergraduate I went to a college affiliated with the Anglican Church of Canada. Muslims, Catholics and Jews were there assumed to speak from positions of error and our instructors found many small, subtle ways of indicating this. None of this was aggressive or openly derogatory. Indeed, discussions of such matters were uniformly civil and often engaging and informed. Still, as a working class Catholic I was religiously and socially 'other' in a number of ways. Did this bother me? Occasionally, but I lost little sleep over it nor did I ever question the right of such institutions to exist. It was just a situation I lived in like any other. I had a narrative about *myself* that did not quite overlap with the University's narrative about *its* self. The institution I attend was dedicated primarily to training a WASP elite for positions of public prominence but secondarily offered a good education for various others such as myself. I had and have no real problem with that.

I suppose part of the reason for this was that I felt then and feel now entirely secure in my rights as a Canadian citizen. For instance, I can vote, work, access medical care and receive due process if accused of a crime. I can travel under a Canadian passport and, so long as I am discreet about my theological proclivities, not face any discrimination at work. The world would look very different, however, if my identity were more visible and more hotly contested. This is the situation Ms. Curlew and others find themselves in. From such a perspective free speech is a rigged game. There are many in Canadian society who speak from a position of assumed powerlessness. These are people who belong to ethnic, linguistic and sexual minorities whose status in Canadian society is contested. For such people the speech of dominant groups is so constituted as to shut down their own. Under a libertarian regime of free speech such voices cannot be heard as bigots or others who question the status or even the reality of certain groups are, whatever their intentions, taking all the oxygen out of the room: *they*, like an obnoxious uncle at thanksgiving dinner, use their power of speech to create an atmosphere of intimidation and threat that forces discretion, indeed, extreme discretion on others. Thus, we need a Miltonic adjustment. The libertarian view of speech, as of economics, assumes a level playing field that does not exist. In order that hitherto suppressed 'Catholic' speech be free hitherto dominant 'Protestant' speech must be limited. Free speech is a zero-sum game and, unlike the libertarian position, the circle of speakers is assumed, by necessity, to be closed at, at very least, one point.

Just how this overturning of dominant speech is to happen however seems murky as hardly anyone at all will admit to being in favor of censoring people. What seems to happen in practice is an enforced kind of etiquette: we tend to suppress such speech as can be perceived as slighting or hurtful. Justifying the suppression of speech on the grounds of its falsity is problematic to say the least. However, all of us oppose rudeness and if certain opinions can be classified as inherently offensive then that seems to create an adequate justification for suppressing them. Of course one obvious objection to this is the that the standard of 'offence' is inherently subjective ('offensive' has no objective definition) and if I claimed to be 'offended' by quantum mechanics, say, I would quite rightly be put in my place. Worse, the very act of calling out someone as offensive may cause the very same level of offence in turn: if the Trump supporter in my class cannot offend me it is hard to see why I in turn can offend him. That said, it will not do to simply complain about 'snowflake culture' and the ways that modern institutions attempt to accommodate it at all costs. I think there is a principle at stake that goes deeper than the narrow, subjective and ultimately incoherent category of 'offense' which, after all, does not really convey what 'Miltonists' are trying to do, which is to define the circle of speech in a fashion that it is closed rather than open. We want to define people who labor under certain misconceptions about the world as 'out of the game' because they get something about its rules fundamentally wrong. This is in the name of changing society *not* on the principle of politeness but of the principle of justice (which far being identical to politeness may demand the harshest invective).

Let me elaborate: all of us spend our lives elaborating what might be called foundational narratives. These are the root stories that contextualize our thoughts, actions and ideas. Sometimes these narratives are common to a community. One of these might be called the 'conversion' narrative. I will give some examples of it. One of these we might term the religious: I once was "lost" and now am "found" . Mr. Smith, for instance, may have many frustrations in his life from addictions to stress in his family and at work. At this point Mr. Smith feels lost and alienated and may be at his wit's end. Then he encounters a member of the Watchtower Society who tells him that the end of the world is immanent and that if he is among Jehovah's elect he will shortly spend all eternity in an earthly paradise governed by God's deputy Jesus and various other Old Testament figures. Looking past the eccentricity of these images we can easily see how Mr. Smith's entire outlook changes: with the *eschaton* on its way Mr. Smith can now view things *sub-specie aeternitatis.* Problems that were once huge are now small, indeed Mr. Smith can now see the smallness of his own petty concerns when compared with the grand cosmic drama about to unfold around him. Events and people in his lives are now radically re-evaluated from an entirely new paradigm: a new perspective is adopted that radically reshapes the entire environment in which Mr. Smith's life transpires. The arch or *ur* narrative behind this tale is, of course, Augustine's *Confessions* which sets the template for all subsequent conversion narratives: a period of wandering which issues in a crisis and a resolution. The *ur* narrative for this may well be Homer's *Odyssey.*

Through the influence of Protestantism, the conversion narrative has almost become *the* narrative for the contemporary world. For this reason, there are innumerable secular versions of it. For instance, Mr. Smith might well become disenchanted with waiting for an apocalypse that never seems to arrive. He might notice that the community to which he belongs, the Jehovah's Witnesses, make many demands upon him which over time become increasingly irksome. Mr. Smith may find a book or video of Richard Dawkins that precipitates *another* crisis and *another* epiphany which issues in yet another conversion. From this new standpoint he will again re-interpret everything from a new perspective even his own past: he will tell us, almost certainly, that he has *always* been an Atheist deep down and has only just caught up with his truest, deepest self. He will say this though, from an empirical point of view, the assertion may well be meaningless. If Mr. Smith had lived one hundred years ago this might have been the end of the matter. He would live in a world where people contested his life stance from every pulpit in the land. Where teachers might make snide cracks about atheists and where some would even question his sanity. Atheists at a certain point were 'Catholics': people who were not part of the circle of speakers because they rejected a principle thought fundamental to it. If they were part of the circle they would not be able to assume politeness or fairness from their interlocutors. They would, to use the current lingo "have to grow a pair" and not be "snowflakes" . Many Atheists have in fact done this quite successfully and almost certainly became better thinkers for having their 'identity' constantly questioned.

Now though we get to the heart of the matter. Unlike even a hundred years ago we face the demand not only for universal tolerance but for universal recognition. My deep narrative is just my deep narrative until someone *else* recognizes it. If my deep story (and this is frequently a 'conversion narrative') concerns my sexuality for instance, I not only name myself 'queer' or 'fluid' or what have you but I expect others to name me as such too and at least publicly defer to my chosen identity and unconditionally affirm it as valuable. This demand stems from the Kantian principle that humans are objects of unconditional respect though Kant might well be puzzled by this particular use of it. Respecting the inherent value of a person means giving unconditional respect to their deep narratives. Now philosophically I cannot see how this is true. Surely it is, as Kant held, our autonomy as moral agents that grounds the demand for respect not our founding narratives. Any narrative is in principle contestable but personhood is not.[11] We ought, in principle at least, to be able to differ about the stories we tell while still respecting each other as persons. It should not affect my moral status in your eyes if you happen to be skeptical about my claim that I am currently (and have always been) writing under the inspiration of the Holy Spirit. However, the problem is a bit more complex than this. Certain identities are not just contested: they are actively discriminated against and the people who assume those narratives pay a heavy price in social exclusion. Add to this other issues like poverty or substance abuse or violence and you have people who are in very vulnerable positions indeed. In the contemporary world we want not to exclude these voices but bring them into the conversation. We want to *liberate* people hitherto *oppressed*. To do this, as Ms. Curlew said above, we must create spaces (such as classrooms) where they feel free to express their thoughts, feelings and opinions. These spaces cannot include anyone who questions the fundamental equality of these repressed identities with others either in word or deed. They are, as it were, breaking the first principle underlying the conversation: exactly as atheists, Catholics, dissenters and Jews broke the principle underlying free discussion in the 17th Century by denying the supremacy of the English Church and Crown, the *fons et origo* of all truly "free" speech.[12] This, by the way, is why the suppression of religious dissent in England tended to focus on the threat

---

[11]The assumption here seems to be that to stop violence against certain groups of individuals we have to teach everyone or affirm their identities as valuable. I tend to the view that whatever I happen to think of someone else's identity I should not beat them because beating persons is wrong. Also, while I may not like to affirm your story it belongs to the dignity of humans to tell their own stories to whatever extent is consistent with law, reason and sanity. Of course, the reason this question is as vexed as it is that in our current form of society some persons get to speak louder than others and that a 'free-speech' society must also be a just and equitable society at the same time and in the same respect.

[12]The colonial history of England both in the British Isles and abroad may make us less than misty-eyed about 'English liberty' in hindsight. "Free" England always had its 'unfree' others (Scottish, Irish, Indigenous) who needed to be taught 'freedom' by starvation, massacre and theft of land. Nor is it exactly clear to what degree England under the Tudors, say, was a 'freer' society than Spain under Phillip II. Did Shakespeare have more liberty to write than Cervantes or Calderon? That is for historians to judge. As a philosopher I will point out that it is better to have a myth of freedom than not. Further, we may freely grant the English people a latitudinarian spirit that bore real fruit in the 19th and 20th Centuries in the form of bourgeois civil liberties which, again, are better to believe in than not (whatever their limitations).

of sedition and the fear of 'fifth columns'. In this way courts like the Star Chamber differed from the Inquisition in Spain which was more bound up with concerns about the racial purity of *conversos*. One of the remarkable things about current anti-Islamic sentiment in the West is how it manages to combine the worst aspects of both positions.

The problem with this is obvious even if we do accept that our times demand greater sensitivity than the past when Catholics, Jews and non-believers were liberated to the possession of full civic rights but not to freedom from insult or criticism. All three groups still had to endure plenty of both. We do this by limiting speech to only those assertions that do not touch on the fundamental identity of other persons in the room. By doing this we of course repeat the original gesture of defining an inside and outside to the circle of speakers based on their recognition of an underlying principle that cannot be questioned. This means that Jehovah's Witnesses, say, cannot make assertions about sexuality or biology in an open classroom. This is no problem, perhaps, as Jehovah's Witnesses avoid universities knowing full well they are not welcome there. Further, they freely admit that the contempt is mutual. Mormons, however, do attend university as do Pentecostals, Baptists and Traditionalist (as opposed to Liberal) Catholics, Orthodox Jews and so on: it is hard to see how they could defend these points of view *as positions* even in response to attack from others without violating the rules of the current 'speech game'.[13] This may be tough luck to those individuals but their ancestors have endured far worse. Less inured to scorn than these religious minorities though are campus conservatives who will indeed complain loudly and generally effectively against the double standard employed against them. The problem, and there is no way to spin this away, is that their complaint is entirely valid on the libertarian model. They are being subject to a Miltonic exception.[14]

If you are fine with Miltonic exceptions this is not a problem (except that you want to be careful not to end up on the wrong side of one yourself). Every society, it seems, has some version of this exception. In 17th Century

---

[13]Though the author considers himself a progressive broadly speaking he must point out one thing on which his side is completely and disastrously wrong. The assumption made by many of us is that the people I have listed above exist only out of perversity and ignorance and will go away if ridiculed sufficiently. Progressives hereby commit the cardinal sin of being willfully ignorant of their enemies which is always a recipe for defeat. Protestantism, Catholicism, Judaism and Islam are not foolish contraptions ginned up by yokels but world historical movements involving some of the greatest minds in history. To regard them with the contempt liberals and progressives generally do shows astonishing historical ignorance and an abject inability to grasp the substance of positions not their own. This secular arrogance got its comeuppance with the election of Trump, to which it contributed mightily.

[14]One complication here is that there are live and dead questions. The question of whether people ought to be slaves is not currently (and hopefully never will be) up for discussion. However, a class room does not always work this way: a theoretical understanding of the wrongs of slavery might well entail considering what people like Aristotle said in its behalf even though no one is taking his position up as a practical proposal. Questioning things that are not currently 'open to question' has, in the classroom at least, a serious pedagogical purpose when done correctly.

England the freedom and prosperity were based on the English Crown and its national church. Free discussion could range around a host of issues scientific, religious or otherwise but this bedrock principle could not be touched on: free speech could discuss anything but the Crown itself. William Blake was not free to say 'Damn the King'! Similarly, in an Atheist who questioned the existence of god questioned the foundations of morals, the very principle on which freedom rested: other things could be freely discussed but not the divine origin of freedom itself. Similarly, the fundamental equality of all identities in the 21st Century is the principle of free exchange of ideas: it is the principle behind the discussion which cannot itself be discussed. Everything can be questioned only in light of the one thing that cannot be questioned. Conservatives from right to alt-right to Nazi all fall (partly or fully) under this exclusion. They are the point at which the discussion constitutes itself by some fundamental act of exclusion.

Thus, we have within the contemporary world no place for r*adical* *s*kepticism. In a progressive society, as in most others, everything can be questioned but that society itself. To complain about this may only be to complain about how the world is: the most futile complaint of all. Strauss tells us, after all, that there are things the wise author will (in most times and places) not openly say (504). I suppose he means by this that he will not put the ultimate principles of order in his society to a public test both for his own safety and that of others: he will not challenge the civil theology of whatever society he lives in. Still, I want to say that the proponent of the Miltonic exception pays a cost for that position, a cost she might well want to consider and that Strauss' pessimism may not be the last word. The first is that the libertarian stance guarantees that *you yourself* will not end up a Miltonic exception. It is dangerous to play a zero sum game as you might lose. I believe it was General von Moltke who identified the problem with military planning as the perversity of the enemy: his failure to react rationally or predictably to the application of force. We may institute a regime where certain opinions are proscribed within a classroom setting say and the people who hold those positions told to keep them to themselves. The expected result of this is that the 'deplorables' will comply; altering their behavior and ultimately their attitudes to conform with the accepted boundaries of communication. What though if the 'deplorables' fight back? What if *they* cast themselves in the role of excluded groups whose liberties are being denied? Well, their opponents will huff and puff and declare the notion ridiculous. Unfortunately, the double standard is the hardest one to defend: Evangelicals who hear their beliefs attacked over and over or CPC members who hear the same may decide that their feelings are as tender as anyone's. They will appeal to the same rules that protect others and they will almost certainly be successful in doing so. The circle of speech which shrunk from one side will now shrink from another. At that point we will seriously have to ask whether it has shrunk too much. We might well ask if the reign of sensitivity has itself become stifling and oppressive as applied rigorously it would shut down any discussion as soon as it came within reach of moral, metaphysical and theological ultimates. If we are only allowed to question the secondary or tertiary aspects of anyone's identity, then discussion is of its very nature confined to the superficial. In effect, the Miltonic exception applies to anyone and everyone!

There may be an even deeper cost. We may then be faced with the problem that in an egalitarian society either everyone is a Miltonic exception or no one is. This is as much to say that it is a contradiction and an impossibility to affirm all narratives and all identities. As societies in the past played favorites, protecting some positions and suppressing others, so too we may in the end simply play favorites. If so our society will run on no different principle at the end of the day than 16 Century Spain or 17th Century England. The state will foster truth and suppress error. It may do so with a passive aggressive smile rather than a rack of course but the thing will differ only in degree and not kind. Of course, people of a progressive stripe may not be overly exercised by this as they assume that they will pick the winners and not their opponents. Progress after all is the guiding genius of history and assures that people who are progressives must ultimately win. The cynic in me however suspects two things. First, that nothing at all guarantees the ultimate victory of the left and second, that if reactionary forces do indeed triumph many in that community will experience a sudden conversion to libertarianism (as we have defined it here) and start espousing Mill and Borovoy once more. The great thing about the liberal tradition in the end is that it does *not* in fact assume the apocalypse but lays out articles of peace for all to follow given that we will never all agree on fundamentals. It opts not to play the zero sum game of ending history and eliminating our ideological opponents.[15]

At this point we touch upon what is perhaps the most crucial argument for the libertarian position: that our enemies do us an enormous service and that it would harm *us* if they were to disappear. Let me conclude with Mill on this point: "The greatest orator, save one, of antiquity, has left it on record that he always studied his adversaries' case with as great, if not still greater, intensity than his own. What Cicero practiced as the means of forensic success requires to be imitated by all who study any subject in order to arrive at the truth. He who knows only his side of the case, knows little of that. His reasons may be good and no one may have been able to refute them. But if he is equally unable to refute the reasons on the opposite side; if he does not so much as know what they are, he has no ground for preferring either opinion." (511) All who dream of totalitarian

---

[15]Of course the position of Milton rests implicitly on his sense of providence; his trust in free speech (minus the exception he cites) depends on trust that God's hand is working in history. Mill similarly can rely on an implicit faith in progress though he may understand this largely in secular terms. In the current discussion of course we can call on no such background notions or tacit beliefs. This is no doubt why authors like Borovoy emphasize the dangers of empowering fallible human beings with the authority to censor others. (10-12)

solutions (whether soft or hard) should meditate on this text and on the fact that the other, even the hostile other, is an essential element of one's own intellectual growth. I cannot in this essay, if I can in any, tell people what position to take. I only ask that whatever position you take you recognize clearly and fully the cost of adopting it. There may be extremities that make these costs supportable and I'm entirely sympathetic to the argument that at times it is necessary to sacrifice freedom of speech to preserve public order and safety. There is speech that is equivalent to lighting a match in dry brush. I also recognize that different societies will draw this line in different places. The German attitude to free speech cannot, because of the sheer weight of history, be identical to the Canadian or American one for instance. Still, I stand with civil libertarians in counselling that such interventions need to meet a high bar of skepticism and that if they must exist at all it is best that they be rare.

3 Indigenizing Humanities: Preliminary Reflections

Can a program in interdisciplinary Humanities be indigenized? Specifically, can the Humanities program we have constructed at Grenfell be indigenized? To put it bluntly, can students attracted to Plato or Dante or Woolf be attracted to indigenous thought? Can indigenous students be attracted to Classical Antiquity or the writings of Descartes? The presumption of an indigenized Humanities program is that a significant portion of students will be willing to undertake both. This question must be asked for two reasons. Firstly, the operating assumption behind the question is that Indigenous learning will not be pursued in a separate academic ghetto which would, in effect, function as seminaries currently do on campuses with religious affiliations. Secondly, it is assumed that many other forms of knowledge will be pursued on the Campus besides indigenous knowledge. Barring some cultural cataclysm this will include such standard European knowledge forms as the physical sciences or the study of literary classics. The assumption on which I will proceed then is that our task in the humanities is to integrate indigenous discourses into other discourses. This is on one level very easy. A humanities program may include a course on Indigenous history besides the other histories it tells. However, my assumption is that indigenous knowledge will not simply be pursued on a parallel track with other knowledge. As H.G. Gadamer teaches discourses do not simply clash but through dialogue their horizons merge. Each becomes part of the self-understanding of the other. This leads to a number of issues which I will raise in turn. Let me note though that the culture of Western Europe is no more one thing than all indigenous cultures are one thing. The conflicts noted below may not reflect an absolute division. I note them simply as flashpoints where indigenous and Western European cultures may interface in a conflictual manner even given all the good will in the world. I would also like to emphasize that in this piece I speak for nobody but myself; both my indigenous and non-indigenous colleagues may make of these comments exactly what they will and I do not assume to represent the views of either.

Firstly, it is very likely that pushback will occur from both students and faculty when it becomes apparent that indigenous traditions are of-

21

ten sacred traditions. It is common to find people of European descent committed to the notion that 'secularity' is a boundary that must constantly be policed to prevent the encroachment of religion on the realm of 'scientific' knowledge. How then will sacred narratives and traditions find a place in the 'secular' structure of knowledge? How will rituals such as smudging be integrated into the classroom, a space hitherto regarded as indifferent or even hostile to religion?

Secondly, it is very likely that some indigenous persons will be less than thrilled by a Gadamerian fusion of horizons with the traditions that have hitherto colonized and oppressed them. Dialogue as Gadamer conceives it leaves both sides in some sense altered. Yet one of the aims of indigenous education is to preserve indigenous traditions from dissolution. This is especially problematic as one of the core components of the western university is a culture of critical reflection. This is a much broader thing than the uttering of criticisms whether of colonialism or any other oppressive institution. It implies, for instance, putting our own stories under the microscope as much as the stories of the other. Universities with denominational commitments struggle with this question for reasons that seem analogous: can, say, a Catholic university question Catholic truth? That this problem is exacerbated by the current power imbalance between colonists and colonized goes without saying.[16] One of the possibilities that a 'speculative' project like indigenous humanities must face is that indigenous people themselves may see no point in it. Though I try to find some possible synergies here between indigenous and other discourses I have to face up to the fact that I may fail.[17]

Thirdly, in Western traditions knowledge is produced by the giving of arguments and evidence usually through some formal process involving scientific method, logical construction of deductive arguments, induction and so on. It does not involve direct appeals to tradition or the knowledge

---

[16] As Daniel Salée puts it in a review of recent works on the place of indigenous peoples in Canada: "Widdowson and Howard pay virtually no heed to such considerations (much to the detriment of their own credibility as historical materialists). Had they done so they could see that the movement for Aboriginal cultural preservation that they castigate reacts a long-standing practice of resistance and re-empowerment, a strategy of political affirmation against power structures that marginalize and oppress Indigenous peoples." I, as is no doubt apparent to the reader, am not writing within the framework of historical materialism or any other such directly post-Hegelian stance. As such, the dialogue I propose goes beyond seeing indigenous cultures as modes of resistance however important those might be. (see "Indigenous Peoples and Settler Angst in Canada: A Review Essay" 321)

[17] To put it bluntly neither I nor any other Western scholar is in a moral position to demand dialogue with indigenous people however much we might think it a good idea. It a basic option for any human person or society to remain within its own categories and not engage with the other and for some it may be the sensible option. It may well be that, as Tim Lilburn asserts, "We are therefore in state that precedes conversation. . . precedes even the state of pre-conversation." (2017; 15) Lilburn counsels European descendants to look within their own contemplative traditions to find a ground on which they can profitably engage First Nations beyond the "imperial ploys" masked by "an evolutionary philosophy of history" . (15) This is entirely in line with what I suggest in this piece which is, just as Lilburn says, a gesture towards a possible conversation.

of elders. Knowledge in such a paradigm is fluid, following the give and take of argument. I suppose that like others indigenous communities have processes of argument and justification. To what extent though do these involve appeals to tradition, the telling of stories and so on. Can both of these processes be used in the same classroom? What if they produce conflicting results?

Like a good Medieval teacher, I will begin with my general reply before addressing the specific objections. Why does a program in indigenous humanities make pedagogical sense? Well firstly it reflects a legitimate moral demand of those of us who have benefited directly or indirectly from the mass expropriation of lands and resources (both natural and cultural) from indigenous peoples. This is a matter on which there should be little controversy: acts of restitution need to be made and one of the areas where these acts need to start is education. This is both a pragmatic and intellectual/spiritual necessity for indigenous students and an opportunity for moral growth for non-indigenous ones. Of course this does not by itself answer the question of how or indeed whether a project as apparently heterogeneous as Indigenous humanities would work. Surprisingly, for me at least, it may work far better than it seems at first blush. I will begin by citing indigenous scholar, Jaqueline Ottman: "Decolonization of teaching practices begins with educators asking: who am I? Where did I come from? Where am I going? What are my responsibilities? These 'identity' existential questions begin a 'mining' and a deeply introspective journey for the teacher." (15) Ottman continues by citing T.S. Wilson to the effect that: "A decolonizing education for white teachers involves "bringing forward" the storied history presently subsumed within their teaching but in relation to post-colonial or counter stories for the purpose of provoking a different story that can open and shift their horizon." (15) Further below we read (again quoted from Wilson): "Teachers need opportunities to reclaim their own stories or 'landscapes' so as to recognize their "standpoints" . However, reclamation becomes a truncated process of reification if touchstones are not recognized as formative, are allowed to re-subside into the unconscious, and fail to be counterpoised with stories that challenge them with an alternative them with an alternative perspective." (15)

This is an excellent description of our own program: we too attempt to tell a deep story about western culture occluded by our current academic specializations. We too eschew an 'unconscious' relation to the past that hides deep structures of thought and experience. We too invoke a narrative approach to uncovering unexamined assumptions about 'European heritage' and what has gone into its making. As I advert to below this archeological or genealogical approach can take Hegelian, Marxist or existentialist forms (as in Heidegger's 'history of being'). It can also take the form of internal critique (i.e. immanent critique which is to be distinguished from the superficiality of polemic). Western modernity has uttered many critiques of itself both from traditionalist and radical standpoints. Of this I can say that our program has in fact been structured as an implicit defense of freedom in its Western bourgeois forms (particularly its Anglo-Saxon forms). This is deeply imbedded in the tradition of 'great books' education whose origins lie in the cold war.[18] I offer no opinion on whether this is a good or bad thing *sub specie aeternitatis*. I simply note that as a conversation it is inherently limited. Grenfell humanities has already recognized this to some degree as a consideration of post- modernist and post colonialist critique was factored into the curriculum. However, the next logical step would be to extend this conversation by rooting it in the actual community in which we live. This means that the specific form of our conversation should address a living question with which many in our community are deeply concerned: how indigenous and non-indigenous cultures can interact productively given that both must inhabit a common geographic space and indeed given that many partake in both heritages at once.

Having penned my *respondeo* I will now proceed to address the three objections I have noted. To the first I reply that I think it is dogmatic secularism that needs to bend here, if only in this instance. I am quite aware that this is a floodgate that many do not want to open and with good reason. Western Secularity, however, must come to the realization that it is not a 'transcendental signified'. Secularity is a theological construction of the modern west: it is always already its theological (and Christian) other. It has no universal necessary form for all times and all places. Europeans invented 'the secular' as a way of framing questions of temporal politics in a world where humanity's primary focus was on its eternal salvation. The secular was the realm of secondary and natural as opposed to final good. This meant that social relations became, to some degree at least, questions of practicality and power and not sacred concern. By the 20th century this notion of the secular had broken free to a great degree (though his divorce was never total) and became a realm not distinct from and subordinate to the sacred but one that encompassed and supplanted it. Thus, while Europeans and especially North Americans assume that the concept of the secular is immediate and naturally given (simply reflecting the direct 'natural attitude' on which the sacred has been overlaid) it is in fact historically mediated. This is why cultures founded on religious law (like Jewish and Islamic culture) or sacred custom (many indigenous societies) do not reflexively share our 'secular' posture which many of them see (correctly

---

[18] As I say below: "The story of humanities was the story of freedom, particularly of Western freedom as it issues in the modern state. This is the story Hegel told in his Philosophy of History and it runs from the birth of subjective freedom among the ancient Greeks and culminates in freedom objectively realized in the nation states of modern Europe and North America. This story is not negligible and many critics of colonialism, for instance, assume some version of it: after all the West has, in their view, selfishly kept its freedoms to itself and refused to extend it to 'others' in the third world and elsewhere. Many of these thinkers turn to the development and extension of Hegel's story in the writings of Karl Marx." In this paper I am going beyond even the traditional 'progressive' iteration of the western triumphalist narrative (as is still propagated by traditional Marxists like anti-indigenous scholar Frances Widdowson).

it must be admitted) as an imposition of the *Christian* west.[19]

Nowhere is this truer than in Canada. The secular modern society we have built is not a creation *ex nihillo*. It is built on an act of expropriation and part of that expropriation involves the suppression not only of the sacred traditions of indigenous people but of the sacred itself. We may think this a triumph of science and instrumental reason over base superstition. People like Frances Widdowson and Margaret Wente still justify colonialism on exactly these grounds.[20] (see Simmons for a decisive critique http://uppingtheanti.org/journal/article/11-residual-stalinism) But this is an act of profound and destructive forgetting. For generations the animistic and holistic viewpoints of indigenous peoples were part of Western European culture as well as the forgotten conceptions of Neo-Platonism, Magic, Alchemy, ancient physiology, medicine and folk belief all attest. The west had a culture of sacred symbols and conceptions that was eclipsed by the scientific revolution exactly as indigenous beliefs were. It is not my intention here to tote up the many ways in which this was a gain and in which it was a loss. Nor is it to refight the battles of the past.

---

[19] 'Secularism' is something that ought to be distinguished from what I would call 'secularity'. Secularism is an assumed solution to a basic human problem that claims permanent and universal validity. As such it is doubtfully defensible. Ten thousand years from now will the galaxy be filled with societies that conform to our current definitions of 'secular'? Secularism is a provincial solution to a regional problem: the place of society and politics in a world defined by Christian revelation. 'Secularity' is the opposite of this for it is not a purported final solution to an age old problem but a simple denial of triumphalism. Secularity simply means 'everyone speaks' while secularism tries, among other things, to define the circumstances under which a person can claim the status of a knower and hence speaker.

[20] Simmonds notes "My particular interest here is the way in which science has been reified by Widdowson and Howard and used to legitimate state decision-making on behalf of oppressed peoples. Science is counterposed to indigenous traditional knowledge, which by way of a children's parable (The Emperor's New Clothes) is denounced as mere superstition in the service of a corrupt "aboriginal industry." The state is called upon to harness scientific rationalism in the old colonial interest of "civilizing the savages." In the words of Widdowson and Howard, "It is not clear how the remnants of Neolithic culture that are inhibiting this development can be addressed without intensive government planning and intervention" (252). Nothing is shallower and more irksome in the discourse propagated both by unreconstructed Marxists and new atheist neo-cons than the notion that 'Neo-Lithic' cultures can have no complex or vital perceptions of the world; presumably because copper and bronze impart some magical wisdom? There are entire academic discourses, like anthropology, that these so-called 'intellectuals' and 'rationalists' are either ignorant of or willfully ignore. Marx himself, too little too late where subsequent history was concerned, came to qualify the negative view of indigenous societies he took in the German Ideology. Pursuing this insight might have led to a very different kind of 'Marxism', one less enslaved to the very notions of bourgeois political economy it sought to critique. Alas, pursuing what ifs of this kind turns Marxism into a form of idealism, the very thing it purports not to be. Marxism as a path to a rational utopia has failed the only test it recognizes, history, as bourgeois liberalism is failing now. This is not to say, however, that either the Marxist or Liberal traditions are standpoints from which nothing useful can be learned or appropriated. On this question though there seems to me a problem that is fundamental and cannot be fixed simply by finding quotes in Marx that are nicer about indigenous people; that is that in Marxism nature is the dialectical other of humanity which, right or wrong, is not readily squared with the indigenous view of the matter.

Many things in these ancient traditions must seem strange and bizarre now because they either *were* strange and bizarre in their original form or because we have lost the key for understanding them. Evaluating the beliefs of the distant past is no easy matter when we are missing so much of their context.

Still, we may make a few generalizations. Before the scientific revolution the human body, as all things, was embedded in a sacred cosmos structured according to a scale of value[21]. The health or order of the human body was predicated on an attunement or alignment of our physical structure with this sacred order. (see Tillyard,1942; 66-69) This meant that medicine, for instance, was a symbolical or liturgical process as much as a strictly scientific one: these two elements existed together in what now looks to us like confusion.[22] What is more, the typical conception of the universe was monistic. The cosmos was systematically interconnected in surprising and awe inspiring ways. Hidden bonds bound the most disparate parts of the universe together with what we would now call 'spooky action at a distance' features. Then of course these were called occult properties and their existence expressed the broadly accepted fact that the world was a living organic whole in which the least part was connected to every other part through its participation in the totality. In the renaissance this insight was given elaborate and detailed scientific expression in bodies of knowledge, like alchemy, which we polemically term 'superstition'. [23]

There is neither the possibility nor even the need to revive these older

---

[21]The reader may here consider one of early modernity's most remarkable literary performances Robert Burton's Anatomy of Melancholy. This work gives us insight into an enormous body of medical thought and practice stretching from antiquity to the renaissance. At the same time, it is an exercise in reflexive irony, a moral and spiritual exhortation, a wry spoof of pedantry, a sincere tribute to learning, a paean to the power of imagination for good or ill and all and all a witness to the all-encompassing power of the written text. We are not currently used to seeing 'medical information' embedded in such a 'context' that fundamentally challenges our interpretation of it. This is the kind of difficulty that faces us in understanding the cultural monuments of the past.

[22]One might consider, for instance, the English physician Robert Fludd who held that 'airy demons' were the basic cause of illness but that demons could operate through secondary natural causes that a physician could counteract using drugs, chemicals and so forth. (18-20) Clearly, Fludd saw no problem in using naturalistic and spiritualistic categories at the same time in cheerful defiance of Occam's razor! How then are we to classify him? As a superstitious magical 'healer' or as a modern scientist who worked with William Harvey and was among the first to recognize his theories? It is crucial to study the past for just this reason: that distinctions we take to be natural or rational are in fact constructed. For instance, is the rejection of divine interference as a cause for epilepsy by the Hippocratic doctors an assertion of naturalistic 'science' against magical 'superstition'? If so what should we make of the fact that the Hippocratic author's primary argument is an appeal to the (Platonic) theological principle that evil must not be attributed to the Gods? (The Sacred Disease in 1978; 240).

[23]A good introduction to this point of view is the essay On the Sacred Art by the Athenian Platonist Proclus: "Just as true lovers move beyond the beauty perceived through the senses until they reach the sole cause of all beauty and all perception, so too, the experts in sacred matters starting with the sympathy connecting visible things both to one another and to the invisible powers, and having understood that all things are to be found in all things, they established the sacred science." (https://www.google.ca/search?q=proclus+on+the+hieraticart)

forms in all their over-profuse detail yet contemporary science may be groping its way towards some of their underlying insights.[24] It occurs to me then that there are aspects of a humanistic education which indigenous people need not undertake simply for the sake of polemic or 'understanding error'.[25] There are 'genealogical' projects in which western and indigenous scholars can *assist each other* in recovering lost or superseded aspects of their own traditions. Indeed, Indigenous scholars make liberal use of European theory in the negative task of *deconstructing* western colonialism. Might there be other layers of 'theory' useful in constructing a positive alternative? I don't know the answer to this question but Indigenous humanities might be one way of finding out. Examination of the excluded knowledges of Europe might help Indigenous scholars enrich their own self-understanding. They in turn can help Western scholars to a less destructive relationship to nature and a less reflexively antagonistic relationship to the domain of the sacred. This may well be a waste of time. The thoughts I have expressed here may annoy my western colleagues without striking the least spark in the minds of my indigenous ones. That however is a risk I am willing to take if in some way it moves the discussion forward. Thus, it is not necessarily the case that every discussion between a European and indigenous scholar has to be cast in an oppositional framework or that the only purpose of contemporary scholarship is to frame all questions as polemic. The purpose of polemic surely, is simply to free the ground so that *positive* exchanges can in the future be free and not compelled.[26]

Here, perhaps, is one way of stating this possible synergy. Neo-liberal

---

[24]Which it must do in its own way and at its own pace. The author no more desires to interfere in the scientific domain than he desires interference from it in his own. Thus I leave aside the question of holism in biology, the significance of quantum entanglement, the Gaia hypothesis and other questions from the fringes of current science. As an intellectual historian I only note the traditional provenance of such notions.

[25]Here I must declare a sort of bias: I favor a hermeneutic of charity over a hermeneutic of suspicion. This is not because the latter is not sometimes necessary and useful. What is more there are great polemics in the world such as the first half of Augustine's City of God or Burke's Reflections on the Revolution in France. It is a fact however that if one wanted to understand either Roman religion or revolutionary politics one would not rely on these as sources. This is because polemic of its nature eschews complexity and ambiguity.

[26]Polemics have the purpose, perhaps, of undermining the status of any narrative as the default one. What it means to be 'post-modern' is (in its positive sense) that no position has automatic default status. This means that we are no longer in a situation where a western scientist say, can assume his ontology without argument whereas an indigenous person would have to justify her eccentric life choice. The one position has now to bring forth its grounds as much as the other. This is because defining the 'default' position on any question is an assertion of social not rational authority. The default position on any question is simply that of the person in charge (except in narrowly defined circumstances such as presumption of innocence in a court of law). On this model the western scientist could not simply use the assumed authority of archaeology to tell an indigenous person what she ought to think about autochthony. He would also have to bring forward a consideration of archeology as a form of life and its virtues and benefits for various communities. I do this sometimes with students of a fundamentalist persuasion. Instead of simply, and pointlessly, telling them their literal reading of Genesis is wrong I ask them whether a different hermeneutic might better achieve what is, after all, their goal; respecting what is given in the text.

and Marxist critics of indigeneity assume a supercessionist narrative that begins with the 'childhood' of indigenous and other historical beliefs and ends with the 'maturity' of the bourgeois (or possible post-bourgeois) west and its technocracy and culture of 'reason' with reason identified with the western sciences or, if you are a Marxist, the western social sciences. This 'rationality' in its most extreme expressions will not even tolerate the hermeneutic culture of the humanities let alone the beliefs of indigenous peoples. However, this account of 'reason' is seductive precisely as it is puritanically (and incoherently) narrow. What we now have to face is the glaring fact that neither in its Marxist or nor its liberal form is this 'maturity' compatible with living on a finite planet. Nor is either ideology compatible with an appreciation of the diversity and complexity of human or natural life which are all to be sacrificed to a mania for universal rational form. We have to face the fact that we in the west *may* have made not a trivial, easily corrigible error (that could be corrected by a better reading of Marx or Smith or Locke or some other source) but a *deep* error.[27] There is a greatness to erring greatly of course yet we should not be so blinded by the genuine grandeur of modern European civilization as to refuse to look at the shadow side of its achievements in which the so-called 'right' and 'left' are both implicated. This shadow side was evident almost from the start to indigenous peoples who were among the first victims of it. As Rome burns around us we might start to listen to them as a possible alternative to fiddling.[28] Also, from the other side, the enormous scholarly resources mobilized by the historical and cultural

---

[27]What is this error? Why is western freedom literally burning up its natural, material basis? Is this, to use the current catchphrase, a bug or a feature? Behind our current secular culture of course lie the theological and philosophical structures of Latin Christendom. As a western scholar I can, of course, convey my knowledge of these sources to anyone who may find it useful. This may be of some benefit to the 'genealogical' project outlined by Ottman adverted to above. I say this because the way Western Christendom (as opposed to Eastern Christendom) has constituted itself theologically may be one aspect of the problem. People like Phillip Sherrard have argued so in the past (see Greek East and Latin West) and if his treatment of the problem has been justly criticized the problem still remains: does the Western figuration of the life of the Trinity elevate the moment of the logos or reason in a way that prepares for a universal technocracy of instrumental reason to which the moment of natural life (the spirit) is subordinated? The question is vexed because it is equally apt to ask whether the eastern tradition has so naturalized the spirit (which does not pass through the moment of reason but is begotten directly of the Father) as to lay the groundwork for a destructive and violently anti-Christian ethnocentrism. Theology is an important endeavor because it is a dangerous one in ways that a shallow 'secular' criticism has barely any inkling of.

[28] There are of course going to be people who think that a Marxism or Capitalism or Socialism tweaked to take more account of ecological responsibility will move us forward. Frankly, if what the climate scientists are telling us is true, I think that ship has sailed. At any rate, whatever concessions these traditions might make to parks and greenery the fact remains that in both bourgeois liberalism and its Marxist epigone the human realizes itself through a dialectical opposition to the natural realm as its 'other'. The struggle of the human with an indifferent and hostile natural realm is inscribed in the very foundations of both traditions, a fact it was a great virtue of Marx to make clear. I tend to the view that we are currently called to think past such conflictual, dialectically antagonistic accounts of the natural word.

sciences of Europe (of which Grenfell humanities is one expression) are as essential to any genealogical project as the outsider perspective which can see past euro-centric perspectives others might take for granted.

Finally, let me note something about procedures of justification. Though this is not an easy question to resolve I think we can say that one solution at least is not the correct one. We do not have a single valid procedure for producing justified beliefs. The belief that 'scientific method' constitutes this is simply wrong for two reasons. Firstly, 'scientific method' does not describe more than fraction of what even scientists do. Many scientists rely on narrative procedures to reconstructs past events such as paleon-tologists. Others rely on detailed observation and field notes such as in zoology. Secondly, what we might broadly call hermeneutic studies neither need nor can make any use of experimental testing except in an indirect way. Many times citing an authority is fully adequate to resolve a question even in the sciences where practitioners must trust the conclusions of people in smaller subfields of which they have no direct knowledge. Thus there is no inherent problem in indigenous peoples appealing to their own 'experts' to justify their assertions. However, this can only be at the start of the conversation not the end. All may introduce their own authorities and positions in whatever form they like and use their own justificatory procedures. If they then merge on a conclusion it will not be because one has surrendered to the external authority of the other but because inter-secting lines of reason giving and justification have merged in a consensus. If they do not, we still have a better comprehension of our differences. Au-thority is one of the things contested in democratic discussion as when one person relies on *CNN* and another relies on *Fox*. I don't think adding in-digenous perspectives to this mix changes the equation except in a positive and more egalitarian direction.

In sum, there seem to me no compelling reason why indigenous ap-proaches to learning and indigenous content cannot be integrated with other traditions of learning. There are challenges and potential flashpoints to be sure but why not regard these as opportunities rather than dangers? Nor is the potential failure of such a rapprochement a reason not to try. If we are serious about living in a post-colonial context one of the things that must inevitably be questioned is our traditional stories about how epistemic privilege is distributed to some claimants and not others. This, I think, would in fact be liberating for everybody. This is a crucial point to emphasize for it is very difficult to convey to non-indigenous people that gains for indigenous people are not losses for them. Acceptance, say, of indigenous medical practices is *not* an *assault* on western ones or a sys-tematic suppression of 'science' and 'reason'. This is no easy task but one I hope I have begun here.

4 Humanities: Queen of the Sciences

Well actually theology is the queen of the sciences or at least it was in the Middle Ages. It is useful for us to parse what this meant. It meant that knowledge was vertically integrated. It did NOT of course mean that theology was the only form of knowledge or that it could colonize or replace the 'lower' sciences. It simply meant that the sciences could be ranged hierarchically according as they dealt with more or less universal principles. Physics then might deal with the world insofar as the world was material. Arithmetic and geometry might deal with the world in so far as it was quantifiable. Mathematics was the 'higher' science insofar as the category of 'mathematical being' was broader than the category 'material being', including but surpassing it (i.e. angels still had number whether dancing on pin heads or not). In this sense the science that dealt with God was the highest science because the activity of god is the broadest and most universal category (as God is the principle of all things). This did not mean that theology dictated to geometry any more than geometry dictated to biology. It meant that biology rested on principles known properly to mathematicians as mathematics rested on principles known to theology. In the 21st century we are not challenged as the Medievals were to integrate knowledge in a vertical hierarchy culminating in natural and then revealed theology. Still, we are, as much as ever, challenged to integrate knowledge. That, in some sense, we want to do this horizontally rather than vertically only makes the challenge greater. No longer inhabiting the medieval chain of being or its epigone the clockwork world of modern science (where all knowledge culminates in physics rather than theology) we face the practical task of coordinating and integrating a wide diversity of discourses from an increasingly pan cultural and global background. Let's use a metaphor from medieval astronomy. An astronomer of those times had to account not only for the regular, circular motion of the planets but for the oblique motion of the sun (source of generation and decay). For us, there are various oblique motions. A physicist might structure the world exactly as a medieval would by ranking the sciences from biology, to chemistry, to physics on exactly the same hierarchical principle (particular to general). However, there are 'oblique knowledges, indigenous knowledge is one, which cannot be placed vertically in this scheme. These are knowledges that cross the path of other knowledges but do not move in direct synch with them. We live in age of such oblique knowledges. This means that every vertical movement of integration is challenged by a horizontal movement across its own path by *something other*, something that challenges the universality of the hierarchy.[29] It is not my purpose to say how the sciences should deal with such challenges as that is for them to decide. It is my purpose however to point to ways in which humanities in the broad sense, and in the specific sense of our 'humanities program' might try and meet them.

First things first: What is humanities in the second sense? We are all familiar with the individual disciplines such as English literature, history or philosophy. Humanities, however, takes a little bit of explaining. Beginning in the 19th century and moving into the 20th and 21st centuries we (in the western world at least) have come to think of humanity, nature and even perhaps god in terms of their 'historicity'. What do I mean by this? I mean that we do not conceive truth or reality as simply static and timeless but as developing in and through a process of change. Our awareness has developed and changed over time through various landmarks and watersheds that occur in history. There is a history of the human intellect and a history of the human spirit that manifests itself in philosophy, religion, the arts, politics and science as these alter and develop over time. Humanities is the discipline that tries to tell this story in an integrated way and as such crosses the boundaries between disciplines. Its aim is a comprehensive knowledge of the history of intellect and sensibility of human beings in the west and beyond and a critical and reflective attitude towards the historical dimension of experience. For instance, in humanities we not only think about history, philosophy, fine art or religion as specialized disciplines but think about them in relation to each other. It takes a certain breadth and flexibility of mind to see the deep interconnections between science, music, philosophy, theology or literature yet throughout the length and breadth of western culture these endeavors have mutually sustained and influenced each other. Musicians can think about Bach and philosophers about Leib-

---

[29]Of course my 'dominant' non-oblique view is oblique to the other. The problem is that I cannot as a 'non-oblique' person occupy the oblique standpoint any more than the other can occupy mine. I am still stuck with saying that the other is oblique to my path as I am oblique to hers. All one can really do is strive to lessen the negative impact of this difference through acts of imaginative sympathy (which is a basic component of joint action). This entails, in my view, a humanistic outlook which does not posit ethnic or other distinctions as absolute. What we need, to continue the metaphor, is a new astronomy that accommodates simultaneous, multiple frames of reference as an astronomer (even today) may use the geo-centric system for some calculations and the helio-centric system for others. As Cusanus had already figured out at the dawn of the scientific revolution there is no Archimedean standpoint from which anything (strictly speaking) goes around anything. Ancient science of course (except for certain special calculations) assumed the standpoint of the observer as a fixed point from which to describe the heavens: the relativistic implications of placing the observer at some assumed point outside the heavens (which is nowhere at all) may provide a useful model for our current discussion.

niz but humanities gives us the opportunity to think about them together. Thus, Humanities gives us a better more rounded picture of our intellectual and spiritual heritage than any specialized discipline can give on its own for it allows us to take an extra step in reflection that asks how the arts disciplines can be thought of contributing to the larger whole which is human self-understanding.

Of course, the presupposition of such a discourse is that there is a narrative structure or framework that synchronizes the perspectives of various disciplines. Otherwise there would be no integration in humanities above and beyond the specialized disciplines. Let me then explain how I came to perceive the necessity and value of such studies. My background is in classics and classics is founded on a set of exclusions. Classics deals with Greek and Roman antiquity. Near Eastern or Egyptian antiquity were the under the purview of 'Orientalists'. Hebrew antiquity was the purview of Biblical studies. The Church Fathers, who produced an enormous body of literature in time, place and culture *identical* to the Greco-Roman classics were the purview of *yet another* group of scholars. None of these distinctions are grounded in any intrinsic reason. Hebraic and Patristic studies were separated from other antique studies on the grounds that they were propaedeutic to theology and ultimately ministry. Egyptology was distinguished from Classics by the racialized categories of Orientalists. Studies of the Mesopotamians and other peoples of the fertile crescent did not even exist when the boundaries of classics were defined. Geographically, temporally and even ethnically and culturally these divisions are at bottom arbitrary. This is on two levels. Firstly, despite the desperate denials of Orientalists, Egypt IS crucial for understanding Greece. The Romans knew all about the Hebrews and the Hebrews early on absorbed Greek philosophy. Culturally, as commercially and militarily, ancient cultures in the Mediterranean basin interacted constantly. Secondly, this interaction was not a clash of incommensurable 'paradigms'. A common concern for articulating divine and human order animated all and this issued in a number of striking convergences as a comparison of the *Memphite Theology*, the prelude to the *Gospel of John* and the surviving fragments of the middle Platonists and Platonizing Stoics attests.

I was fortunate in that as a Canadian scholar (at Dalhousie University) I was able to study in a program in which these boundaries and exclusions were not operative. To a philosophically minded student the study of Classics offered an enthralling alternative to the dull scholasticism into which Anglo-American philosophy departments had, according to my state of mind at the time , then degenerated.[30] This was something akin to the

---

[30] It is not any part of my intention to the deny the virtues of lucidity and clarity that mark the best sort of analytic thought or to deny that people grounded in that tradition like Putnam (whom I quite admire) and Davidson address the same fundamental problems that should animate all philosophers. Plus, as you will have noticed, I value clear direct exposition in a fashion that does not exactly derive from the continental tradition. My general complaint is that it evades rather than confronts the question of history (as we are all tempted to do). My specific complaint at the time concerned

spirit in which a contemporary student might turn from the one hundredth paper on the analytic/synthetic distinction and, to the despair of his older instructors, take up Gilles Deleuze. In retrospect I was, of course, stiff necked and full of the arrogant folly of youth though I retain from those times a certain marked bias towards a historical approach. At any rate, one of the books I pored over at that time was by a Canadian, Charles Norris Cochrane, entitled *Christianity and Classical Culture*. It was, as indicated by the title, a comprehensive account of the emergence of the Christian culture of late antiquity from its classical background. More important than its thesis (in retrospect) was the way in which it proceeded, synthesizing philosophy, theology, history and literature to tell a comprehensive story about a crucial epoch in, western, and indeed (for better or ill) human history. This was the approach that Cochrane's student James Doull had instituted at Dalhousie. There one might study Greek drama and lyric, Thucydides and Tacitus but also previously disreputable things like Neo-Platonism. Plotinus and Proclus were presented to us without Euro-centric cliché. They did not represent the 'surrender' of Greek (and by implication 'Western') rationalism to the 'indefinite' of a mystical and irrational 'Orient' as earlier scholars had thought but the culmination of the Hellenic spirit.[31] This liberal spirit was (thanks in part to the excellent Dr. Dennis House) extended not only to Patristics but to the study of pre-Greek civilizations and (albeit cautiously) to Jewish and Islamic studies.

I do not say this because the Classics department at Dalhousie was a bastion of enlightened progressivism. It was anything but. Still, *vis a vis* the older exclusions there was a great liberation of mind to be had there. There was also the sense that in Cochrane, James Doull and George Grant as in other thinkers like Northrop Frye, Emil Fackenheim and Charles Taylor there was a legitimate national tradition distinct from dominant English and American modes of philosophy.[32] This allowed an openness to con-

---

a cavalier but all too typical treatment of the textual monuments of the past. It will just not do reduce the arguments of Descartes, say, to some spurious formalization which one then pronounces 'bad'. Nor, having done so, will it do to claim that one has 'dissolved all the problems of metaphysics' forever and for all time. Yet academic philosophers in England particularly produced mountains of such pseudo-commentary on Plato, Augustine and other thinkers of central importance. I thought at the time that if ever there were books destined for the privy it was these. At any rate, a cartoon I recently saw sums up the problem of trying to reduce philosophy to a process of formal ratiocination: a student is looking at a shelf underneath the caption "books of analytic philosophy that have changed my life" . The shelf is empty.

[31] The first translations of Plotinus, Iamblichus and Proclus were made by Thomas Taylor in the 19th century and were immediately subject to virulent attack. This was because they undermined the 'pure' 'neo-classical' vision of antiquity as asserting 'reason' and 'moderation' against 'Asiatic' formlessness. For such as vision mysticism could not be a 'Greek' interest and had to be attributed to the infecting influence of an 'intuitive' and 'irrational' (dare one say effeminate?) eastern culture. This was no doubt helped along by the fact that Plotinus was Egyptian in origin.

[32] To this list could be added the Quebec born Jesuit philosopher Bernard Lonergan, whose major work Insight is a considerable achievement. Or one would were it not that for most of the last century Catholic philosophy was a world entirely onto itself.

tinental thought and German idealism that would have been unthinkable in the typical Canadian philosophy departments of the day (dominated as they were by ex-pat Americans). For example, not long before I arrived there we had hosted none other than H.G. Gadamer. Of course, there were fault-lines (not all the figures mentioned necessarily liked or admired each other) and these developed particularly over how the story was to be continued after the classical period. Doull and his pupils insisted (and still insist) that Hegel's history of freedom was the lens through which previous epochs were to be viewed. Some pushed back against this from a traditionalist Anglo-Catholic perspective. Others, such as George Grant, saw western secular modernity as culminating in a nihilistic universal technocracy inimical to reason and freedom. It was Nietzsche and Heidegger who laid bare the form of this society not Hegel. These were and remain fundamental questions and whatever we say at the end of the day about Grant and Doull it was a significant achievement on their part to create an institutional context in which they could be addressed both at Dalhousie and (later) in the school of religion at McMaster.

Now, however, I return to the present and its very different demands. Humanities at Grenfell remains in its fundamental conception a historicist project as I have laid this term out here. It uses, for instance, periodization as its fundamental pedagogic structure as it must if it is to avoid pointless eclecticism. Of course, the downside of this is that the diachronic perspective is developed at the cost of the synchronic one. The result of this is that we have a long story to tell before even getting to the 'oblique knowledges' mentioned earlier by which point we are pretty much out of breath! It is easy to say at this point that humanities should restructure to accommodate more things and this is all well and good but of course it is a council of perfection that ignores the fact that this restructuring must happen without new money and with minimal institutional commitment. How does Humanities get better without getting bigger? How will we include Asian or African knowledge in our story given that no one will ever be hired to teach those things? Shall we have one faculty member who functions as a universal dilettante? Unfortunately, we have to pick which oblique knowledges we are going to interact with synchronically and this will not be all of them. This is complicated by the fact that humanities is not a local discourse any more than philosophy is. We are bound as philosophers

---

Thomist inclined thinkers at Dalhousie did not, as far I can discern, ever interact with their counterparts at St. Mary's though they were just down the street. I should also say a word about Frye who I read very early. At the time I knew (vaguely enough it was true) that there was a group of philosophers called the Vienna circle who claimed that all meaningful assertions had to resolve into the observational language of the sciences if they were not simply analytic. If this was so, then the discourse of Frye, for whom our worldviews were constituted by mythic structures of great complexity, had to be literal nonsense. The rich content he seemed to draw from Blake, Milton and the Bible had to be some sort of illusion. I decided (for better or worse) that this was rubbish and that Carnap and co. had to be wrong. I still tend to the view that the ability to draw content out of mythology and literature is a basic test that any philosophical approach needs to pass.

and historians are to the standards of a pan-institutional and international disciplinary endeavor. This means, for instance, that whatever the community might think we, along with the philosophers, would vote no to executing Socrates. Thus, the opinion I heard one local politician express, namely that Grenfell Campus exists to serve the city of Corner Brook is flatly untrue as it must serve the discussion of an international community of scholars as well.

Still, there is one epochal confrontation that is entirely relevant to the community in which we live and that is the one between European settlers and indigenous people. I recently heard a passionate presentation by a Miq'maw artist who, after detailing the depredations of colonialism posed the question to European settlers "where did you get the idea?" Well, that is a good question and one that academic specialization is ill equipped to address. The sciences cannot address it at all as their realm is nature not history. To the extent that the answer involves 'deep-structures' of metaphysics and theology it escapes the empirical historian (who cannot *qua* historian expound the content of such notions but only note their existence) and, though the disconnect is perhaps less stark, the literary scholar (who must expound aesthetic forms and movements to some degree from *inside*).[33] It escapes the professional philosopher entirely to the extent that he is uncritically committed to a Whig history that engages only in a brisk review of 'canonical' figures before going back to brains in vats. If I might inject a bit of my own research here the story of 17th- 18th Century thought is NOT the story of Locke, Berkeley and Hume. Philosophers seem particularly maladroit at engaging with historical questions. As people who deal with 'timeless' problems they recognize the history of their discipline but not its historicity.[34] The difference between Plato

---

[33] In keeping with Aristotle's observation that myth is higher than history it is part of the literary scholar's task to understand the mind that operates in the text (which is not, please note, always identical to the 'mind' of the empirical 'author') and to this extent she deals with things like theological or philosophical positions, religious devotions, erotic conventions, social/political mores and so on as these animate the art works she studies. It would be an odd account of Milton that said nothing about Protestantism or, more to the point, said any old thing about Protestantism regardless of what was in the sources. To this degree the literary scholar, as a student of 'mythoi', comes closest to what I mean by the humanities scholar.

[34] I don't mean to be facetious here as the question is as fundamental as it is vexing. Philosophy does indeed aim at un-tensed knowledge and should aim at such knowledge. It is absurd to expect every philosophical claim about Plato or Locke to be embedded in 30 pages of social history: this kind of 'empirical' historicism is just as much an abstraction as the a-historicism of certain professional philosophers. That philosophy is (in part) a trans-historical conversation is itself a historical fact and for this reason there is a history of philosophy over and above social or material history. At the same time, we cannot act as if historical epochs do not determine what and how we see. It is just not the case that we can pluck 'arguments' out of Aristotle or Plato or Leibniz and evaluate them neutrally without considering our own metaphysical and textual horizons in relation to theirs (as for so long Anglo-American philosophy uncritically did-my own earliest graduate work focused on the basic incomprehension that results when the question of dialogic form is ignored in Plato and he is simply, and abusively, mined for 'arguments'). How eternity is mediated to time greatly exercised St. Augustine and it ought still to exercise us when we consider something even so basic as the fact

and Russell is not that Plato failed at being Russell. Here social scientists have a bit of a head start post-Kuhn. They recognize that the history of science, for instance, is not an uncomplicated tale of progress or regress towards or away from the current state of science. It contains radical shifts of perspective in which the answers alter because the underlying questions and assumptions do.[35] Again, Archimedes is not trying and failing to be Einstein. There is between them an epochal transformation (perhaps beginning with the Baconian equation of knowledge and power) which alters fundamentally what scientists do and how they approach basic questions.

Indeed, Ms. Tremblatt, the artist mentioned above, is in a better position to see this than many an entrenched academic specialist. Indigenous peoples are well aware that beneath their various sectarian differences (conservative vs. liberal vs. Marxist etc.) there is a European settler 'story'. They know this because they have suffered it as an external and destructive fate. They see from outside the very thing which, in Humanities, we are trying to see from inside. If it is true, and I think it is, that no one discipline can answer Ms. Tremblatt's question comprehensively it becomes legitimate to ask in what context they get to pool their resources and under whose aegis they do so. Well, the ideal result would be a cadre of dedicated 'intellectual historians' who addressed these meta questions while the individual specialists went about their work. Some of these people would have a background in indigenous studies others not. However

---

that the immorality of slavery, a proposition utterly obvious to us, was unknown to entire civilizations. Clearly, a moral insight like belief in the equality of women is not an 'object' sitting out there in the world hidden in plain sight for millennia. Such insights are the product of a free creative projection. They do not result from a passive 'registering' of external 'facts' about the world. Where was geometry before Euclid? In the world one might say but the pure lines and surfaces of geometry are most pointedly NOT in the world. Yet at the same time what we bring about in our freedom is not therefore arbitrary or adventitious, there is an underlying necessity or rightness to the moral insights so uncovered. Creation is also disclosure. Reason comes to be in history. Of course, if I could articulate adequately how and why this is so I would be a genuine philosopher rather than a provocateur.

[35]The social sciences, of course, tend to assume the Marxist standpoint for which a cultural 'superstructure' rests on a base of social, economic and other power relations. One might conclude from this that sociology, say, is after all the queenly science, as all the content in the superstructure can (putatively) be resolved into the base. Frankly, I do not think the history of philosophy (to use an example pertinent to my own research) can be explained in these terms. Philosophy may not sail effortlessly above its social substratum but it does not simply sink under it either. Philosophical traditions maintain themselves over the most radical social transformations for centuries and to that extent there is a 'timeless colloquy' that constitutes the conversation that is philosophy (evident in the fact that these discussions have an internal logic which close reading can illuminate). It is to the description of these trans-historical 'traditions' that much of my own work is dedicated. I also have here to prefer Kuhn over Marx (or at least one strain in Marx). Radical shifts in ways of seeing are not the autonomic result of underlying 'forces' but involve as well leaps of creative intuition. Changes in how we look at things happen all the time in daily life and if the new synthesis cannot be resolved into a preceding analysis that does not make the shift arbitrary or irrational as critics of Kuhn often assume. To use an example from J.H. Newman, it is perfectly reasonable to distinguish the twins Peter and Paul though one cannot break down such a judgement into smaller ones.

as this is beyond what Grenfell Campus is able or even willing to do we need a different conception. To use an image from Plato, if we can't have the best city described in the *Republic* we can have the next best city described in the *Laws*. This would be a program in which a rotating cast of specialists would present their material on whatever period was under discussion leaving a 'facilitator' to coordinate to following discussion. Of course, it would be good if there were another (indigenous) facilitator for some discussions. In fact, I would regard it as essential. I must emphasize however that I do not have any pat answer as to how such a project should work or what its result would even be. It would be an experiment in 'melding horizons' with an unpredictable result. This makes humanities (especially 'indigenized humanities') an uncomfortable proposition and it is easy to see why one would abandon it for the direct practical certainty of grooming entrepreneurs. To borrow a phrase from the French philosopher Marcel, 'problems' with 'determinate solutions' are a blessed relief when we are confronted by uncertainty and self-doubt. This is why video games and Sudoku are so popular. The questions posed in humanities may be a 'meta-question' too many especially as the question itself is only imperfectly defined and has to be worked out in process (you can't learn to swim by flapping your arms on land). I conclude by noting however, that I am not interested in imposing on anyone a question they have no interest in asking. It is indigenous students themselves who are asking questions as well non –indigenous students who carry the burden of settler heritage. We might then consider some frameworks in which to address their concerns that make use of our current resources.

5 DIVERSITY IN THE HUMANITIES: SOME REFLECTIONS

The issue of diversity of representation is a vexed one for Universities as a whole but it is more so for programs in fields like philosophy and intellectual history where the sheer preponderance of canonical material written by men of a Greco-Roman or Christian European background creates a deeply ingrained bias against authors of other genders or cultural origins. There are fields where this is not the case. The student of 20th century literature for instance has a great many wonderful writers of a non-European background to call upon. A student of contemporary poetry benefits from the fact that women have produced, over the last hundred years or so, a body of major verse that compares in every respect with that produced by men. Is there anything lost if a professor assigns a poem by H.D. over a poem by Auden? I do not think so. Unfortunately, not all programs are so blessed. Below I will detail the challenges faced by my own program, an interdisciplinary study of intellectual history. To begin however I wish to clarify some basic points. I want to make some distinctions concerning the nature of equity and how I think the concept applies to this question. Further, I want to clarify the concept of diversity, which is multi-faceted and must, as it were, be approached from a number of directions simultaneously.

First things first: What is humanities as we practice it at Grenfell? I will repeat what I said above. Beginning in the 19th century and moving into the 20th and 21st centuries we (in the western world at least) have come to think of humanity, nature and even perhaps god in terms of their 'historicity'. What do I mean by this? I mean that we do not conceive truth or reality as simply static and timeless but as developing in and through a process of change. Our awareness has developed and changed over time through various landmarks and watersheds that occur in history. There is a history of the human intellect and a history of the human spirit that manifests itself in philosophy, religion, the arts, politics and science as these alter and develop over time. Humanities is the discipline that tries to tell this story in an integrated way and as such crosses the boundaries between disciplines. Its aim is a comprehensive knowledge of the history of intellect and sensibility of human beings in the west and beyond and a critical and reflective attitude towards the historical dimension of experience.[36] This means that our program (at least) is historical in focus and that our emphasis is on the history of ideas. This means as well that our concern is with text though text can be taken broadly to mean not only literary text but visual, aural and even material text. Our approach to text is, as befits our subject matter, hermeneutic. An essential question we face is who is to be represented in the story we tell and it is this question I wish to address in this essay.

Let me begin with an axiom. Diversity is a good thing not just for pragmatic reasons or in terms of its effects but because it is a question of justice: the nature of the call to diversity is, to use the language of ethics, deontological rather than teleological. Diversity in a workplace is necessary, for instance, because all human beings deserve a chance at meaningful employment. This 'equality of opportunity' can be said to be achieved when, barring variables, some rough equality of result exists. Now I will lay down another axiom: in education equality of opportunity means that no person should be excluded from the curriculum or classroom discussion based on their gender, sexual orientation, religion or ethic and cultural background. This equality of opportunity can be said to exist when, barring variables, there is some rough equality of voices in the classroom. I say 'rough' equality because not every variable can (or should) be predicted or controlled for. To use a phrase from Plato: this is an area where necessity must be under the wise persuasion of the good. However, it is part of recognizing the full personhood of others to attend to their thoughts and experiences whenever they are relevant to a discussion or line of inquiry and whenever they achieve the necessary depth of insight and power of expression.

Furthermore, the determination of this 'rough equality' is twofold. Firstly, it is subject to a quantitative measure. One oriental text in ten years is not diversity. We can then say very definitely when equality does not exist. However, any quantitative measure of equality must also take into account qualitative factors. The spirit of a classroom cannot always be judged from a headcount of texts. Is a professor who teaches Mary Wollstoncraft only to ridicule her contributing to equality? Is a professor who teaches the *Oresteia* and thereby inspires a deeper reflection on gen-

---

[36]This raises the question of the unity of knowledge. In the Middle Ages knowledge was a pyramid that converged in the apex of revealed theology. All other forms of knowledge were propaedeutic to participation in God's knowledge of himself as revealed in sacred scripture. They were steps on the ladder of a spiritual itinerary. This was a demand both of Hebraic revelation and of the ancient philosophical tradition as summed up in Plotinus and Proclus. Writers like Rene Guenon have deplored the breakup of this synthesis and the consequent degeneration of knowledge into meaningless specialization and dogmatic pragmatism. (2004; 44-45) They may well be correct however it is a given that we inhabit a secular university and in such an institution the integration of knowledge must be historical and not theological: we can do no more than open the possibility of a divine order. This means the order of knowledge is constituted as narrative and if we cannot uncritically employ a Whiggish, Marxist, Hegelian or even Heideggerian narrative in a new globalized context we must formulate an alternative one: we need to articulate, if you like, a new theology of history.

der and power among his or her students not contributing to it? Thus, it will always be easier to judge when diversity is being violated than when it is being honored and this is another fundamental limitation. As Aristotle might say, determining the degree of equality in a classroom is a matter of *phronesis* or contextual judgment. It is matter for ethical reflection not mathematical determination. This however, is a point to which I will recur below. For now, let me point out that much that happens in the classroom depends, by default, on the judgment of individual instructors. What is more, much also depends on the student whose agency and autonomy we are building up as educators: a student may fail to connect with a work of post-colonial criticism yet gain real insight into the dynamics of colonial power from reading the *Tempest*. There is no adjusting or accounting for such idiosyncrasies of personal development.

Now I wish to lay down some more axioms. I have said that diversity is a fundamental value but what do I mean by diversity? This is not an easy question to answer for one often gets the sense that in the contemporary academy some diversities are more diverse than others. I do not hold this position. For me, a diverse program is one where no voice is excluded in principle and it is recognized that any voice can, in principle, contribute to the discussion.[37] In this I stand firmly in the tradition of Mill's *On Liberty*. Again, I think this spirit is clearly manifested in a classroom where there are, in practice, many voices are present. Voices come from many places and so diversity must embrace many different things. Let me lay these out. One demand of diversity is that we include the voices of women. No professor should make the assumption that a female author is, qua female, any less worthy of consideration than a male one. Another form of diversity is racial or ethnic: no professor should exclude a voice on the grounds that it is African American, Japanese, Aboriginal etc. A third form of diversity is cultural. No voice should be excluded on the grounds that it is Islamic or Jewish as opposed to Christian. A Confucian perspective is in principle as good as a western liberal one in terms of its capacity to generate insight on the part of students. What is more, all these voices deserve to be heard on the grounds that they are human voices. Conversely, there cannot,

---

[37] There seems to be an operating assumption that diversity is defined by exclusion; the diversities to be recognized are those which have been objects of conscious or unconscious oppression and exclusion. This is a fine principle as far as it goes though it tends to be selective in operation. Evangelical Christians are not considered 'diverse' in this sense as they loudly and often complain though their perspectives are systematically excluded from the domain of academic discourse outside the special context of seminaries or denominational schools. This, alas, is a considerable component of the 'Trump' phenomenon. It too is reasonable as far as it goes though, compared to other groups, the level and scale of discrimination against Evangelicals does not rise to the level of a moral crisis. They are not going hungry and no one is beating them in the streets. I know some Evangelicals who will resent this observation but as far as I can tell it is a fair and accurate assessment. At any rate, in my own program there is certainly room for 'un-diverse diversities' an example of which is considering the Byzantine culture of Eastern Europe in our courses on the Middle Ages. As Greece and its people have been treated with such contempt by their Western Christian creditors there may be more than historical nostalgia in this consideration.

except under special pedagogical circumstances, be any willed exclusion of voices on the grounds that they are male, western or Christian. Thus, as a regulative ideal, I assert that the best classroom, course or program in one in which the maximum number of perspectives is heard consistent with the course or program having structure and focus and not being a mere cacophony.

Of course no such ideal classroom exists or ever will exist: like Kant's Kingdom of Ends it can be approached only asymptotically and over time. Thus, I have laid out my basic axioms and indicated the ways in which they must be qualified or hedged. All these qualifications and hedges are in light of one deeper principle or fundamental axiom: our ultimate aim as educators is to produce insight into self, society, nature, history and, if our students are spiritually inclined, into the divine. I say this because insight into these things is what our students need from us and what we are obligated to provide them with. Thus, our primary ethical aim is the individuation and self-realization of each student we teach as far as self-realization and individuation are intellectual. For instance, if a student happens to be an Atheist or a Hindu it is one of my aims to make them a more reflective Atheist or Hindu. Personally, I never make it my aim to convert a student from any perspective to any other though naturally, a white supremacist or anti-Semite who becomes reflective about their position will immediately drop it as these positions have no reflective basis.[38]

Now I will address some of the problems and limitations (the variables mentioned above) specific to an interdisciplinary program in the Humanities followed by an account of how these limitations may be progressively overcome. I will consider this from the standpoint of gender diversity though what I say should be taken as applying to other forms of diversity as well. The aim of the program in which I teach is three-fold. Firstly, our program exists to educate students in the basic tensions of human existence: authority vs. freedom. tradition vs. innovation, justice vs. revenge, morality vs. self-interest, liberty vs. tyranny, duty vs. inclination and so on (everyone can make their own list!).[39] Secondly, the aim of our pro-

---

[38]See Wills "Dear Whites" in Believing Weird Things.

[39] Sometimes the critic of traditional Humanities will land herself straight into the oldest questions and the most traditional answers. Linda Smith for instance has a theology of history of just the kind we attempt to elucidate. History (she tells us) "... is the story of the powerful and how they became powerful, and then how they use their power to keep them in a position in which they can dominate others." (35) Hobbes could not have put this better but there is more for Smith also tells us that indigenous peoples are currently struggling to "transform history into justice" . (35) Of course if the first statement is true then the latter task is impossible and it is a good question how anyone could ever have conceived of it. The myth that reason, truth and justice cannot enter history is, of course, the Gnostic myth and it is as ancient as it is powerful. But the acute reader will have noticed that I am struggling with the same question throughout all these essays and trying to give a different answer grounded in a different myth, the Christian one (or at least a Christian one shorn of Gnostic elements). I would begin by pointing out, with Hannah Arendt, that domination is only one iteration of power which can be constellated in many different ways not all of

gram is to introduce students to the body of reflection that exists on these tensions. This is on the assumption that something like Plato's myth of Gyges or his analogy of the sun, line and cave are of proven pedagogical efficacy (having survived over millennia). Thirdly, we try to communicate to students that our knowledge of these tensions is mediated and constituted historically. There are crucial watersheds in human self-understanding where justice comes to be understood as justice or charity as charity and these set the basic context for any informed discussion. Justice is not just a thing in the sky that falls from heaven. It is something that was (in some difficult to specify sense) created/disclosed at a certain date by Aeschylus and Plato as charity and the absolute regard for persons as ends was created/disclosed by the revelation of god as agape in the Gospels. Was there a 'self' in 300,000 B.C.E? No, no more than 'mathematics' exists for those indigenous Amazonian societies who find no occasion to count past three. It was around the third or fourth century of the common-era that people became selves. Does it behoove students to know this? Yes, because otherwise they would assume that justice or charity or freedom or self-hood are simply things immediately given and this is not to be reflective about how the world is.[40] All the values I adverted to above as governing education and diversity have at one point in human history simply not existed. This is true of values even more basic: a fact we are reminded of when we see that the hero of Homer's *Odyssey* sees nothing wrong with a bit of piracy now and then and hangs his maids without protest from anyone.

This raises for us the problem of canonicity. Every discipline has as a matter of practice some rough notion of canonicity however much it may decry canons in theory. Any course on gender theory, for instance, will include Butler or Cisoux before it includes Louisa May Alcott or the blessed Edith Stein. The historical mediation of core questions is often (though

---

which are morally equivalent. If this is true though we may say, after all, that necessity may be the slow birth of freedom and that justice and reason may have, when all is said and done, some historical embodiment in however roughhewn a form. We can't transform history into justice if by this we mean replacing one with the other, that is Utopianism. All that is not heaven, though, is not therefore hell.

[40]Historicity will never be popular as it cuts against both the pragmatism of the technological elite (historicity has no cash value) and the moralism of progressives. Both in their own way are 'whig' historians for whom the past is a diminished version of the present. This attitude is no doubt pre-reflective in most cases but it is assumed in the stance that takes on the past primarily as an object of moral evaluation and (its inevitable corollary) denunciation. Historicity though does not judge the past by the standards of the present because it is asking where present standards came from in the first place. Historicity does not assume that values like feminism or equality simply lay ready to hand and that the Ancients were too churlish or too blind to notice them (though gender equality appeared to Aristophanes and Plato as a comic hypothesis at least). It assumes that such values were the product of a long, slow process of construction and discovery and that it is a waste of everyone's time to put Odysseus on posthumous trial for his piracy when we could be studying the history of the law of the sea. Of course, we must also recognize that reconstitution of the past is only one moment in a dyadic process which also involves bringing the past into the present, a process that does not leave the past untouched: as one of my colleagues put it, T.S. Eliot had a profound influence on Shakespeare!

not exclusively) textual.[41]   Accordingly, students of intellectual history or philosophy will tend to recur to the texts of Plato, Aristotle, Dante, Shakespeare, Descartes, Kant and so on in so far as these texts encapsulate historically epochal movements or events.   Of course canons are never really fixed. We no longer, as the Renaissance did, take the tragedies of Seneca as models of Drama. Few in the 17th Century would have granted Shakespeare the stature we accord him now. Nonetheless there are broad determinations we can make: I can imagine Demaris Masham or Ann Conway becoming part of the philosophy canon if enough students of early modern philosophy take up their work. I cannot imagine Shakespeare being replaced by hacks like Henry Pye or Colly Cibber. Though the borders of the canon may wander like planets it remains the case that a student of Middle English literature today will turn to Chaucer before Gower exactly as in the 19th Century. This is as much as to say that, prescinding from how it is that we arrive at this judgment, some texts are in fact better than others (aesthetically, philosophically, pedagogically and so on).

I am happy to say that where my program is concerned the 'Canon' (which too many people tend to be stiff about) has the opportunity to undergo a marvelous expansion on three fronts in particular.[42]   In this essay I will discuss the first: gender. In Heroic Greece or the Hittite Empire gender equality as we understand it did not exist. It is scarcely possible to say if its absence was felt. Penelope was annoyed at the suitors for sure but was she annoyed by her status as an Ithacan woman? However, beginning in the 17th century (perhaps) women like Mary Astell created/disclosed what we now call gender equity. Having been created/disclosed, its absence has been felt not only by generations of women but increasingly by many men. Indeed, as a moral demand it has become as objective as oxygen or microbes (which were created/disclosed a bit later!). Thus, hardly anyone denies it on a theoretical level however much they may kick against the pricks in practice. Thus, the study of humanities now has a whole new watershed or epochal event to enshrine in its canon. It is no longer conceivable to me that my students can complete their studies without a close consideration of Wollstoncraft or Woolf not to mention more recent theorists. Feminist literature is now canonical and can no more be skipped over than Plato on Justice or Dante on love. This, I suppose, is hardly a controversial point. Perhaps I am even insulting the intelligence of my reader by stating something so obvious but I hope my desire to be

---

[41] I try to understand text in the broadest possible sense to include visual art, music and even tools and artefacts as 'text'. Text is whatever is subject to being read. Humanities then concerns the reading of artificial and conventional signs as science concerns the reading of natural signs. This, at bottom, is the old medieval distinction between the book of god and the book of nature, suitably secularized.

[42] Besides coming to terms with gender students of the humanities must recognize that much of what is deep and vital in contemporary culture is expressed in forms like television or hip-hop which in the past would have been dismissed as 'popular' forms not worthy the consideration of serious minded scholars. The same goes for the insight that Islamic or Confucian forms of culture are not just lesser anticipations of the West but alternative figurations of order worthy of consideration for themselves.

as thorough as I can be in this essay may stand as some excuse.

This, however, leads to a more vexing question: that of representation and here we are on more controversial territory. One natural result of the Feminist revolution is the desire to have more women contributing to the conversation as after all any discussion that includes more voices is thereby rendered less parochial. This is a challenge for our program for it cuts across one of our fundamental goals: to think origins and foundings in their primary depth. This entails a deep conversation with works from Antiquity and the Middle Ages a great many of which have male authors. This is a conversation in which reader and text mutually question each other in the hopes of carrying forward what is vital in the past (and not everything is!) in order to expand our understanding in the present. We might speak here of Gadamer's understanding of interpretation as a melding of horizons. The crucial point however is that conversation is mutual. The text is not a dead, reified object we dissect like a pig's heart in biology class but a conversation partner. It is not a thing to be learned about but a partner to be learned from. This learning is not a dead submission to the authority of the text but an understanding of self and world that is the student's own however much it may be mediated by the encounter with the text. In this process texts from other civilizations and time periods are uniquely effective for their very otherness forces the reader into an encounter with his or her most fundamental beliefs about the world.[43]

How then is a desire for inclusivity to be reconciled with the other pedagogical aims of our program given the fundamental fact that many of the time periods we study are male dominated? We cannot do a headcount of authors for there are some periods and some themes (like epic literature or ancient drama) where this simply is not possible. Moreover, a head count of authors would be an artificial exercise anyway for many of the ancient and medieval texts with which I deal do not have authors in the sense that we understand the term. In what sense was the Hebrew Bible 'written' by an 'author' we can identify as 'a man'? Another problem is that ethnic, cultural and religious diversities must be recognized as well. This may involve hard choices in the limited time-frame of a semester long course and these choices can only be left up to the judgment of the individual instructor based on his pedagogical aims for a particular course. Further there are biases grounded in taste and expertise. A Medievalist who has no time for mysticism and devotional literature will have a rough go of it for figures like Julian of Norwich, Marjory Kemp, Catherine of

---

[43]This of course distinguishes Humanities radically from fields like History or Religious Studies. Practitioners of the latter especially fear that any attempt to interact with 'text' as something besides an empirical object risks collapsing into theology. A 'scientific' stance towards text (broadly defined) is thus inconsistent with a hermeneutic engagement with its meaning which is, I was once told, crypto-theology. This objectifying, non-participatory stance towards objects of knowledge has been severely criticized by feminists like Helen Longino as a poor way to do science. It is, as far as I can tell, no more successful elsewhere. To be fair though, Hermeneutics is not just crypto-theology it is theology re-inscribed as secular practice and the fact neither the natural nor social sciences can effectively banish it ought to give the doctrinaire secularist pause.

Sienna and Marguerite Porette produced an imposing body of work in this area that has no rival in other fields. I myself taught a course on love whose medieval component consisted of a close reading of Dante though Marie de France might have been an equally apt choice. Why? Well, I happen to be very comfortable with Dante but was, at the time, rather weak on romance literature. At the end of the day all of us, and this is particularly true of new instructors, will tend to teach the things we know well.

In a university that has graduate programs these limitations can of course be made good as students specialize later in their program and move beyond the 'classic' authors such as Locke or Shakespeare. My program, however, makes no assumption that its students will move on to graduate degrees. We assume that the education we provide is the education (in the liberal sense) that our students will receive. Thus, we are under extra pressure to 'get it right'. Part of getting things right is of course giving our students the best texts that we can and here we get to the even more vexing question of quality. Is Barbara Strozzi a great composer? Is Ethyl Smyth? I have greatly enjoyed works by both. I have read poems by Anna Laetitia Barbauld that I sincerely admire. Should we be devoting precious classroom time to introducing these figures to first and second year students? Are these figures too 'minor'? Is 'major' vs. 'minor' a relevant pedagogical concern? I do not have pat answers for these questions. With male authors we have a certain intersubjective agreement to appeal to: it is idle to argue Mozart is a bad composer or Shakespeare a talentless hack. Unfortunately, this consensus has had little opportunity to form around some of the figures mentioned above owing to their historical eclipse (due in some measure at least to prejudice against the creativity and intellect of women). [44]

Is the situation then dire? Are we being asked to square a circle? Are we faced with the choice of reproducing the injustices of the past in the classroom or having no real conversation with other times and places except on our own narrow terms? I don't think so. Accordingly, I will now discuss the problem of representation. Of course, I could argue that women are probably represented equally in the classroom proportional to the amount of text they have produced but this would be a pat answer for women have produced what they did under conditions of (sometimes) terrible constraint that did not apply to men. So, how are we to make some just allowance for this in the humanities? This is all the more pressing in that an interdisciplinary program cannot be built on random eclecticism. Some narrative or other must structure our consideration of such diverse material as Platonic dialogues, Shakespeare plays, hip hop albums and post-colonial critiques of the West. In the last century this was more easily done, for instance at King's College in Halifax. The story of humanities

---

[44]Oddly many of these authors were known and admired in their own day. Mary Wroth was considered a superb poet by her contemporaries for instance. Yet when the study of literature is regularized as a university discipline and a canon is formed authors like Wroth or Mary Pembroke disappear from it.

was the story of freedom, particularly of Western freedom as it issues in the modern state. This is the story Hegel told in his *Philosophy of History* and it runs from the birth of subjective freedom among the ancient Greeks and culminates in freedom objectively realized in the nation states of modern Europe and North America. This story is not negligible and many critics of colonialism, for instance, assume some version of it: after all the West has, in their view, selfishly kept its freedoms to itself and refused to extend it to 'others' in the third world and elsewhere. Many of these thinkers turn to the development and extension of Hegel's story in the writings of Karl Marx[45]. There are as well the many versions of Feminism that depend on classical liberalism, psychoanalysis, Marxism, post structuralism and so on. These may also be taken as a continuation and deepening of the 'Western' conversation to include a larger cross section of the human race (50% !). Feminisms which intersect with various forms of anti-colonialism, queer theory and so on may *broadly* be construed in this way too though the question is already becoming more complex.[46]

Yet there seem to me to be factors that militate against telling this story in the straightforward way it was, for instance, told to me at my alma mater King's College. For Hegel there are modes of spirit that belong to the past: religions of Law like Judaism and Islam have, for instance, been superseded by the spiritual freedom disclosed by the Christian revelation. Deep moral relationships to land and environment experienced by indigenous peoples are not accommodated by the bourgeois freedoms of the West. There are cultures that do not even inhabit the secularized liner time of western Europeans. For long as we, as white North Americans, were struggling to understand ourselves this was perhaps not so great an issue. However,

---

[45]Though Marx is having a moment (and rightly so) it is Hegel who is more foundational where a program like ours is concerned. To put it bluntly, historical materialism is a contradiction in terms strictly speaking. To the extent that something is historical it is to that extent no longer material. We are in the realm of signs not things. To revert to the example of geometry: one can explain the use of geometry in terms of social substructures but one cannot explicate one bit of its content or the connections that constitute it as a system. This is why social science cannot supplant hermeneutics any more than biology or physics can. One of the things that has a history will be Mind (whether one wants to tell Hegel's story about that or a different one). One sign of this is the fact that a myth like the story of Oedipus does not lose significance after the social relations that produced it disappear but in fact gains immeasurably in meaning as it is told and retold and adapted and twisted into myriad shapes. Sometimes it is Marx who needs turning on his head not Hegel and here is one case. Influence is not deterministic causality and if social factors shape what we see by predetermining the questions we ask and the answers we will accept they do not do so reductively. Under-determination and openness reign here as elsewhere: freedom and necessity are co-relatives neither of which can be collapsed into the other.

[46]As a student of mine ruefully pointed out "... most of the sources used in this paper for the critical dismantling of Western narratives... are still, for the most part, coming from Western theorists as part of a Western post-structuralist approach." (Dussan,15) It is not the case (surely) that the overturning of hegemony in a post-colonialist context is just the substitution of one iteration of theory (post-structuralism) for another (Marxism or Liberalism). It involves also listening to voices from outside the academic context whose language may be religion or myth as much as theory. (see Wills "Why I am not a Rastaman" in Believing Weird Things)

we are no longer the sole parties to the discussion. The other is now here. There are students among us deeply devoted to the tradition of Islam. There are students of African heritage and indigenous students seeking their rightful place in modern Canada. What is their stake in the triumphalist story of western freedom? The problem is that we do not know; this story is currently writing itself and, as Hegel himself said, the owl of Minerva flies at dusk.[47] This leaves us in the position of not quite knowing what story we are telling and why. Still, we know whatever story we were going to tell will involve more speakers than it has in the past. While the West may have developed the story of freedom it no longer owns it if it ever did. It will involve the historical voices of women in a way that a traditional emphasis on canon has precluded. We must now consider how this will occur.

The first practical step is to use what we have for women have produced many texts recognized as great in spite of all the impediments to doing so. No course on early modern Europe will suffer from studying the *Autobiography* of St. Theresa. This will scarcely get us where we want to go except in the 20th and 21st centuries but it is a start. Secondly, I revert to the discussion above. We should err on the side of generosity in the inclusion of neglected and forgotten female artists and authors. I quite admire Elizabeth Carey's *Tragedy of Mariam*. I could not possibly tell you if it is 'great' as opposed to simply 'good'. It does, however, shed light on the subjectivity of women in the 17th century and might well make an interesting period piece. Why not give it a try? Perhaps we will find it resonates more deeply with the contemporary reader than at first blush we

---

[47]It is Kant, in his third formulation of the categorical imperative, who outlines the notion of a universal kingdom of ends in which each member is both subject and sovereign: responsible only to the self-legislation of their own reason considered as practical. It is Hegel and Marx who seek to understand this notion as the guiding principle of the human world which becomes the self-realization of freedom in history. The author in fact sees himself as broadly in this tradition as nothing in the Hegelian history of freedom precludes it taking a post-bourgeois and even post-European form. That said there are issues of a more fundamental kind when we confront the ontologies of indigenous peoples, say, with the radical demand of modern idealism that the world be a moment in self-positing of 'mind' or 'consciousness'. On this point see Lilburn "The Ethical Significance of the Human Relationship to Place" . Lilburn looks to the older contemplative traditions of Orthodox Christianity and Neo-Platonism to articulate a sense of place as that from which the human receives itself. Here he reprisinates (if I read him correctly) an older platonic notion of soul as that which receives itself from reversion to a higher cause which transcends it. Freedom is a gift received from the other not a radical act of self- positing. These, however, are deeper waters than we need swim in at present. I will note though that one thing humanities does need to be more cautious about are Whiggish claims such as the false notion that Western nations have abolished slavery. Certain capitalist enterprises (especially industrial agriculture) cannot deliver the low prices required by western consumers without slave labor whether that take the form of third world sweatshops, the prison industrial complex in the U.S. or the exploitation and physical/sexual abuse of migrant laborers. These enterprises have always required slaves and will require slaves for as long as they exist. Further, requiring them they will always find them in one form or another. The Ancient Greeks held that, contrary to Marx' dictum, there will always be human beings who exist as conditions for the autonomy of other human beings: no one has yet proven them wrong.

had supposed. Perhaps not but if nothing is ventured nothing is gained. One thing I have noted in my own scholarly work is that scores of doors can be opened if one is willing to risk consideration of the so-called 'minor' authors. One of these things is that 'minor' status has been handed out to thinkers and writers based on prejudices we no longer really hold. For example, the Cambridge Platonists (among whom were a number of female thinkers) have been excluded from the history of philosophy on the grounds that the epistemology of Locke pointed to the 'true' direction of English philosophy which was in essence empirical. Absent this prejudice there is no reason whatsoever to accord the works of Norris, Cudworth or any other committed Platonist *automatic* second class status. In how many instances have un-thought philosophical or aesthetic pre-judgments condemned female authors to obscurity who we would now find quite vital given access to their texts? There is only one way to find out and that is to read them. We may find they bore or repel us but then again we may find they don't.

Finally, we can introduce a measure of realism into this discussion by remembering that the point of it is to help our students: we are not *simply* trying to satisfy some abstract standard of equity but also trying to educate actual people. Even if I intended as an instructor to use the classroom as a venue for presenting the voice of reason and high culture as a male-gendered voice I am not sure what the effect of this would be. My students are not authoritarians. They do not take the voice of Plato or Kant as a voice of authority of any kind and certainly not a voice of paternal authority. Almost without exception I have to win them over to material I am presenting. My students, male or female, show this spirit almost to a fault. My female students face many obstacles to asserting agency and autonomy in their lives but in spite of this they seem able to take or leave from the texts I give them on their own terms. As readers at least they are free to engage with the most ancient along with the most contemporary things. This should remind us that freedom is an event that transpires between reader and text. A liberating text is one that is relevant to the challenges to personal agency faced by a given student. To a woman, say, from a strict fundamentalist background this could indeed be the *Second Sex*. It could equally be a dry work of biblical scholarship or a biography of Albert Schweitzer. Another student struggling with addiction might find liberation in the *Koran*. There are students who are oppressed by factors that are systemic or corporate. For many others forms of oppression might be more personal.

Given that this is the case perhaps we partly mis-identify the problem and the opportunity by focusing overmuch on the question of texts. Equally important is what happens between teacher and student. To what extent do I as an instructor enable or model the kind of discriminating judgment that allows us to make intelligent contemporary use of whatever texts we happen to be reading? What is the kind of judgment that is able to appropriately contextualize the textual monuments of the past in the present with its very different moral demands? This, at least, is the primary issue for me as the study of the past is absolutely intrinsic to our program. This ability to obtain and apply a refined historical sense is an essential part of any critical culture. It is indeed one of the primary forms of freedom as it teaches us to avoid parochialism in time as Anthropology, say, teaches us to avoid parochialism in space. Ultimately, it teaches that any culture of criticism is grounded first in self-criticism which is the first form of critical freedom. This is one aspect of our program that perhaps I have under-emphasized. Chemistry is not a critique of Chemistry in that things fundamental to the discipline are assumed rather than argued for. Humanities at Grenfell has, since its inception, considered itself as a possible object of critique. I have attempted, in this essay, a critique of hidebound notions of canonicity that are still strongly entrenched in my discipline and are still reflected in the program I teach. At the same time though any critique is itself a possible object of critique and notions of canonicity are essential to a program that seeks to tell a coherent story about the past (if the canon is not sacred no particular critique of it is sacred either).

This story includes, of necessity, canonical primary texts as its main locus and history has not distributed the production of these in an equitable manner.[48] History, as anyone remotely cognizant of it can attest, is grossly unfair. It is, as Hegel says, a slaughter bench and like evolution, is prodigiously wasteful. It can elevate the grossly undeserving to places of prominence. This, no doubt, is why certain people distrust the historicist stance as I have laid it out here as a threat to absolute judgements about truth or morality. Scientists and moralizers are not friends of historicity for reasons with which one can sympathize if not exactly agree. There is no way around certain authors if one wants to understand the world in any depth. Still, Humanities is not bound to any particular list of these beyond obvious choices like Aristotle or Jane Austen. Things can drop out of the canon as well as fall into it. This has happened many times in the past. Will Durant's once popular *Story of Philosophy* devoted many pages to George Santayana; a name of which I am sure the majority of my readers are completely unaware. Canons, if I may use an image, can rotate (even cyclically). For this reason and the one's given above it seems to me at least that we can meet what seemed at first to be two incompatible needs: fidelity to textual traditions of immeasurable cultural significance (the *Tenach*, Greek Tragedy etc.) and openness to the liberation of perspective that can result from a commitment to diversity and pluralism. Let me make a final point however. One of the ultimate conditions a free engagement with the cultural monuments of the past is freedom from (to

---

[48]The use of secondary literature is, of course, one way to introduce a more equitable selection of texts. There are two problems here however. We could use such materials to speak about the Greeks (say) generally but then our program would shade into the inquiry that we call history. If, however, we use secondary literature to speak about the texts of Sophocles or Homer then it would be a basic abdication of intellectual responsibility not to read them.

some degree at least) the oppressions of the past. I don't think Marx was joking when he said that in the post-capitalist world we would be reading Homer in the morning and fishing in the afternoon because not only are we now free to fish for ourselves we are free in relation to Homer as well. We may never attain a point beyond history where the entire human past becomes our free possession in this way but any defense of a historical canon must also be a defense of a society where all stand in the same free relation to that canon.

6 DOGMA

Dogma is a word only ever used in a pejorative sense. What is more, dogmas are things that other people have; I, being the rational enlightened fellow I am, have justified beliefs. Some of these beliefs may be certain, others may be only probable or plausible. Still, all my beliefs exist within a structure of explanation and justification. Since the demands of reason are the same for all rational beings it must be that people whose beliefs differ from mine do not have such a structure. Their beliefs must be the product of some emotional or psychological motive, they must have a blind spot, a *scotosis* as it were. Their beliefs are dogmas held only on external authority or personal whim, never examined or critically questioned. This notion is itself a fine example of a dogma (in the negative sense) as even a cursory examination of the matter reveals that there is no human endeavor that does not, at some crucial juncture, rest on a dogma. Dogmas are usually associated with religion though religion is hardly their exclusive domain. No scientist opens her lab without a dogmatic belief in the basic reliability of her senses. No scientist ever questions or critically examines this belief because going through the process of Cartesian doubt before every experiment would be a waste of time. Science could not exist without bracketing such fundamental questions. In the same way the ordinary business of Judaism could not exist without bracketing the question of the divine origin of the Torah. Most of the time both the scientist and the Jewish person are dogmatists. This does not preclude the scientist having fears of a deceiving demon or the Jewish person questioning the Torah in light of the holocaust, say. My point is simply that they will do this at different times and in different contexts. There is no distinction between dogmatic and un-dogmatic people as all of us are dogmatic at some points and undogmatic at others. Of course there is an art to knowing when to be one and when to be the other. The scientist should NOT be dogmatic in a philosophy lecture though she should be in her lab. The Jewish person should not be dogmatic when addressing a holocaust survivor questioning his faith. This comes down, as so many things do, to a fine point of judgment.

A dogma is literally a thing taught or received. The original context of the term is Hellenistic philosophy. To those philosophers known as Skeptics other schools of philosophy such as Stoics and Epicureans were known as dogmatists. This was because they assumed principles like atoms and the void of which they could give no ultimate account and simply asserted them against those who held contrasting positions. To the Skeptics all claims to positive knowledge suffered from this defect. Trace any chain of reasoning back to its first principles and you will find that those principles are such that no rational account may be given of them. Thus between positions that rest on opposed assumptions no mediation is possible and for this reason the Skeptics suspended judgment on all questions. This, of course, is what we now call anti-foundationalism and it is now as it has always been a basic philosophical option. Later, the same Greek word came to be used for the things 'taught or received' by the Christian church. By and large it was thought that certain 'dogmas' were held in the form of belief rather than knowledge because they were un-demonstrable.[49] Such dogmas might be the belief that Christ was both man and god and that the unity of the god-head subsisted in three persons. Note however that few (if any) of the ancient theologians held these doctrines to be unintelligible. Through analogy, negative reasoning or other forms of explication they could be rendered perspicuous at least to some degree. They simply denied that these doctrines could be proved: they remained objects of faith though faith could always seek understanding. Unlike the skeptics, the Christian fathers of the church accepted belief as a valid form of knowledge and proposed their 'dogmas' in this spirit. Again unlike the sceptics they also tended to hold that though these dogmas were un-demonstrable in themselves other related 'teachings' such as the existence of God or the immortality of the soul could be known by human reason. Thus beliefs were not the be all and end all as they existed in concert with rational truths. Thus, the rationalism of later Western culture existed in the context of dogma from the very beginning.

Thus, the discussion of dogma is bedeviled by the confusion of meaning between the philosophical and theological uses of the term. A religious dogma is nothing less than a thing proposed for belief. A philosophical dogma is a thing asserted gratuitously which can be gratuitously denied. Of course it is all too common an occurrence for a religious 'dogma' to be

---

[49] As I said above no scientist begins her work day with a systematic test of her senses by means of Cartesian doubt and, to that extent, most of the ordinary claims of the scientist rest on what Plato calls 'pistis' or opinion. This very same word was used by later Platonists as equivalent to 'faith' as in 'a lively trust in the providence of the gods'. On this precedent I have no problem whatsoever with drawing what seem to me evident analogies between 'pistis' as it exists in different domains: particularly as applying to both our religious and scientific beliefs. Some, no doubt, will object to me using the word faith at all in the context of speaking of science but this seems to me unnecessarily strict: faith, at least the Platonists tell us, is at the end of the day is an assumed attitude to undemonstrated or non-thematic truths and this attitude is a structural part of human experience in any domain scientific religious or otherwise. Plato knew of this centuries before post –modernism: natural science, all natural science begins with an untestable hypothesis and this is the distinction he draws between dianoia and episteme, the unhypothetical science that culminates in the intuition of the Good. These assumptions, we have learned post-Nietzsche, are given culturally and historically and even in part linguistically.

held 'dogmatically' in the second sense. This is the case, for instance, when religious persons use forms of justification internal to their communities in public discussions involving persons external to their communities. There are in fact a couple of confusions that need to be cleared up here. The first is that un-demonstrable propositions can only be held gratuitously. Beliefs that fall short of apodictic certainty can nonetheless be justified and many religious persons use hermeneutical and other procedures to justify the things they claim as when they appeal to the meanings of sacred texts and so on. Thus it is wrong to say that there are no justifications for the beliefs that religious peoples hold. What religious people often fail to recognize though is that this is a two-way street. As they appeal to critical principles so can these same principles be used against them. An atheist may challenge a particular reading of scripture as well as anyone else. Discourse can always generate counter discourse after which a discussion ensues that may go as far as bringing the most fundamental principles into question. At that point the Christian or Jew is no longer engaged in theology or scriptural interpretation but apologetics. Of course no one likes discussing fundamentals or first principles because such discussions so often come to an impasse in which the participants simply talk past each other. That does not however mean that such discussions can or should be avoided (with apologies to the ancient Skeptics!). There are in fact any number of moves that can be made in such discussions. One might think that the gulf between a lover of Keats and a hater of Keats would be unbridgeable. This need not be the case however as the Keats lover always has the 'taste and see' option: "you disdain Keats so much but perhaps you have read him with a jaundiced eye... why don't you look at him again!" . Thus, an atheist may say: "Are you sure the Bible is such a good book... read it again with its graphic violence in mind!" .

Of course the elephant in the room here is the question of authority. It is often assumed that the argument from authority is inherently fallacious. It is not as can readily be demonstrated (do you diagnose your own aliments on the internet? You are a fool if you do!). As H.G. Gadamer points out in his marvelous essay "Authority and Critical Freedom" authority is an essential component of any critical culture religious, scientific or otherwise.[50] This author would think it a huge cultural loss if the traditions of Judaism, Christianity or Buddhism were to disappear.[51] This is because

---

[50]It of course seems iconoclastic and bold to say the purpose of education is to 'challenge authority' but without authority we have anti-vaxxers, birthers and climate change deniers. Clearly Gadamer is right that one of the purposes of education is to teach us to value legitimate authority and to challenge illegitimate authority and to give us the critical tools to distinguish the two. There is no way to restore the authority of science, say, without restoring the authority of authority. Authority, like tradition, peer review and perhaps even censorship is founded on a gamble: that over time and in aggregate bad ideas will be weeded out in spite of individual misjudgments.

[51]This is a point wonderfully illustrated in a poem by Robert Frost called The Black Cottage. In this poem an 'enlightened' minister muses about removing the words "descended into Hades" from the creed. He does not do so for the sake of an elderly widow who would, he thinks, regret the change. The image of the nodding widow

a good deal of the inherited wisdom of the human race would disappear with them and time is tragically misspent re-inventing the wheel. That said the over-extension of the principle of authority seems actually to be a significant problem in many religious traditions. It is not hard to see why: if I challenged a Buddhist to justify the four noble truths she might well wonder what more fundamental principle she could appeal to in order to justify them. To her they might seem self-evident and not in need of any justification. In this they would be like the principle of induction for a scientist: a scientist may well ask what procedure more fundamental than induction could be used to justify induction. What is more, in both cases there is a social need for stability of doctrine or content. The world is not a debating society and neither religious doctrine nor scientific theory can be at the mercy of faddishness: epistemic and moral boundaries have to exist in the life of any institution. This is clear in the case of political parties which police heresy and dissent in their own ranks without complaint or comment in ways that might get churches or scientific institutions in considerable hot water! It is simply understood that if you don't support the platform you cannot be a member of the party.

The problem is that authority in all these realms is too often its own worst enemy. It is as clear why Rupert Sheldrake is not a member of the scientific community as it is why Hans Kung was not a member of the Catholic Church. Everyone decries the ability of the Vatican, say, to censure a theologian but Catholics cannot give it up for if a theologian declared himself a neo-Nazi they would immediately want that same power to exercise itself. The fact that Universities cannot simply fire right wing cranks is often urged as a criticism of them. We are very much of two minds on the question of authority both desiring its exercise (on others) yet resenting it when it goes against our own predilections. This may be one of those circles that cannot be squared this side of heaven. I think this is because we see the need both of having heretics and of policing them. Boundaries must be enforced exactly as they must be challenged: life is under two conflicting necessities! It is also true that differing institutions will have differing standards on this depending on their priorities or (alas) their sources of funding (as with the news media). One solution to this problem is Liberalism in the broad sense. Institutions like churches or political parties cannot become coterminous with the state. If someone dislikes the Liberal Party or catholic doctrine, there ought to be some-

---

expands in the minister's discourse into the idea of a haven where all unfashionable truths await their turn to become fashionable again. It is striking that barely a few years after this putative conversation between Frost and the minister Owens' Strange Meeting was descending, along with European civilization as a whole, into Hades once more. Indeed, without this phrase of the creed it is hard to say what Owens could have been descending into beyond a foul tunnel in a trench. The previously meaningless symbol was now horrifyingly real. It is the job of the conservative element in a society (the nodding widows!) to protect such indispensable images from the aggressive (and misplaced) self-certainty of discursive consciousness which asks if they are true not according to the valance of symbols but according to the ordinary categories of the understanding.

where else to go. This allows institutions to enforce their own internal standards while allowing heretics someplace to go. In some respects, this protects authority from its own abuses. What is more, the general culture of liberalism creates demands within particular communities for a more latitudinarian outlook. It is hard to think of a modern bishop coming up with the anathemas of the Athanasian creed! Of course, no one likes liberalism except as it applies to themselves: we are all self-interested in that respect. Still, as a means for striking the impossible balance between authority and freedom there may not be a better answer.

7 CAN THE STATE WITHER AWAY? A PARABLE

Cloud-Cukoo land has arrived. The dreams of Marxists, Neo-Liberals, Anarchists, libertarians and far-right Patriots have all come true: there is no state. What does this look like? Well I will assume what Aristotle says about the *zoon politicon*: we have not degenerated to beasts or metamorphosed into gods. We live together in some form or other. But what form? Well I suppose the most basic determinant of this question would be geography. At its very simplest the human community (if I may borrow from Swift) will divide between the Big-Endians who live by the river over there and the Little-Endians who live on the Island over here.[52] In the forest there may be a community who have nothing to do with soft-boiled eggs at all. We can assume then that each group will exercise some kind of claim over what they can practically appropriate. Thus, the Non-Endians will make use of lumber, the Big-Endians will construct mills and the Little Endians will, no doubt, fish. Actually this is too complicated because the last thing we want at this point is for the Endians to begin trading: we don't want to give the argument to the neo-liberals right off the bat! Suppose then the Non-Endians live off the meat of forest animals, the Big-Endians get by on trout (and one assumes chickens!) and the Little-Endians have just enough wood to construct simple boats. As in Plato's city of pigs each community has what suffices for its own sustenance and basic material for tools and handicrafts. The Endians have little reason to bother with each other positively or negatively. Assuming nature to be stable there is little need for anything to change. Plato, of course, who thinks it is human nature to want limitlessly, assures us that no humans will rest happy in such a state of equilibrium.[53] (*Republic* III,

---

[52]Swift's image suggests that the ground of social distinctions is some form of arbitrary determination that shuts down a possibility: I may do x or y but not both so I do y. In other words, at the base of any social structure lies some irreducible contingency. Thus, Britons will drive on one side of the road and North Americans another. Lilliputians will eat their eggs one way, Blefuscudians another. Lilliputians and Blefuscudians, of course, are heavily invested in concealing the arbitrariness underlying their differing habits by inveterate warfare.

[53]Plato's City of Pigs we may take as functionally equivalent at least to what modern theorists call the state of nature, that hypothetical pre-civic condition in which humans

372-373)

We don't need to contest this question yet though. Rousseau goes further to the root of the matter when he notes that nature itself changes and us along with it.[54] The Non-Endians are finding their customary prey is becoming scarce, perhaps from over-exploitation perhaps from other factors. The Little-Endians are running out trees, never very plentiful on a wind-swept island. Assume too that climactic changes have been favorable to salt-water fish. Is there any way to stop the inevitable from happening? Surely not. The Little-Endians have surplus food while the Non-Endians have surplus building material, the former will send food and the latter will send lumber in return. The inequities of nature can only be rectified by trade. Meanwhile the Big-Endians have not been idle. One of them, a clever fellow, has invented a way to refine some of the wild wheat that grows near the river into a much finer product: flour. This is a pure contingency of course but contingencies happen. Making bread is not the expense of labor and time fishing on the ocean is. Nor do the Big-Endians have quite the same need for lumber as the Little-Endians. Still, houses of wood beat houses of straw and the Big-Endians have a very fine product, bread, which they can trade for lumber. The Non-Endians are in a good situation and as long as their lumber supplies are healthy they can easily trade for both and enjoy a more varied diet as a consequence. Nothing, however, can alter the fact that they are now supplying lumber for the needs of three communities not one. Introduce another contingency of nature, like a parasite, and things alter again.

Suddenly the Non-Endians do not have all the lumber in the world. The sensible thing to do would be to stop buying bread which is probably a luxury compared to fish. Unfortunately, the Non-Endians have developed a liking for bread, a want has become a need. What's more, they have just received a shipment of fish on which they owe payment. Worse, a new player has arrived in town, the Vikings, who do not see the need to trade for lumber at all given that they can simply take it. The situation has now become chaotic but there seems one clear way to resolve it. The Endians need to form some league in which the interests of all parties

---

no longer subsist and perhaps have never subsisted. The difference (or at least one difference) is that Plato has no story to tell about how we are forced out of this state. Rather, it is the intrinsic force of human desire (not external nature) that multiplies human wants and generates the opposed classes of which the city is composed. It is not as the moderns (Marx included) would have it that we struggle with nature (which is presumed here to be beneficent) but with the infinity of our own nature. Further, as 369-372 make clear, the City of Pigs does anticipate the later divisions of the inflamed city and to that extent is not 'natural'. It is pre-civic as the life of the autonomous village or tribe is. This essay, is, I must confess, an attempt to work out what Plato is saying in this passage.

[54] "In proportion as the human species grew more numerous, and extended itself, its difficulties likewise multiplied and increased. The differences of soils, climates and seasons succeeded in forcing them to introduce some difference in their way of living. Bad harvests, long and sever winters, and scorching summers which parched up all the fruits of the earth, required a new resourcefulness and activity." (Discourse on the Origin of Inequality, 213)

are guaranteed. This will be an endian league as they share a common language, common customs and a mutual dislike of Vikings.[55] The Endian league will have several features. First it will be a mutual defense pact against Vikings which entails the mutual construction and maintenance of walls, fortifications, and a force of armed men to garrison them. A second feature is that the Endians will now interact more closely. The Non-Endians will need to go farther afield for lumber but can contract with the Little-Endians for shipping. In this way they can meet their debt. However, this means more resources will go into transport and less into fishing. In the meantime, though, the Big-Endians have domesticated wheat and are quite capable of making up the shortfall. Their bread is now essential to the functioning of the league as it frees up transport capacity for the Little-Endians. But with what can the Little-Endians buy bread now that they fish less? Well, I suppose they could trade services or bodies. They could offer to assume more of the responsibilities for mutual defense in exchange for bread. If they have surplus people, they can also trade labor. However, these relations are beginning to get complicated. All three groups now find themselves part of a system of exchange on whose smooth and consistent operation they all depend. Everyone depends on everyone else holding up their end of the bargain. This means the Endians need more than a handshake, they need an explicit contract with penalties stipulated for its violation. Throw a few more products in the mix like wool for clothing and dyes from shellfish and you have a market that would function so much more smoothly if currency replaced barter. Then a man would not need lumber in hand to get a wool jacket or a woman need a bucket of shell-fish to get some planks. We would have something that represented abstractly the value of these things and trade would occur more smoothly

---

[55]Vikings we shall always have with us. This is something neo-liberal anarchists recognize because while being libertarians they also support a violent, punitive state apparatus. Of course part of the reason for this is that the security state is a major customer of their enterprises and it may be, as someone once suggested to me, that it is a fundamental limit of the neo-liberal dream that it needs the state to buy large ticket items like jet fighters that it is difficult to imagine any private entity acquiring. This, though, is just one example of what I am tempted to call the paradox of anarchism which in some way effects both left and right wing forms: that all anarchisms founder on the question of authority and force. Let me give an example. Suppose a reporter filming a clash between white supremacists (our 'Vikings'!) and black bloc anarchists. There may be many reasons why neither group wants a media presence. Suppose one of the black bloc people comes to the reporter and tells him to leave. By what authority does an anarchist, of all people, tell another human being he cannot stand on particular spot? Well presumably by the authority of moral suasion (we are fighting in a good cause!) and, failing that, the authority invested in the bat he is carrying. But of course these are precisely the forms of authority invested in the traditional state which the anarchist simply appropriates to himself entirely on his own say so. He becomes the state on that particular side walk. What is more, having named himself king, he might well develop a liking for monarchy. He will then become one of the legion of revolutionists who decide that they, after all, ARE the revolution and form the new hierarchy of power that replaces the old. To fight the state, you must become a new state, it seems. What is worse, supposing we have succeeded in over throwing the state what, except another state, will prevent new forms of exploitation from emerging exactly as they have emerged in the past? How do you make salvation permanent?

and reliably. Thus we have the basis for a common currency, a legal system and mutual defense. The reason we have all these things is that we have to adapt to contingencies and one of the ways to do this is for smaller communities to become bigger communities and for custom to turn into law. In essence villages who develop systems of mutual interdependence will (barring some insurmountable ethnic or religious difference) tend to merge into small states to insure the predictable operation of those systems in frameworks of accountability. There is too much at stake for them to do otherwise.

All of this of course assumes communities that depend directly on nature for survival under conditions of natural scarcity. Marxists will protest that of course under such conditions states will develop but that these conditions are contingent: they belong to the beginning of history not the end. In our scenario people had interests to protect in things they did not own but depended on access to. This lead to commerce, law, and potential warfare. An advanced technocracy though will eliminate natural scarcity and all ground for political, military, and commercial institutions. Of course Plato would repost that while people's needs can be met their wants proliferate without limit so that scarcity of some kind will always exist.

Again though let's give Marxism a pass on this and assume a very different situation. The big endian and little endian folk are now workers who have assumed direct control over an endian league that has grown far more complex in technology and culture. What to do now? The Little-Endians now own an advanced fishing fleet and have constructed fish farms. The Big-Endians now engage in full blown industrial agriculture producing vast surpluses of food. Bread and fish are no longer an issue for anyone as there is more than enough and there is no capitalist class to confiscate a disproportionate share for conversion into private capital. Moreover, the Non-Endians now have metallurgy and the capacity to produce advanced alloys, plastics and so on. This obviates much of the need for lumber as there is now a vast array of materials out of which things can be constructed. One immediate problem is that these communities are still differentiated by having distinct resource bases. It seems they still have to trade: no community can produce every single thing required by an industrial society with complex needs and wants. For one thing people like to be entertained and entertainment often requires novelty. A fad for big-endian films or songs may sweep the Little-Endians or vice-versa. Be that as it may there is one thing I want to discuss here and that is elevators. Medicine is wonderful but it cannot eliminate contingency from life. Workers will have accidents from time to time and some of these may limit the ability of certain people to climb stairs. Plus, humans will still age. Yet horizontal space is finite so the Endians will have to build up. This will require mechanisms to help the old, the lame and perhaps small children ascend to the higher floors of buildings.

I suppose the Non-Endians are the people best able to meet these needs as they have the materials and know how to build complex mechanisms like elevators. The question now is (given the superabundance postulated by Marx) why would they? If scarcity is overcome in every local instance no motive would exist for exchange or trade. It must be that scarcity, then, is overcome *en masse* by an interlocking system of communication and exchange. Mere differences of geography dictate that there will be local shortages of, say, farmed salmon or wheat. Presumably the sophisticated machine tooling of the Non-Endians (who I can't see making elevators for the fun of it) will now be exchanged for food stuffs of various types.[56] The Non-Endians will find it worthwhile to construct an elevator factory though the problem remains that elevators cannot be rolled to market down a hill. These products must travel on some kind of communication grid like a rail line. Yet again the Endians will have to co-ordinate to construct, maintain, and defend their rail links, making sure that they are well maintained, safe and protected from bored teenage vandals.[57] Moreover, the Little-Endians and their suppliers need the rails to be working as and when they require them. These links would need to be regular and predictable so that it seems inescapable that there will be some common body overseeing them and agreements governing their use. Yet again these problems will only proliferate until all the Endians are once again under a common governance founded NOT on the contingent fact of inclination but upon binding agreements as to what must be done by whom.

So, to this extent the post capitalist situation does not really differ from the pre-capitalist one (unless we abolish nature and chance altogether). To the extent that there are accidents of nature and geography there are still forms of scarcity (to the extent that we still have bodies nature and geography will shape our choices). These will have to addressed through trade as well as the maintenance of conditions for trade involving binding

---

[56] To put this problem in a nutshell; what happens if the free impulses of individuals to express themselves in craftsmanship and labor does not supply the actual needs of individuals? Things like elevators are not lovingly hand-crafted items and presumably must be created by the command of an administrator, the force of custom or religious sanction, or under the impetus of a market (at very minimum of a simple pre-Capitalist kind like barter). A final option I suppose is making elevators out of charity or goodwill but this is something over and above the individual free self-expression in work that is supposed to mesh seamlessly with the needs and the freedom of all. It may well be that not all labor can be undertaken freely, that a moment of alienation exists in even the freest work and that the Ancient Hebrews were correct to regard it as the curse of Adam.

[57] Of course there are those (such as Mark Bray) who will insist that a post capitalist society will have no vandals or at least so few as can be dealt with easily. (The Antifa Handbook, 149) I have no doubt that capitalism exacerbates many of the tensions between people but some degree of violence exists in all other social forms the human race has tried from simple tribal societies to city states to monarchies. If there is a reason to think that the end of capitalism will be the end of human aggression and violence I confess that I do not know what that reason is. As the Underground Man puts it there will always be those who poke their tongue out at the crystal palace precisely because it is there to be disrespected. Of course, different evils have more or less latitude in one type of polity or another. It is equally clear however that violence and other evils will not simply cease with the disappearance of one type of society, which type of society they predate by millennia.

agreements. Thus, it seems at the end of the day that the early liberal theorists were no a pack of fools: they recognized the centrality of contract or covenant to any functioning social order.[58] Higher and freer than the immediacy of self will is the general will embodied in social covenants to which we all bind ourselves. Rousseau seems to be on the mark about this. Perhaps, to be fair, Marx saw this as well. Perhaps all he meant was that a certain oppressive form of the state would wither away, one that embodied interests opposed to those of the citizenry as a whole or, for that matter, the citizenry taken as individuals. I will leave this for Marx scholars to argue over. To conclude though there is one principle on which all the dreamers we began with, from anarchists to right wing patriots to libertarians, come to grief on and that is the ultimate fact of contingency: the fact that a. is over here while b. is over there. Utopian ideas all involve some final overcoming of contingency by planning or some principle of spontaneous self-organization (communism vs. neo-liberalism/anarchism) yet it seems this idea can't get past even the basic facts of geography. This leaves virtual reality and cyber space as the only possible site of Utopian space, time and corporeality being insuperable barriers.

---

[58]The moral idealism of the anarchist (of whatever stripe) finds the social contract an impossible constraint. The moralistic zeal of the ideologue however cannot establish an objective body of right. What gives the neo-liberal anarchist the right to his property? By what authority does the black bloc anarchist tell any human being he can't be a racist? If we (entirely on our own say so) suspend civil rights of various problematic people by, say, beating them we do, exactly as Hobbes says, revert to a pre-civil state in which there are only empty moral appeals and threats of force. Propaganda and violence are not substitutes for law and objective right. As Arendt points out the compliance produced by violence (though sometimes necessary) is no substitute for the consent to legitimate authority whether of persons or laws and is a by-product of failed governance. (On Violence, 45-47)

8 The Sect: A Tiny Parable

Let me resume my Swiftian metaphor in another context. Institutions from time to time fall into serious scandal. One response to this to clean up after them. The other is to form a sect. Let us take the Big-Endians once more. The leaders of the Big Endian clan have been caught with their hands in the cookie jar. They have taken massive numbers of cookies and resorted to every conceivable subterfuge to hide their theft. Moreover, these crimes go to the very top of the Big Endian hierarchy. What happens if I take the sectarian response to this problem? What happens if my next move is to gather like-minded folks together and become the Little Endians? Two rhetorical stances become necessary. My move is predicated on the fact that the Big Endian clan is not just corrupt as all institutions are but corrupt beyond redemption: ITS problems are inherent not accidental features. If this were not the case, then the *raison d'etre* of the Little Endian sect would disappear. Thus, I need a maximalist rhetoric about the wickedness of the Big Endians. Now every sect faces the problem of the routinization of charisma. Once our reforming zeal settles into the everyday business of paying the Little Endian bills and painting the picket fences we will find that Little Endians like cookies too. Inevitably, some Little Endians, will steal cookies. Concerning this I need not a maximalist rhetoric but a minimalist one. Unlike Big Endian crimes, Little Endian ones are accidental expressions of human failure and do not express an underlying viciousness in the character of the sect. Of course, eventually, it's only a matter of time, Little Endians will commit a theft on a scale comparable to the original crimes of the Big-Endians. This argument will then become harder to maintain. We now have the basis for another sect, The Original Pure Endians, who will begin the entire process again.

Some though, might well feel they have been burned enough. They have the sinking feeling that the Original Pure Endians will eventually have cookie thieves among too. They are now done with institutions which are too corruptible and too fallible and disappoint those who place their trust in them. Indeed, the path to innocence may now lie in not associating with any corruptible grouping of humans. A pox on all their houses! I suppose now they are anarchists of a sort. But really, there is no such thing as anarchism in the strict sense. Minimally there is one ruler, myself, and one subject, also myself. One day, I will probably (secretly) steal a cookie and at four AM alone before a mirror have to confront the question of my own dubious governance.[59] Unfortunately, I cannot separate from myself except by suicide (which is always an option). I do though, have one mechanism left short of such an extreme. I need someplace to put my guilt and humans actually have an excellent device for that: the scapegoat mechanism. From the standpoint of my sect of one I will relieve my own guilt by placing it on someone else. Perhaps this is, once more, the Vikings. I will now become the investigator and denouncer in chief of the crimes of the Vikings who will take on the appearance of all evil in my eyes. My crimes are petty next to theirs, mere peccadillos, and even though I do have the odd skeleton or two in my closet the real force of my goodness and the purity of my moral nature (only trivially and accidentally stained here and there) are evident in my hatred and detestation of vice as it appears in the form of Vikings. How could I be a bad person? Look how I hate Vikings! My hatred of Vikings expiates my own small (very small!) moral failings!

We have seen evil and the consciousness of evil bounce about like a ball till it has finally landed someplace safely over there which is always where we wanted it to be. Finally, we have achieved innocence if not quite in the way we originally thought. Of course we might decide that 'purity' whether of people or institutions is not the solution to evil as we can never effect the desired separation of the wicked from the good either in society at large or in ourselves. Then I suppose we return all the way back to 'cleaning up' what currently exists and forgetting about sects altogether. That or we plant bombs in longhouses to kill not only Vikings but their evil spawn as well.

---

[59] I take the Biblical history of the ancient Israelites to illustrate this uncomfortable truth: after all the slaughter and sacking of cities, after all the 'ethnic cleansing' it turns out that the real Canaanites are those within. The prophet Amos was one of the few men rude enough to point this out. The sectary has great trouble with this point for, if we were to put his error in theological terms (and all errors are at bottom theological ones), he is more interested in where the spirit isn't than in where it is.

9 Has the Nation State a Future?

Things come and go. Some have wondered whether an exception to this truism might be the form of society created by western Europeans and North Americans. Others have opined that this form of society is no exception to the course of time according to which all things (trees and societies alike) mature and die. The whole form of society we belong to may indeed be on the point of collapse for environmental and other reasons. Many seem to think or at least hope that it will be replaced by a better society. Some like myself suspect it might not. Philosophers are not prognosticators however. I can only talk about the present and what seems to be going on on a day to day basis around me. Let me comment then on what I see when I look out my window. One thing I see is the dissolution of the nation state. The nation state is constituted by the idea of an indivisible sovereignty diffused (like the soul in a body) throughout a territory. The claim to sovereign territory is asserted by the presence (and implied threat) of militaries, police, border services and so on. At the same time the nation state is constituted by legal and constitutional frameworks as well as popular sovereignty embodied in legislatures and parliaments. Alongside these we see auxiliary institutions such as the press and schools and universities which shape the perceptions and thoughts of citizens. Nation states so constituted have a number of ways of failing. One we can see right before our eyes. One aspect of the state can turn against the other as when military coups dissolve elected parliaments or overthrow presidents. This is familiar from Latin America and other troubled spots around the globe.

A peculiar version of this is happening in the United States. In the period of national decline into which that society appears (on the surface at least) to be entering we do not see the Generals throwing out the president. Rather we see the populace (or at least a large chunk of it) losing faith in all public institutions *except* the police and military. The police and military will no longer be at the behest of courts and legislatures but directly at the behest of 'popular will' as embodied in a demagogue who articulates their anxieties and resentments.[60] Political and legal institutions are perceived

---

[60]This is why voters are unswervingly loyal to the demagogue no matter how corrupt and incompetent he turns out the to be and no matter how much damage he does to their own material interests. His function is cathartic and so long as he embodies the

as under the control of a cabal who thwart the will of the people. Their sole function on this view is to protect the privileges of elites by giving the mask of legal sanction to their naked class interests. To a considerable extent this is a true perception however much one deprecates the gross misjudgment that would replace these flawed institutions with a 'great leader' who wraps himself in the symbols of militarism and national glory. Plus, to the frustration of leftists, populists, stubbornly contradictory as they are, do not seem to disdain the primary instrument of Capitalism, the corporation, as they do the politicians who serve them. I suspect, however, that there is a very simple reason for this. People's jobs and livelihoods depend, or at least appear to depend, much more directly on corporations than on governments so that workers in the private sector tend to view their interests as bound up with those of their employers. This is obvious to anyone who lives in a mill town where workers will make abject concessions simply to keep their wealthy patron from leaving them and their pensions in the lurch. Thus, faith resides in business (as in any patronage system) and in the relatively 'uncorrupted' symbols of national strength and glory like the army even as faith in other (far more fundamental) institutions withers.

When the state fails people turn to other things, either other organs of the state or private bodies like churches, mosques, street gangs or even private armies in the pay of a local warlord. They also fall back on notions of ethnicity and family, especially in rural areas where less than privileged people depend much more directly on extended family structures than elsewhere. This is why leftist rhetoric about family, to use one example, has little traction even with people who might in the long term benefit from more equitable family structures and fluid gender norms. When I can't afford a plumber I need a cousin with plumbing skills and when I don't have childcare or a drive to the hospital I need an aunt or sister or at least a live in boyfriend (in an area where choice is limited). In a failed state people turn to what they know, even to the devil they know, and no amount of hectoring will make them do otherwise. Thus, sham as they are, the appeals of the great leader to faith and family are simply logical to those whose lives center around churches or families. His appeals to militarism are equally simple to those whose jobs depend on defense contracts or who view the armed services as a means of modest social advancement. His corporatism is equally comprehensible to those who work for corporations (or small businesses that depend on them) they cannot afford to offend any more than a renaissance sculptor could afford to offend a Medici. Finally, and no doubt frustratingly to many here, there is an absolute double standard asserted by populism. The corporation is free to roam the globe and has every right to do so if it feels insufficiently bribed by governments and increasingly ineffectual unions. Workers from

---

people's will to revenge he will be forgiven literally anything. This can be seen in the fact that one of the primary appeals of right wing populists which is that they 'own' or 'trigger' liberals. A leader who upsets people the demos feels look down smugly upon them can literally do anything else (like rob people of health care).

other countries however are not. They are greedy 'economic migrants', not true citizens, despised for the crass materialism of wanting to flee poverty and violence. Of course workers are not blind to the fact that this is mild compared to the greed of global corporations and a bit of anti-corporate rhetoric does not hurt the great leader one bit. However, workers know they cannot really hurt their corporate masters and focus their ire on an easier target. The great leader is always happy to help them in this as he, after all, is invariably in bed with capital himself.

This logic can be illustrated on the other end of the political spectrum. Please note that I am NOT asserting any moral equivalence between radicals on the left and radicals on the right. The former are manifestly better intentioned people than the latter (though we all know where good intentions lead). However, animated as they are by a similar problematic it is inevitable that they will come to comparable conclusions. This case in particular is one where the analogies are glaringly obvious to those who stand outside both groups though invisible to those within them as water is invisible to a fish. The black bloc radical and the right wing militia man have come to a common conclusion: that the state is corrupt and that the very idea of the state itself may be vitiated. Both make an uncompromising claim to moral authority and regard themselves as sanctioned (by their ideological purity) to dole out physical punishment to others. In other words, the instruments of violence that once belonged to the state now belong to them. Looking through the pages of Mark Bray's *Antifa Handbook* this seems to be justified on the basis of superior knowledge and moral integrity. A persistent theme in his book is that we cannot trust the state but we *can* trust him and his comrades. This "trust us we know what we are doing" argument is one he uses on any number of occasions. Do we worry that anti-fascists will assault people who are not actual fascists? "Trust us" he says for we are better trained to identify and oppose fascists than the police or politicians. (155) Well actually the combination of self-righteousness and violence is one I think toxic and for that reason I don't trust Bray and his friends at all.[61] The worst police

---

[61]Bray's claim that anti-fascist radicals are morally and intellectually superior to the corrupt organs of the state (and thus to be preferred to them) is not always borne out by the radicals he quotes with seeming approval. One of these 'Luis' informs us that: "... you need coalition building to allow yourself the tactical space to achieve the political goal and to send the message to the government that if they protect Nazi demos we're going to burn your city to the ground." (198) This is jarring indeed as 'Luis' is speaking from Dresden, a city literally "burned to the ground" in the last great anti-fascist struggle. Could 'Luis' possibly have been ignorant that his own words evoked the memory of a monstrous war-crime? He is remarkably unreflective if this is so. This is on the charitable assumption that he is not speaking literally. On page 150 we are introduced to a certain 'Job Polak' (I assume these names are fictitious) who has a novel theory concerning free speech: "You have the right to speak but you also have the right to be shut up!" I confess I have never heard of a right to be shut up nor do I have any idea on what principle such a right could be grounded. Bray himself keeps speaking of opposing Fascism "by any means necessary" . Really? By poisoning children? By rape or torture? Herein lies a fundamental problem. Bray, I have no doubt, has a civilized definition of "any means necessary" and is not counselling his

in the world may still be better than self-appointed militias responsible to nothing and nobody but their own hubris. At the same time though, this is the simple and logical outcome of the problematic outlined above. When police are infiltrated by right wing lunatics and will not drive white supremacists from your neighborhood it is entirely natural to fall back on some pre-civic organization if not on your own vigilante spirit. This is why the Taliban become the default rulers of Afghanistan and ISIS of the Sunni areas of Iraq. It is why the church became the de-facto ruler of medieval Europe. Nor can we particularly blame Bray and company for falling back on *everyone's* default solution for social breakdown, violence. When we feel impotent and feel that we are incapable of genuine action we fall back on myths of action and our primary myth of action is violent intervention.

These are despairing reactions to the death of the sovereign nation. If they represent the end of the nation state it is the end in the sense of its decay. Might there be something better than the nation state with its undivided sovereignty and uniform conception of citizenship? I don't raise this question lightly because there are many dangers, perhaps unsupportable dangers, to the deconstruction of the state. Plus, it is hard to see how falling back on smaller local associations is consistent with the demands of a global society. Still, I have no desire to be a prophet of gloom either. As there was a time before the state there will be a time after it. In some ways this future may resemble the past, specifically, the medieval past hopefully shorn of its oppressive hierarchical features. This, of course is the era just before the rise of the nation state. It is commonly thought of as an era of authoritarian oppressiveness though this is only partly true. It was also an era of experiments in living. This is evident in the institutions of monasticism which offered the broadest range of life options to those (too few no doubt) able to exploit them. These ranged from mendicancy to strict communism to hermetic solitude and the worldly holiness of beguines. It included the option of same sex communities. It was also an era rich in dissent with many competing 'heresies' vying for attention and allegiance with the official powers of church and state. The authoritarian middle ages were also the anarchic middle ages with the latter tendency no doubt exacerbating the former. In comparison with this we might think the life options of the citizen of the contemporary liberal nation state comparatively impoverished. One is by and large a producer/ consumer with hobbies and private distractions! More importantly the medieval world did not have a realized conception of indivisible sovereignty. Royal and ecclesiastical courts operated together. Local cultures and languages flourished. Sovereign entities intersected and clashed with other sovereign entities within the same 'state'. This often produced an anarchic mess and the clarity and logic of the modern state with its uniform conception of the rights bearing citizen was no doubt a necessary

fellow activists to commit exactly the kind of war-crimes states commit on the exact same principle: that the end justifies the means. His enemies though, have no such restraint and in open warfare will sink to depths ANTIFA cannot.

historical phase for Europeans. Still, it is possible to wonder if this phase has reached its terminus.

It is clear for instance that we need new models of sovereignty to deal with the aspirations of hitherto oppressed minority groups such as indigenous peoples. I cannot say what form these should take as it is not my call but theirs. What is clear however is that indigenous peoples cannot be 'citizens' of the modern 'nation state' in a neutral sense without being disadvantaged and reduced to second class peonage.[62] This does not entail, as the right complains, giving indigenous peoples 'special status' within the current system but rather giving them a form of sovereignty that *within Canada* permits them to live not under alien institutions imposed on them from without but their own. To put it bluntly, indigenous peoples do not have a bourgeois liberal view of the world and cannot exist as indigenous peoples within the bourgeois liberal state. Nor, by any feat of prestidigitation, can they acquire a sovereign territory of their own (such as the Jews have in Israel) to rule themselves as a classic nation state. Indigeneity is not portable in that way. Plus, having a Canadian passport is a desirable thing as is using a relatively stable currency and banking system. There are advantages to the virtuous mediocrity of Canadians. Clearly we need a concept of indigenous sovereignty that *intersects* with Canadian sovereignty in something of the medieval manner. As I say I cannot tell you what this looks like and I have no right to tell you because it is not up to me. I simply point out that one cost of this move will be the traditional concept of the nation state as absolute within its own territory. In defense of this one might simply point to facts on the ground. This MAY be the direction in which we are slowly and painfully moving anyway.[63] Indigenous people may well become not 'integrated' in the way liberals once imagined but form alternative societies as Mennonites and Hutterites already (partly) do. The precedent set by this (if indeed there is a precedent set by this) might inspire other forms of alternate community that might claim some limited (or not) form of sovereignty.

---

[62]This is as much as to say that in neither a Lockean nor even Rawlsian social contract can an indigenous person appear or assert their rights as indigenous. They can only appear as a neutral, disengaged rational actor to whom personal identities are 'private' constructions of no status in the public sphere. This rational actor has all but only those rights that belong interchangeably with all other rational actors who have formed the social contract from a presumed point of neutrality, the so called 'veil of ignorance'. There are, despite the polemics uttered against it, many virtues to the social contract tradition as I have adverted to elsewhere. However, the problem of indigeneity seems to me to be one place where it breaks down decisively. What has the liberal tradition in this form have to say to those attempting to restore suppressed and colonized identities that disappear in the social contract?

[63] Of course we do have conceptions of limited government which may apply here though limited government is not the same conception as limited sovereignty. It applies not to sovereign entities within other sovereign entities but to the rights of the 'private' sphere as defined and enforced by the state (as when the judicial branch stops an overreach of the legislature). As such 'limited government', though the notion has many legitimate applications, tends to the protection of corporate interests above those of the public at large especially when it comes to concerns over environmental damage wrought by industry.

Liberals will not like this. There are good reasons not to like this. It seems superficially at least to undermine the regime of human rights by replacing the authority of the state with the whims of local communities who, presumably, could use the cover of 'special status' to roll back gender or other established rights.[64] After all, do we have here an argument that would justify other forms of ethnic or religious enclaves that would function as a kind of state within a state? One need only look at certain polygamous Mormon communities to see how unattractive this might be. At the same time, and here is the dilemma, people will not give up their religious and ethnic specificity or their prejudices because liberals hector them about universal values. Both Canada and the United State are roughly divided 40/60 between those who lean to so-called 'conservative' values and those who do not. This spilt is hardening with each passing year with both groups living increasingly in incommensurate worlds. To put it bluntly, Liberal societies contain substantial populations of people to varying degrees illiberal or at least non-liberals not greatly engaged by the values of liberalism. Liberals of course are confident that demography will solve this problem as younger people tend to be more liberal and conservatives can consequently be expected to die off in the next few decades. Others wish to use alternate voting systems to prevent the minority from having an outsized influence on elections (which they currently do- 36% of Canadian voters can elect a majority government). Alas, people may change their political stripes as they age and seemingly disenfranchising roughly 4/10 voters is also a dicey proposition especially as many in that group are already dangerously alienated and increasingly paranoid.[65] Our cur-

---

[64]What for instance if I wanted to found a community on the very notion of gender discrimination? Tori Truscheit writing in The Slate (https://slate.com/human-interest/2018/10/man-hating-lesbian-insult-reclaim-anger-metoo-activism.html) muses about just such a thing. Ms. Truscheit is a lesbian who not only feels no sexual attraction for men but does not like them as people either. In fact, she claims that she has some difficulty regarding them as worthy of 'mental sympathy'. This raises an interesting question. People do indeed have sympathies and antipathies that are often pre-reflective and stubbornly personal. Religious communities used to be one place such people (or at least such people whose negative feelings focused on the other gender) could find a 'comfort zone'. Ms. Truscheit does not ultimately endorse this solution (separate is too rarely equal) but is it intrinsically wrong? In a liberal society someone with a prejudice is expected to deal with it. They are not (except under special circumstances i.e. with vulnerable groups) granted the right to an exclusive space free of the 'other'. But is this always the best solution? Would a liberal society with at a certain range of 'opt outs' be less tense overall? This raises the specter of white ethnic enclaves and so on but might there be advantages to allowing such people to isolate themselves? We have long operated on the assumption that 'prejudice' is something to be uprooted but is this working or backfiring? Might we say to Richard Spencer "here's a plot of land, go ahead and have your stupid ethno-state without sushi" ? This might founder though on the fact that without an 'other' to suppress there may not be a 'white identity' beyond things like Verdi, single malt or Romanesque architecture, the study and appreciation of which will almost certainly bore the typical white supremacist energized as he is by anger and conflict not opera or English gardens.

[65] This is a much more serious problem than many progressives realize. Many of the gains of which they are justly proud have come from the imposition of change on a recalcitrant minority. This is a formula for temporary progress only as people have long

rent form of governance is thus in increasing danger of fracturing between the majority and an increasingly alienated, angry and dangerous minority (Fascist revolutions, like others, do not depend on majority support). The United States is in particular trouble here as its liberal/non-liberal divide is clearly geographic and threatens to result in an actual split of the country into 2-4 different entities. Then again, if this only reflects the reality that there are indeed two countries (at least) are Americans going to undertake another civil war to keep the U.S. together?

It is clear then that we have come around to the problem we began with. People are disinvesting from the state yet we have no clear model of what can replace it. We have some models of what new kinds of sovereignty might look like but no clear idea of how they should be applied beyond the specific circumstances that have brought them into being. Everything I've said here may be unprofitable speculation but we need a way to decompress our societies quickly before they explode. I do not however think the state is something to be given up on quite yet. There is one untried option that may yet save it and render the musing I've engaged in here about the end of the nation state moot. We *could* reverse our current course and, say, make large investments into reversing some of the inequities in income, internet, access to education and health care, clean air and water and so on that divide North Americans often along urban and rural lines. Minus these irritants we would have a new situation, not the Liberal dream of a mass conversion to Liberalism perhaps but a situation in which people would be more inclined to keep a respectful distance from each other because they are not eaten up inwardly by social resentment.[66] It is easier to be on some-

---

memories and the resentment created sows the seed for later disaster. The most glaring example of this is the red state/blue state divide in the U.S. which is a legacy of the civil war and particularly of Sherman's earth scorching march through the south. Even over a century later these ancient resentments can be stoked to life by a clever populist which indicates, at very least, that one way NOT to settle a profound social issue is war. I mention this as a problem to which I wish I had a clear solution but alas I do not. We do though need a formula for social change that does not depend on a zero sum showdown between 'modernity' and 'tradition' though the legalistic framework of the charter makes this challenging in Canada. This problem is exponentially more grave in the U.S. which will, in all likelihood, disintegrate once again into northern and southern halves. That Canada is in a better state in terms of divisive social issues is perhaps a testimony to the fact that it is not a product of a war of independence and has never had a full civil war (though there have been a number of rebellions).

[66]This may be heretical to utter in Canada but I think the demand (uttered by our Prime Minister!) that people with incommensurate world views be forced to love each other is tyrannous, love not being a thing that can be compelled. Certain people should not be in each other's hair. At the same time though distance (i.e. keeping yours) is one form of respect and respect is much more important to a functioning society than 'acceptance'. Thus, there seems to me no point in demanding that a Pentecostal baker bake a cake for a same-sex couple out of affirmation and love. After all, no one is being asked to affirm him. There is, however, every point in demanding that he bakes a cake out of respect for the neutral character of commercial space which cannot be closed to people simply because they adopt alternative life styles. He must make his customer a cake exactly as an LGBTQ baker would have to make a Christian themed cake for him and the reason for this is that discrimination of this kind if universalized would leave unpopular people without access to cake.

one else's side when someone is on yours. It is easier to view concern for 'others' as non-threatening when one is an object of concern oneself. The perception in many rural areas and small town areas that these are being 'neglected' in the name of helping 'the other' (a blessed status most of the rural population can never attain- they are only the same never the other) is not entirely inaccurate though the populists who exploit this feeling to bigoted ends have no intention of doing anything about it. They cannot for economic and social alienation is their bread and butter plus they want tax cuts and deregulation of the fossil fuel industry not investments in rural healthcare or improved internet access.[67] In such a situation white rural or small town Canadians (I don't know about Americans) might actually realize that the forces that oppress indigenous peoples, migrants and others are the same forces that put obstacle after obstacle in the way of their own advancement and the coalition of resentment constructed by the right in a divide and conquer strategy might actually begin unravelling. Unless you are a right or left wing anarchist or someone crossing their fingers that the immanent collapse of everything is the prelude to a glorious new dawn (and I have no idea why you would think that) you might want to consider this as the one viable option. Somewhat ironically it is Trumpian populism that makes this possible. It is dangerous in the extreme to shred the unspoken norms of governance and social relations but it does create space for previously unthinkable options one of which is the final abandonment of the neo-liberal project which, after all, is no more permanent and necessary than any other revolutionary project. I have considerable sympathy for the conservative instinct to regard hypocrisy as superior to shamelessness as the former pays lip-service to norms which the latter simply destroys. At the same time though the fact that "... large sections of voters turned their back on his (Obama's) intended successor, the new makeover candidate Hillary Clinton. They saw through the role-playing. They preferred, even if only reluctantly, the honest vulgarity of naked power represented by Trump over the pretensions of Clinton's fakely compassionate politics." (https://mronline.org/2018/11/14/long-read-the-neoliberal-order-is-dying-time-to-wake-up/?) does raise the question of whether the unmasking of neo-Liberalism for what it is (Fascism) is the prelude to its overthrow rather than a new age of barbarism. The jury, however, must remain out on this. I may at this point say only that I am neither enough of an optimist to think we are at the end of neo-liberalism rather than the beginning of fascism nor enough of a pessimist to give up on that possibility.

---

[67] Of course rural and small town people regard the fossil fuel industry as a source of ready cash and tend to look past the price their communities pay not only in the areas of health and environmental damage but in prostitution, violent crime and rampant substance abuse.

10 Thoughts on Conservatism: A Response to Adam Riggio

I must preface my comments with a short statement on myself. I was educated at King's college in Halifax and as such exposed to what we might call Red-Toryism. This was the outlook one could find expressed with great eloquence in the essays of George Grant and to a considerable degree I made this underlying attitude my own. When I speak of conservative thinkers like Grant or Leo Strauss then I refer to the thinkers I cut my teeth on. The tradition I found in these thinkers sought in the classics a kind of antidote to the worst aspects of modernity, an account of reason in public life and enshrined standards in culture and religion that rejected the relentless and thoughtless pragmatism of the technological society that came out of the Puritan conquest of North America: a society where the open ended quest for means trumped any rational or humane ends and things like goodness or beauty or truth could not be public goals except where they could be shown to contribute to the GDP or to the expansion of technocratic control over nature. This was a cultural conservatism that was compatible with notions of ordered freedom and the common good and led Grant, for instance, to align himself with the left on questions like the Vietnam war. Oddly, I came to internalize this stance almost at its end. Shortly after Grant died the Progressive Conservative government of Brian Mulroney was wiped out in a federal election and that government (which no one should be sentimental about) was the last gasp of any Tory tradition in Canada.[68] Manning's reform movement was populist

---

[68]I must emphasize that there is, as I have argued elsewhere, no effective conservative stance in current politics. Red Toryism like any Toryism now belongs to history. It is idle to speculate on whether this is a loss or a gain for it is a basic fact. At any rate the Tory account of politics took for granted a religious and ethnic homogeneity which we can no longer assume. Coleridge, for instance, addressed his arguments to a white protestant gentry (the 'clerisy') assumed to be capable of philosophy. However, it is now American evangelical Christianity (with a smattering of 'New Atheists' and mentally colonized Catholics like Rick Santorum) that carries the banner of white Protestant hegemony and American Protestantism is, at its core, hyper individualistic, rampantly utilitarian and founded on a doctrine of ethno-nationalist exceptionalism. Where Coleridge assumed the clerisy capable of reflective faith evangelicals have (with some honorable exceptions) abandoned Christianity for Christian identity. This doctrine (national Protestantism) will meet the ugly end that awaits all attempts to fuse religion and nationalism: the

not conservative and we see it now, in the form of the CPC, veering to the ugly populism that, I suspect, was always its root principle. At the time too I read American conservatives. I bought Buckley's *National Review* semi-regularly, but I could never stomach the free-market fundamentalism of Buckley and Paleo-conservatives like Russel Kirk never seemed to me effectual and southern conservatives of course were utterly disingenuous on the subject of slavery. Plus, it was obvious that the patrician 'elitism' of Buckley was an empty sham and the Republicans themselves preferred the hucksterism of Reagan (and after him Bush, Palin and Trump in descending order of crassness). So when I speak of an end of conservatism I am simply adverting to this fact. I am also adverting to the fact if anyone in 21st century Canada wants to make a difference politically it is the radical tradition they must work in which is not to say that it is the best tradition or the only tradition but that it is ours. So politically I cannot call myself a conservative though I think there is a kind of prudence and realism in that tradition that I try to bring to political problems. Like Plato's demiurge you have to work with the matter you are given.

Of course for years and years I was a grad student and had no reason to confront the soundness or lack thereof of my political attitudes. I am however a rural Canadian by extraction and even now I do not live in a major urban center. When you are young and ambitious of course you are trying to tell the world "I am not one of them" but at a certain age you realize that you are of course 'one of them' and if you eat the bread, as it were, of rural Canadians and then go on to become some Pinkeresque apologist for the managerial class I think you are in a very compromised position. So, if you decide the people you grew up with are the people you are in the most direct solidarity with then you have say that you are some species of progressive as the right is interested only in keeping rural and small town Canadians angry and alienated and resentful of 'others'. I think, for a number of reasons, that we need a new deal for rural and small town Canada the chief of which is, that if services are concentrated in centers miles and miles away then you are less invested in services and indeed the whole notion of a public good. This is a redistributive project involving a transfer not just of quick cash (the oil patch can do that though at considerable cost in terms of addictions and domestic and sexual violence) but of essential social capital. For this reason, it is a socialist project and I think any fair minded person now has to consider themselves a socialist not in the vanished radical Tory tradition but in the current one. I see this redistribution as good in itself obviously but also it is essential to tackling the rise of populism and when people like Mark Bray talk about, say, doxxing white supremicists or dressing up for street battles as the vanguard of the revolution I tend to think that is trifling. If you are going to be radical, I think you need to be radical in your acts of solidarity and for me that's solidarity with the 'left behind' whoever they happen to be and however unpleasant or unevolved you think they might be. Solidarity also starts at

---

nationalism will empty out all pretenses to religion.

home so the left behind I start with are the left behind I grew up with and I work outwards from there. I think the cost of failing in solidarity here is populism as it is very easy to pit marginal people against other marginal people and you will do very well with that politically. This is not to say by the way that rural and small town alienation in the U.S. and Canada is the only driver of populism but that it is a key driver of populism (look at the states Clinton lost for instance) and without it populism loses a great deal of steam (though it may never go away altogether). [69]

Arnold Toynbee once used the phrases 'internal proletariat' for a persistent theme he had noted in human history: that societies contain classes of people, of various kinds, who are not invested in the civic theology (with all its hierarchies and rituals etc.) or in the existing power structures. Such groups of people can be the majority of the population but they do not need to be. Historically they have sometimes functioned as fifth columns as with the Copts in the Byzantine Empire who made common cause with Islamic invaders and indeed transmitted to them much of the cultural heritage of antiquity. An internal proletariat is of course an object of suspicion and contempt ('deplorables') to the ruling class and those invested spiritually, culturally or materially in it. One of the things that gives the populist movement energy is that rural and small town people are becoming an internal proletariat and thus a subversive element within the liberal order. The demagogue, of course, is historically the master at using the resentments of the mob of the internally displaced to further his reach and power though of course he will never really address their concerns in more than a superficial way, i.e. with bread and circuses rather than real reforms. One thing I agree with Bray about is that these internal emigres do not need to be anything close to a majority to wreak havoc as we see white Evangelicals doing in the U.S. (140-141) Thus we face an old political problem, what to do about those who don't mind wrecking a society they have no real stake in either emotionally or materially. It is a problem of inclusion to use the current buzzword though more on this below. I must note (for now) something that is, after all, Marxism 101: rural Canadians live under different material conditions and will naturally have very different attitudes on social and religious questions than their

---

[69]Of course figuring out who exactly this 'internal proletariat' is (in Canada) challenging in an intersectional sense. Rural and small town white people over the age, say, of 50 would seem to be at the core of it. However, Evangelical Christians chafing at their loss of cultural cache are also a part and they can be urban and suburban people as well. A diminishing number of these people seem also to be traditional Progressive Conservatives oblivious to the fact that their party no longer exists. All the above are, of course, heavily courted by the fossil fuel lobby which sees ethno-nationalism and even out and out racism as its ace in the hole in terms of evading ecological responsibility. Of course there are rural people, particularly indigenous people, who don't factor in the equation in the same way: if they are an internal proletariat they are a distinct one. In the department of small mercies, however, this effect seems to be less pronounced in Atlantic Canada at least in terms of the ethno-nationalist component (https://policyoptions.irpp.org/magazines/june-2019/urban-rural-divide-atlantic-canada-myth/?fbclid=IwAR0UZirnTV5_kYOCERnsMyF2z3JBG0verMUrj1CckVi-6eN8yeBPOQJTClg)

urban counterparts.

And herein lies a fundamental issue that cannot be ducked: that of social authority. Let me frame the problem this way. Minimally, people are the stories they tell about themselves. These stories, in a modern western context at least, are often a version of the conversion narrative whose founder would appear to be St. Augustine. At a crisis point in one's life one becomes aware of some underlying force or necessity (whether divine or natural) that issues in a profound personal change. This necessity can be divine necessity of course and then we have a religious or perhaps ethical conversion. It can concern things like diet or mental well-being or a host of other purely personal issues where some kind of 'will' is summoned to do what before had seemed impossible. Narratives about sexuality and gender also seem to have this general character though the underlying necessity here may be framed in biological, psychological or purely introspective terms. Note I am only speaking here about how such stories are structured though at some point we may have to confront the question of the truth of these narratives. This can wait however. Now there are two problems here. The first is that with the best will in the world not all of these narratives are logically consistent. If I discover my deep true self to be a big game hunter and you discover your deep true self to be to be a PETA activist we are on a collision course. The second is that these narratives are taken to be self-authenticating by those who tell them and that there is no body of scripture, religious or scientific, that can externally adjudicate them. There was an old way of doing this of course and that was to give external public validity to such narratives as could render themselves in secular terms and exclude those of which the sacred was an essential element. Not many people have noticed but this is now a dead option because we cannot do justice to the identity of indigenous peoples on these terms for sacred narrative is part of their conception of the world.

So, if you like, we have Leibniz' monads without the pre-established harmony. You have people whose base categories will be 'other'. You will have a Dawkins or Pinker who loudly asserts the supremacy of instrumental reason and the utilitarian rationality of the managerial class (deified as 'science' and complete with conversion narratives) and you will have others completely disinvested in that. You will have the *God Delusion* and you will have the Creation Museum in Kentucky or NBA stars and rap artists who think the moon landing was faked. Some people will explore transgressive sexuality and others speak in tongues. This is because people are not disagreeing within a given framework as say, a Catholic and a Lutheran might have in early modernity. You have people who disagree about the frameworks themselves or at least appear to. Logically of course, any disagreement at all has to be within SOME framework or it could not be a disagreement. We don't need to go all the way to deep incommensurability. Still, it may require a deep conversation to reveal this but deep conversations are not the norm and you need to create the right conditions for them to even occur. So one thing I ask is what conditions need to be in place for 'horizons to meld' as Gadamer would have it and I think part of the answer to this is material. To make new conversations possible we need new material conditions. These conversations may not produce unanimity or anything like it but that is not their purpose. What they produce (and inter-faith dialogue is a good example of this) is the ability to contextualize and humanize our differences and that may not end in us hugging exactly but it may at least end in us learning to keep out of each other's hair if that's what social peace requires.

I suppose this problem has occurred in the past and the time honored solution is force. One side suppresses the other and so if you live in Ancient Hippo you have to accept Augustine's theology not that of Donatus because somebody will assault you physically if you don't. You can even create 'conversions' this way by destroying people's mental resistance though we are talking about things like torture with racks and hot irons here not just being punched in the snout by Mark Bray's pal Gator. (167) This is what China is now doing to Muslim Uighurs. One of the problems the anarchist stance has there is that ANTIFA and organizations like it cannot actually summon the depths of violence necessary to make racism unthinkable and remain a progressive movement. But on the subject of Bray let me make one point. In my previous book I actually addressed arguments to white supremacists and Islamophobes and this is generally considered a foolish and naïve thing to do.

I would like to dissent from this judgement however and to do so I will appeal to one of those 'Tory' authors I began by saying are a thing of the past S.T. Coleridge who not only wrote the *Rime of the Ancient Mariner* but lectured and wrote extensively on metaphysics, theology and political economy. Here is what he says on the matter of freedom and it is quite radical: "An injurious system, the connivance at which we scarcely dare more than regret in the cabinet or senate of an empire, may justify an earnest reprobation in the management of private estates: provided always, that the system only be denounced, and the pleadings confined to the court of conscience. For from this court only can the redress be awarded. All reform or innovation, not won from the free agent by the presentation of juster views and nobler interests, and that does not leave the merit of having affected it sacred to the individual proprietor, it were folly to propose, and worse folly to attempt." (1972; 217). On one level of course this a defense of property: the owner is sovereign of his estate. On another level though it is the principle behind any radicalism anarchist or otherwise: the individual is radically autonomous. Kant worked out the consequence of this morally: any appeal to the other must first and last be an appeal to autonomous judgment, hence the notorious Kantian proscription of lying.

So ethically it's a problem of what to do with the middle. I address arguments to deplorable people because it an ethical necessity to do so otherwise I am treating them as means not ends. What then of force? Well when the police physically assault people to produce short term external compliance we universally denounce that. So, if a black bloc person does that how are they different from police? How are they not acting as a 'state' in precisely the sense that anarchists decry? Well they might say "our ENDS are nobler" (205) but here I think Dr. King is right. Ends pre-exist in means. Means and ends only have a neat separation in reason. In reality means subtly influence the end achieved in myriad ways and as Arendt points out means can even replace ends. If your means of protecting freedom is ICBMs then freedom is no longer the end you are protecting for there is no freedom on a dead planet. If the means to peace is war, then you have a society totally devoted to preparation for war not peace as in the post war military industrial complex. So, this seems to me naiveté of an unpolitical kind and that's my critique of Bray; he is not political. He is an abstract moral idealist who think in terms of Manichean conflict and ideological and moral purity established through rituals of violence (perhaps the most primitive ritual of all).

Our problems though have to do with institutions and policy. Now of course, as Alan Borovoy says, any democracy contains means of legitimate intimidation like boycotts and strikes and so on but no one seriously thinks ANTIFA should torture the children of racists (that's ICE), say, so morality sets a fundamental limit too. I say physical assaults are one of those limits and I know that enrages certain people who feel I am disarming them and I am called all kinds of names but that's how I see it. A friend of mine observed to me that people don't understand non-violence because they don't understand violence for which there is no excuse because there is a vast body of theoretical reflection on violence from Arendt and Simone Weil, King and myriad others. Here too I have to be blunt: is rural internet service going to get better because Bray's friend Gator threatened a local skinhead? No, because ANITFA can't follow anyone into the ballot box to make sure they vote NDP or for a progressive democrat; that is their basic limit and threats of force are, at any rate, subject to a law of diminishing returns.

So that being the case I have a working proposal: a new deal for rural and small town Canada. This has to be done and done now. So far as I can see it has to be done within the existing structure of state institutions by a party like the NDP or Liberals being pushed by the NDP. To that extent I'm an ameliorist rather than a revolutionary. The kind of intervention we need here and on climate seems to be the kind of thing only a state (of some kind) can do so I guess that makes me a left-of-centrist. Will this for certain work? Perhaps it won't. Perhaps it is a null hypothesis and I am misreading the sources and strength of populism. But consider the example of climate change. What do we lose long term by switching to renewable energy? Nothing. What do we lose by redistributing social capital in this country? Again nothing and we might convince a critical mass of people to reengage with the civic project. This would force the CPC in particular to disengage from populist rhetoric that instead of appealing to a 30/40% chunk of voters appeals to 5/10% . The parties would realign to the left and we would have a healthier democracy because of it because this would be a shift to responsibility from reckless ness. Of course there would still be many nagging problems to deal with but the atmosphere for dealing with them will improve drastically.

11 Human Nature Post Irony: Why the Left Should Abandon Performativity

In the Social Sciences it is a sound and useful procedure to point to the way in which we 'perform' certain roles and identities which may have no underlying natural or biological basis. Good social theory is not necessarily good politics however and this is a case in point especially if one is a progressive. I will be brief and to the point. If there is no human nature, there is no progressive politics for there is no liberation if there is nothing to liberate. A sound account of human nature grounded in solid and tested philosophical principle is a deadly weapon against the right and one before which it will wilt. Unfortunately, even a cursory glance at social media will show that what many younger progressives seem engaged in is a war over identity: to wit, which of two groups is performing the 'cooler' one, themselves or the alt-right. This is a battle they will lose every time because they are fighting the opponent's fight. The alt right pseudo-Nietzsche crowd gathered around Peterson and others are 'performers' through and through and in a battle of theatrical self-display will always come out on top. 'Performativity' is their core principle and deploying it polemically is their basic weapon: deploying it they quickly show their opponents to be *earnest* which is the kiss of death. On the contrary, I will argue, they need to be confronted with a robust account of human nature especially as they the one they typically employ, grounded in pop Darwin and outmoded traditions of political economy, is so vulnerable to critique. This will not be an insurmountable challenge as progressivism has an implicit philosophy of human nature within it and it is a matter of asking progressive people to simply attend to the real implications of what they are saying on a daily basis: that there are core human values and needs right wing politics cannot fulfill because their market driven ideologies and crude Social Darwinism make that impossible.

Of course it will sound odd to some of my readers that something so cutting edge and pomo- iconoclastic as 'performativity' turns out to be (potentially at least) a reactionary principle and something so old and boring as 'human nature' turns out to be the true basis of progressiveness.[70] Bear with me though as I make it plain. Social science performs the useful function of describing the arbitrary construction of certain social behaviors such as driving on the left side of the road as opposed to the right. On this basis one might be tempted to elevate the social construction of identity into an absolute principle and say that 'performance' goes all the way down and that there is no underlying structure we can call 'human nature'. In the Anglo world especially, founded on the empiricism and nominalism of Hobbes and his successors, this will seem as inevitable and natural as witchcraft to the Azande. One might be tempted to say with Faust 'in the beginning was the deed' or, as I heard it put recently "there is no doer prior to the deed'. [71]

---

[70] Historically absolutist or reactionary political stances have often appealed to nominalism and anti-essentialism as their foundation. Hobbes stands out as an obvious example: if there is no nature, no reason, no order then it is up to the sovereign to create these things. Skepticism in early modernity was often used to justify the existing order of things as in the traditionalism of Joseph De Maistre or the Catholic apologetics of Pascal or Charron. Pascal is interesting on this point. Does a man seek faith? Then take a little holy water! Altering our habits and patterns of behavior will alter our minds for the mind is a product of our behavior as much as behavior is the product of our mind: habitual or repeated actions alter our perception by imposing regularity on the chaotic flux of experience. Following on Pascal are figures Maurice Blondel who also conceived action as radically self-positing. He rejected 'irony' and 'performance' (concepts quite familiar to a 19th century Frenchman), however, on the grounds that (if I understand him correctly) action that posits itself in time and space generates certain non-arbitrary conditions for itself and that a transcendental philosophy was concerned with describing these conditions as they apply in ethics, politics, religion and so on.

[71] This phrase was inspired by Judith Butler. Butler believes that origins are copies and copies origins though the dialectic by which she comes to this conclusion raises some interesting questions. (723) It depends on the claim that the origin depends logically on the copy as the copy depends logically on the origin. Thus, exactly as left is both origin and copy of right so one might say theft is both origin and copy of honesty. This allows Butler to say that homo-sexuality is both copy and origin of heterosexuality thus undermining the entire 'origin/copy' dichotomy which has been reduced to self-contradiction. Butler has taken the logic of opposites (old as Heraclitus) and applied it to all copy/origin relations. However, this logic does not apply (for instance) to privations. A thing does not depend logically on its privation but the reverse because a privation is nothing in itself: for instance, in the moral sphere psychopathy is not a condition of the possibility of empathy. 'Originals', then, do not depend on 'copies' that are reductions in some sense or which they include by excess (like Judith Butler and a photo of Judith Butler). Of course, Butler is entirely free to argue that same sex desire is not the absence of hetero-sexuality in the sense that it is a positive good in its own right and not simply a 'deviation' that dialectically overcomes its corresponding norm. This problematic is analogous to the ancient theological question of whether God needs the world to which one might answer 'not as a necessary logical correlative' though there are other kinds of necessity and other kinds of need. It is tempting to stand with the Neo-Platonists and say that the One produces out of the 'necessity' of super-abounding productivity and goodness and not because it must conform to some purely extrinsic logical scheme that belongs solely to lower determinations. John Scotus Eriugena (an early medieval 'deconstructionist') assures us that the 'origin' as NOT a moment in a determinate binary is beyond representation and is indeed a sort of 'nothing by excess' out of which all 'somethings' proceed. Whether one calls this theology or atheism or both might well be a matter of preference. Butler seems to conceive the psyche as an excess that grounds (725) but in naming this 'psyche' she is considerably more positive than Eriugena is prepared to be. At any rate that deconstruction always tries but never quite succeeds in disengaging itself from negative theology is the subject of an interesting

I will now explain A. why this is wrong and B. why it is a disaster for the left. It is simply not true that every person is the identity they perform for prior to the deed is the hierarchy of needs of the doer. Human nature is grounded in human need and human desire as Simone Weil showed in one of the great progressive works of the last century *The Need for Roots*. At the core or origin of this hierarchy of needs is the desire for recognition: the core need of every human person is to be an object of ethical respect and all our other natural needs such as food, housing or meaningful work follow upon that basic recognition of person-hood.[72] As the dull pedant Kant said persons are ends in the themselves and it is the basic desire and the basic demand of all persons to be recognized as such.[73] Absent this principle there is only the performative leftism of things like 'call-out' culture where using certain words or making certain prescribed gestures becomes the whole content of politics. Call out culture is leftism reduced to behaviorism; Karl Marx to B.F. Skinner. A progressivism that attends to its ethical and human core will ultimately prefer the language of authenticity to that of irony and performance however much the latter may be useful on occasion as a tactic for those who lack real power or are unfamiliar with its responsible exercise.

But, you might ask, isn't performativity an important weapon against essentialism and isn't essentialism the root of all oppression.[74] Well, false

---

exchange between Derrida and Jean Luc Marion.

[72] The phrase 'hierarchy of needs' belongs, of course, to the psychologist Maslow but it Weil's account I am thinking of here. To recover a sense of what is natural and appropriate for humans we might go back to the pre-Socratics and begin with the nurturing elements of earth, air, fire and water: "Is it not easy to conceive the world in your mind? To think the heavens fair? The sun glorious? The earth fruitful? The sea profitable? And the giver bountiful?...The clouds and stars minister unto us, the world surrounds us with beauty, the air refresheth us, the sea revives the earth and us." (Thomas Traherne, Centuries of Meditations 189-191) At any rate, Weil recommends we start with food as the one truly basic need and proceed by analogy from there (1952; 6) and however one might quibble with her subsequent account that seems to me a sound way to begin.

[73] Here a hard thing needs to be said. Politics is essentialism. Politics is concerned with the orderly (and equitable) satisfaction of core human needs. This involves identifying which needs are core. Public policy cannot be customized for every individual want and so must typify as when we assume a 'rational agent 'standard for people in comas. We must say, at the end of the day, say that water, air and companionship are core needs and having a billion dollars is not no matter how essential the billionaire FEELS his fortune is to his own self- worth. Nor would we change our laws on slavery if someone expressed an (apparently) sincere, deep seated wish to be a slave. Thus, at very minimum human nature is a necessary political construct; it may be a necessary ethical or metaphysical construct too but that is another discussion. I prescind, then, from the question of whether 'human nature' is innate (whatever sense we attach to this word) or a habit so quickly and persistently formed that it makes no practical difference. Nature may (or may not) be no more than 'first habit'. Alas, one difficulty here is distinguishing the proper philosophical sense of the word 'nature' from the notion of biological determinism with which a contemporary reader will unfortunately (and wrongly) associate it.

[74] A close connection between anti-essentialism and freedom is often simply assumed in contemporary discussions but even a cursory glance at history shows how tenuous this connection actually is. In the 18 Century it was abolitionists who asserted a

essentialisms certainly are oppressive but in our current political wars performativity is a pop-gun. It always astounds me how people on my side of the political fence can stare into the abyss and see only liberal values starting back. On performativity, though, the right is way ahead of the game. If all identity is performed, if there is only the deed and no doer, then I can construct a reactionary identity with exactly as much and exactly as little justification as a progressive one. I can then perform this identity publicly and walk off with bags of money laughing at all the people I've tricked into taking me seriously: all the earnest dullards who didn't realize they were being trolled. I can construct new gender roles, true, but I can also with equal validity or invalidity perform all the old ones.[75] I do not even need to do this in an anxiety fueled reactionary sense but in the spirit of an ironic "screw you" as in the current fad for over the top 'gender reveal' parties that revel in the thoughtless celebration of pink and blue. I might well, like the oversophisticated hipster, come to the point where I simply like velvet Elvis paintings and perform a naïve appreciation that has overcome mere *sophistication* as yesterday's news. It seems to belong to human freedom to negate any negation and that is why the Underground man tells us that there will always be those who poke their tongue out at the crystal palace because it's there.

What is more, if I choose to perform this pose of ironic reaction I can with perfect conscience impose it on my children for there is no underlying structure or nature or need I am violating by doing so. Indeed, one of the things I can perform is 'populism'. I can note that privileged people like the Clintons or Trudeau perform a pretty empty, ineffectual brand of liberalism and then express my contempt for them by performing the opposite. Indeed, the more liberal values are insisted on the more flouting them becomes a means of rebellion. As St. Paul noted long ago the law is an occasion for sin. With manners comes the possibility of rudeness. With political correctness in speech comes new ways of being offensive and racist and a whole new incentive for doing so i.e. defiance, rebellion and contempt for elites. This is why the 'great leader', unlike

---

common nature between Africans and Europeans and empiricists like Hume who were unapologetic racists (See my essay "Dear Whites" in Believing Weird Things). At any rate one thing I note about current discussions of gender and sexuality is the degree to which they use not the language of performativity but the language of authenticity: their appeal against conventional gender norms is that they cannot be their true selves within them. This of course assumes that the notion of a true or authentic self has some content and that others are required to recognize its demands. In other words, we are, as a society, in search of an ethics of authenticity (to borrow a phrase from Charles Taylor). The argument against strict gender roles is, it seems to me, that they close down legitimate pathways of human self-expression and that is a moral argument about freedom as a basic human good.

[75]Let me put it this way. We can perform any role we want until an Adam encounters an Eve or a Gilgamesh encounters an Enkidu. At that point we encounter the hard limit of another performer and if we cannot perform our identities fully in the same time and same space we must either kill or subdue each other or recognize the dimension of the ethical; where the well-being of another subjectivity makes an irreducible claim on my own. I use the phrase human nature as a kind of shorthand for these 'hard limits' but I won't quibble over the phrase if the reader prefers another.

others, is not punished for rudeness and vulgarity but rewarded. The 'left' of course will think I am a fool and that I am trying to bring back God or the categorical imperative or biology. Contact with hard core people on the right however has convinced me that they are a step ahead on this: they don't invoke these things at all except (very effectively) as triggering gestures. They are throwing performativity back in our faces and laughing at our reaction. In tradition of the Ancient Sophists they have decided that truth is whatever serves power and advantage. Their stance is ironic and performative through and through and their bag of rhetorical tricks (contemptuous gestures, fake outrage, ad hominem attacks, verbal aggression, shameless gas lighting, projection and so on) ancient and time tested.[76] On this point see my essay "Notes on the Rhetoric of Trolling" . (https://social-epistemology.com/2019/05/02/notes-on-the-rhetoric-of-trolling-part-1-bernard-wills/)

Fortunately, there is a solution and that is philosophy well taught and internalized as a way of life starting with Plato and moving on to Kant, Hegel, Marx and so on. This will frighten your alt-right opponents far more than whatever the latest iteration of 'theory' is as they know exactly the procedure for mocking and ridiculing the latter (as it employs easily mocked and parodied jargon) but will be wrong-footed by the former especially if it employs the virtues of direct and clear expression. When such people, purported 'defenders' of 'Western civilization' are confronted with what thinkers in that tradition *actually say* the results will not often be in their favor. We can then regard 'performativity' as a useful tool for a certain kind of sociological and/or literary analysis that reveals the underlying arbitrariness (the lack of 'origin') of certain constructed social roles. To erect a metaphysics, a morality and a progressive politics on this basis however, is a dicey proposition and, to be frank, betrays the a-historicism which is the ubiquitous disease of North Americans. Perfomativity (at least as an *all the way down* thing) seems to negate any politics progressive or otherwise except as an ironic parody to be taken up or dropped at will. Where 'performativity' and other nominalist doctrines are concerned we should say 'thank you' and move on.

---

[76]Of course there are dupes who actually believe the things put forward by right wing activists Evangelical Christians being a prominent example. All cynical, nihilistic movements depend on 'true believers' who internalize every lie put forward by the 'movement'. This is something I have pointed out in the past concerning the secular authoritarianism of someone like Daniel Dennett: "Dennett must persuade us that science teaches a behaviouristic account of meaning and intention which, if true, would make science itself illusory, for descriptions of fact cannot provide justification. Yet if naturalism cannot be stated discursively without self-contradiction it is still for Dennett the central moral and political project of our age, to be enacted as public policy and defended by every trick or rhetoric and persuasion in our arsenal. There is no literal truth of science. There is no literal truth of anything. There are only the agonistic arts of the sophist and polemicist. Thus, Dennett shares with certain Straussians a penchant for insult, invective and hyperbole along with an apparent disregard for scholarly standards of evidence." (Wills and Hynes "Biologizing Religion Part II" Toronto Journal of Theology vol.27. no.2 2011. 235-248).

PART 2

12 God, UFO's, Numbers, and Things that Exist

It's finally happened! Professor Smith, after toiling in his basement for years has finally finished a twenty- page modal proof of the existence of God. What is more he has found a journal to publish it in. He has even gotten some good reviews along with a blurb from Alvin Plantinga for his forthcoming book. In this book he has anticipated and answered a range of objections. Things are looking up for Theism. We may expect in short order empty churches and mosques to fill. We may expect constitutions hitherto silent on the matter to invoke the supreme being. Scientific hypotheses hitherto excluded from serious consideration, like intelligent design, will suddenly become live options attracting grants and other forms of public recognition. Indeed, the world would see a flowering of spirituality without precedent in history! An outpouring of mysticism, sacred poetry and works of love! Alas, as we all know in our heart of hearts, Professor Smith's proof will have no such effect. The world will go on exactly as it did before with at most a handful of atheists (all of them academics in Philosophy of Religion!) becoming theists. We would be in the same situation as we are with climate change, evolution and a number of other well proven things that many are inclined to ignore or regard as egregiously false when they think of them at all. People, it seems, are just not that into proof. This is a hard pill for philosophers to swallow but such is life. Or is it? Are there forms of proof that actually persuade people of X, Y or Z? Psychologists and social scientists no doubt have a good deal to say about this. I, alas, have only one test subject, myself (philosophy, alas, is stuck with the hideously unscientific process of introspection). What kind of proof would convince ME that something was true? I have read any number of professor Smiths on God and other questions. Rarely if ever do they change my mind or intensify my current beliefs one iota (except perhaps negatively!) The assumption seems to be that a line goes from inquiry to theory to belief. Another line however goes from inquiry to belief to theory and this may well be the more common one. Indeed, even more common would be a line that goes straight to belief skipping inquiry altogether. We must also take into account the fact that, as Lakatos reminds us, there is no straight line (though there may be crooked ones) from experience to theory which is to say that theories are not *inferred* from facts.

Be that as it may I return to the question: what kind of thing WOULD change my mind? I will begin with something I don't believe in, that is aliens, and consider what might convince me of their existence. Seeing them, though a popular option, will not do. Merely seeing something should not convince us of anything. The reasons for this are all familiar. We could be lucid dreaming, hallucinating, the object of a hoax or simply mistaking a for b as when our alien ship turns out to be a weather balloon. Generations of philosophy have taught us to question our senses and we should surely do this here (it is for this reason odd that observation is so often taken as the gold standard of knowledge). Still, seeing aliens does pertain to believing in them: we would expect any indirect proof offered by an astronomer to be supplemented at some point by a physical sighting of some kind before we put the capstone on our belief (as occurred with the 'discovery' of Neptune). Indeed, with a theory in place we can go *back* to our senses and revaluate those funny lights in the sky and abduction tales. They now have a context in which they appear possible and even plausible. Seeing PLUS a theory seems more credible then either are separately (with apologies to string theory). Still, I'm not sure seeing an alien vessel once or twice and having a theory that makes intelligent aliens likely rather than unlikely would be enough to create in me a firm and persistent habit of believing in them. The sightings could still be mistaken and the theory wrong (see Fermi's paradox). If I have a strong incentive NOT to believe in aliens, I can still say to the devil with them.

The universe however does not simply consist of sense objects and theoretical entities; it also contains partners, friends and enemies. It consists of relationships as well as objects. My belief in aliens on Proxima Centauri is a much different thing than a carpenter's belief in her tools. The latter belief is costly to change for one thing. I can, on the other hand, flip back and forth on the subject of aliens with little difficulty. Things would be very different however if I *interacted* with aliens on a regular or semi-regular basis. Things with which I trade or fight, say, attain status in *my* world. Then the problem is not with believing but with not believing: a chemist can no more disbelieve in chemicals than a carpenter can disbelieve in saws. On the same ground the Azande cannot disbelieve in witches any more than the !Kung can disbelieve in ancestors (if we are in the morally compromised position of colonizers we have to work to make them NOT believe these things). To use a fictional example, the porter in the Emerald City believes in the Wizard because his life revolves around him. My world is stocked with things and I act in such a fashion as to recognize the objectivity of these things. Thus, the ultimate ground for believing in aliens would be reached when aliens became things in my world. This seems to be what Ian Hacking is getting at with his notion that things attain ontological status by being the objects of interaction. We can now tote up the results of our brief inquiry. I would believe in aliens if and only If a. there was empirical evidence of them b. a theory or account which put that evidence in some kind of intelligible context and c. some form of interaction or relation (with the depth of my belief increasing with the depth and extent of my interaction). Thus, we can see that one of the problems with climate denial is that most people are not climate scientists and not apt to believe in concepts they don't work or live with.

Now let's think of the subject with which we began. It would seem that a proof of God 's existence capable of actually persuading people would have three moments. Firstly, there would be an empirical sign. Here we labor under a fundamental restriction: while we may hold out some hope for photographing a quark all our observations concerning God's activity will be indirect and inferred. The experience of mystical union claimed by a small number of persons (such as Plotinus or St. Theresa) may be an exception to this but it is surely too rare and high a thing to serve our purpose here. However, a large amount of inferred evidence may be said to make up for a lack of direct observation. Gravity was a widely accepted concept centuries before graviton waves were observed (whatever observed means in that context). Still, there are the many miraculous or otherwise odd or uncanny events that people attribute to God. There are transcendent moments in art, acts of charity or unlooked for consolations that people attribute to the same source. There is the meticulous fine tuning of the natural realm or even the raw beauty of sunsets. There are ennobling experiences like love. Moreover, there are the various moments of historical revelation which founded the Abrahamic faiths. If I follow the process laid out above these would be 'sightings' of a divine power though often more introspective than the sighting of an external object. They would be, as the Stoics might have called them, determinate presentations. They would be evidence which we could dismiss in each single instance but which might become compelling if accompanied by a 'theory' or 'account' that made them plausible. In other words, observation is a complex process that entails a great deal of theoretical construction whether conscious and unconscious. No chemist grounds his experiment on language like 'green, here, cold'. Observational language is sophisticated and sophisticated language is theory laden language.

There is of course such a theory or account: indeed, there is only one though it is expressed and developed in a multitude of ways by a multitude of authors. It is that 'holism' is systematic and complete. In the ancient language there is a *Logos* or fundamental principle of rational order such as might be exemplified, say, by Plato's ideas. As Plotinus tells us, and he is followed in this by Christian, Jewish and Islamic theologians, these archetypal ideas, the forms and patterns of all natural things which constrain events in time and space, form a living intelligent totality. All finite events flow from the productive power of this totality (the *Nous*).[77] It

---

[77]Of course Plotinus and even more so the later Neo-Platonists (Iamblichus, Proclus and Damascius) posit a first principle above intelligence and its presumed distinction of subject and object. This is the 'one' or 'good' which is a hyper-unified auto-intuition inexpressible in the categories of language and conceptual thought. Though important

determines the sensible world but is not determined by it. Its acts flow freely and without external necessitation from its own nature as creative mind and as such we call it 'omnipotent' however inadequate our determinate conceptions of power are to convey the unconstrained nature of its productive activity. Now, you may reject the theory put forth by the Neo-Platonists and carried forward in Western thought from Augustine to Hegel and beyond. You may think it is mystical nonsense. If you are a philosopher in the Analytic tradition you will almost certainly think this. If you are an idealist or even a continental philosopher, you may think very differently. However, if you have had some of the experiences mentioned above you now have a theory that puts them in an intelligible context so that they are not simply isolated bits of dissonance.[78] There is a metaphysical context in which they now make sense. Observation, experience and theory now mutually re-inforce each other though you can certainly toss aside the whole ensemble just as in the U.F.O example. As one of my favorite students once said, if reason proves the existence of God then it is reason that is the problem. As Dostoevsky's Underground Man puts it, $2+2=5$ has its charms as well!

Here we face an interesting problem. There seems to me a sense in which the Underground Man is entirely correct. Theories are embodied in ways of life. Outside this context they make little sense. Mathematical theory is irrelevant to people who do not count.[79] Anthropology informs us that there are such people: some people have an imprecise number term meaning 'a bunch' which they use to designate any assembly of things over

in itself, this distinction will no doubt strike the general reader as arcane and so I omit discussion of it here. Those who wish to perplex themselves on the matter may consult the excellent chapter on Plotinus in R.W. Wallis' Neo-Platonism. In a Christian context they might consider the Corpus Dionysiacum and its development in subsequent Orthodox spirituality through such authors as Maximus Confessor and Gregory Palamas. The ur-text for all this reflection is, of course, Plato's analogy of the sun.

[78] One of the challenging features of ancient Platonism is that knowledge of the first principle is (in its full evolution at least) experiential; the culmination of a moral and intellectual discipline and the terminus of applied meditative techniques. In certain later Platonists this knowledge is even tied to material rites and cultic ritual. To this extent there is in their positions a certain appeal to authority as knowledge of the 'one' is not an isolated bit of neutral, disengaged 'information' sitting out there to be appropriated by just anyone. One has self-authenticating experiences of the first causal principle though, like Eriugena, one might make this principle a moment in the unfolding of a comprehensive 'division of nature': a beginning justified in the totality of the result.

[79] Perhaps I can put the problem this way. There may be no way of life in which $2+2=4$ is false but there are ways of life in which $2+2=4$ is neither true nor false. To revert to early modern debates about divine power (which are quite relevant here) it does, as Descartes indicates in the Letters to Mersenne, seem to lie in the power of God to create a universe in which the basic truths of mathematics do not apply. Thus, the Pythagorean theorem would not be true (though it would not be false either) if god had created the universe using only points. An interesting analogy here would be that of computers for if there were conscious computers their universe would only consist of zeroes and units making all sorts of mathematical propositions not so much false as irrelevant. Such voluntarism (whether theological or secular and whether one accepts it or not) seems at least one viable metaphysical option. An entertaining treatment of this possibility is the film Flatland based on the novel by Edwin Abbot.

3. This is true of a number of indigenous cultures in the Amazon region. In their world the proposition denied by the Underground man cannot even exist. Of course these people hunt and mate and raise children as successfully as many more numerate cultures do. Moreover, their *languages* are sometimes complex and expressive far beyond our own (containing many fine grained distinctions in vocabulary, tense and case that we lack). To make higher mathematics meaningful in their world they would have to begin *operating* with such concepts and this would involve a fundamental change in how they live. For instance, they might have to start sharing food differently. The mathematical world is one which they would *choose* to enter though they might not. Ballistics is a reality only for those who want to kill at a distance. If we decline the world of rockets, cannons, artillery shells and catapults it is not for us an operative concept. In fact, if no one were interested in slaughtering opponents five miles away it would be hard to say in what way existed at all except perhaps in the mind of God.[80] Absent some absolute objectivity like a divine mind the Underground Man may well be within his rights to prefer $2+2=5$ if he is content with a practical form of life consistent with this principle.[81] To be frank, we have living examples of people who have made just this choice (practically speaking) and are no worse for wear. Indeed, they may rejoice that artillery duels with neighboring tribes are not a visitation they must suffer.

Indeed, suppose I wanted to convince an Amazonian of the existence

---

[80]Not entirely a bad option as the career of Bishop Berkeley suggests. Indeed, as his eccentric contemporary Arthur Collier manages to points out (in spite of his almost impossibly prolix style) the claims of modern 'realists' about 'objective truth' cannot rest on the correspondence of propositions to states of an external material substratum which could only be unknowable and inconceivable. If absolutely objectivity exists at all (and we may piously hope it does) this would lie in the 'divine ideas' or 'forms' not in 'things' outside the mind. This may be taken to explain Berkeley's later turn from immaterialism to Platonic idealism. Here though we face a challenge which is that while we have a philosophy of mind few if any see the corresponding need for a philosophy of matter though the latter notion is far from intuitively obvious. Berkeley's early idealism is a correct conclusion drawn on the basis of Locke's notion of substance as 'substratum' but there are of course other iterations of matter in the history of philosophy including Plato's dyadic quantitative flux, Aristotle's steresis (the moment of potentiality in a substance which is receptive of change) and Descartes' res extensa absolutized as external 'matter' by Malebranche.

[81]One might say that anyone who grasps the first three numbers has, virtually, the knowledge of the rest as all they need to do is repeat operations which have already occurred. Why this does not happen among people like indigenous Amazonians is an interesting question. Perhaps it is a matter of ontology: perhaps they simply do not perceive groups as aggregates divisible into discreet quantity. From such a holist perspective they might be reticent about counting beyond the bare minimum. My immediate point though may be illustrated by the passage in the Meno in which the slave boy discovers the square twice the area of a given square. This process involves a leap of intuition that leads to discovery: the decision to view the problem in terms of diagonal lines within the larger square. This change in perspective that leads to a solution is not a necessary inference from what has gone before but a decision to look at the problem in a new way. In the same way we might shift our ground and start counting given some incentive (possibly social) to start doing so: the mathematical realm is both a sphere of necessity AND a free production.

of the laws of ballistics? I could explain to him the wonderful process by which a naval gun can strike a moving ship twenty miles away. I doubt our Amazonian would do anything more than shrug as he has no ships of his own and has no reason to even think of destroying those of other people. We could then change tack and explain to him that these laws explain the action of the arrows and spears he uses in hunting. I suspect he would reply by saying that he understands perfectly well how these things work: you point the bow at the target and (allowing for a bit of lead) release the arrow![82] At any rate he probably has a far greater knowledge of tracking and hunting his prey than the western scientist trying so desperately to convince him he is ignorant of the matter (it would be a foolish biologist who investigated the fauna of the Amazon without inquiring of the locals) . This of course is *operative* knowledge: he, unlike his interlocutor, *handles* the bow and spear. He is like the craftsman who, Aristotle tells us, may know far more than the man of pure theory though this knowledge is in the form of accumulated experience rather than science (though even science contains much of its knowledge in the form of know-how). In fact, our hypothetical encounter seems to end in a standoff. Depending on our outlook we can prefer the superior theoretical knowledge of the scientist or the greater practical knowledge of the Amazonian. As a last desperate measure the Scientist can tell the Amazonian that a knowledge of the principles of ballistics will allow him to design better arrows that will kill more prey from greater distances but here the conversation will end with the Amazonian's perplexed question as to why he should kill more prey than his family or clan can eat. Indeed, if he had some knowledge of the follies of our 'civilization' he could turn this question around and ask (as I once did an engineer) why we didn't develop *less* efficient (and hence less destructive) methods of hunting and fishing.

What implications might this have for our topic? Well, religious concepts, outside the realm of magical practice, are not typically operative concepts in the sense that we operate *with* them. God is not a tool for

---

[82]This is hardly the naïve answer it seems. If a child asks how a microscope works it is a perfectly respectable answer to demonstrate its use. If the child persists and wants to know why the microscope works, responding to each answer with a more fundamental question (as children are wont to do) he may well be told that ultimate whys are for philosophers and theologians and that he should stop his questioning and just use the damn tool. "Shut up and do the math" is sometimes the scientific answer. Indeed, one account of science, the instrumentalist account, holds that the meaning of all scientific assertions is at the end of the day operative. Science simply doesn't bother with why questions or causes. This sophisticated Humeanism arrives in the end at the same position as the hypothetical Amazonian who answers the question about his bow by simply using it. Of course if the Amazonian chooses to dabble in theory he actually has a rather good one. Arrows, he might say, like all things, have within them a spirit that disposes them to do all that they do. The arrow has something akin to a personality or inherent disposition. The virtues of this theory are something I may well elaborate elsewhere. I note it here to show that it may in fact be Amazonian who tries the path of explanation where the scientist may simply do contrary to what might have been our initial supposition. Nothing necessarily forces us to the standpoint of theory (mathematicians DO the operations and do not worry about Platonic realism or conventionalism).

instance (at least as theology has tended to conceive him). We might say rather that religious concepts *operate on us* or perhaps that we *operate within them*. It is easy to see that this is the case with respect to confessional religion. A Catholic or High Anglican participates in a sacramental liturgy in which actions and phrases are repeated with suitable variations on a weekly basis. A Muslim or Jew observes dietary and other ritual prohibitions. Religious belief is in each case grounded in bodily action and continuous observance. Beliefs and principles and laws become braided with the world of things with which we interact. As Pascal pointed out long ago this is the high road to believing anything: a man who takes a little holy water may well come to faith thereby just as teaching a biology class is a potent incentive to believing in biology.[83] (2005; 45) How many biologists believe in evolution because their *work* would be impossible without it? In each case the concepts, abstract in themselves, become the boundaries of our world through constant interaction. This seems to be the third element to coming to a belief. It is indeed easily the most powerful one as it is able to operate without the other two. This is not to say that it should: intellectual responsibility dictates that we do our best to invoke evidence in the context of a theory though this is not possible with every single thing we happen to believe.

Amusingly or not, it seems that Phil Robertson's quaint argument that one cannot be an Atheist because the calendar is based on Christ seems not so wrong after-all. Christian conceptions of time order our lives on a daily basis and while this may not be an adequate warrant for belief it is a not insignificant component of it! After all a person's belief in science may have as much to do with her telephone as with her understanding of nature. However, let's recapitulate. To go back to the beginning, what would a persuasive argument for the existence of god look like? Well it would seem it would appeal to some evidence. This might range from an answered prayer to a complex appreciation of the order of nature. It might simply appeal the not uninteresting fact that there is anything at all as opposed to nothing. However, all this is mere musing if it does not express itself in some theoretical form which gathered and synthesized this evidence in some coherent form. Speculative theology in its various expressions is the venture which gives religious experience this theoretical form. Finally, this argument would appeal to the concepts with which people work on a daily basis showing their theistic implications. For those not directly involved with confessional practice (and that would seem to be most people) ethical concepts daily recognized would be an obvious

---

[83] As in the ancient epics most of us start in media res. We are in the process of acting with things, persons and concepts whose beginnings and foundations we don't ordinarily reflect on. I for instance engage on a daily basis with the process of interpreting artificial as opposed to natural signs usually in the form of written texts but sometimes in the form of visual images or music. As this is my daily practice I repose a certain faith in it though the meaningfulness of meaning may be no more demonstrable than the rationality of reason (unless, perhaps, we use demonstration in a special dialectical sense).

candidate: there is 'practical theism' as much as there is 'practical atheism' i.e. living *as if* there were a god as opposed to living *as if* there was not. This, I suppose, would be a considerable task and not one I will be undertaking here. However, the beginning is the important part of any work as I always try to impress on my students. Consider this my preface to any possible theism. One result of it that seems a happy one to me is that it seems a convincing account of anything would be empiricist, rationalist, and pragmatist at once involving an immediate presentation, a theoretic mediation of that presentation and a practical synthesis in action. And, finally, this illustrates why it is useful to think about the question of divine existence as it bears on the existence of other things as well. Indeed, as American philosopher Charles Hartshorne once quipped, it touches on all the basic metaphysical and epistemological questions.

13 What is the Rational Critique of Religion? An Open Letter to Anti-Theists

I am Bernard Wills. Who is Bernard Wills? I am a professor at a small (very small) liberal arts college in a northern location. I have a background in Ancient and Early Medieval (late Ancient?) philosophy. This means I am not an anti-theist (that not being not much of a thing in that period). It also means I have a certain professional interest in talking to people who are as one can't live in an echo chamber. I am a Christian though probably the world's worst one. I am not a conservative Evangelical Protestant and generally find their theology alien to my own. I don't give a fig for things like biblical inerrancy or other typically fundamentalist doctrines. I have put my thoughts in a book available on Amazon entitled *Why Believe* and a second book entitled *Believing Weird Things*. As according to Blake "Without contraries there is no progression" I would like to start of discussion about these books not with people who like them but with people who don't. In the latter category I would put Secular Humanists, anti-Theists and the like in whatever permutations they happen to exist. I do not put 'casual non-believers' in this category as I am concerned not with Atheism per se but with a certain ideological construction of it. I disagree deeply with this construction not because I disagree with the notion of criticizing religion but because I do not think its adherents understand what criticism is nor how the practice of criticism is relevant to something like a body of religious belief. As this seems to me a very serious error I thought I might say something to address it. I preface my comments with an introduction as some of you will have no interest in taking on this question. Some of you have no interest in talking to anyone who is not a fundamentalist because you have all your arguments about Noah's Ark prepared and are eager as puppies to use them. I'm fine with that. Your self-understanding has come to depend on your chosen adversary with whom you seek conflict on the narrow ground both of you have chosen. Shifting the ground of the discussion may put you in a less comfortable place. If you are up to it however, there is a basic point I wish to make about what is wrong with current discussions of religion as you and others practice it. This point concerns the concept of 'critique' not in the narrow and surely improper sense of uttering negative comments about something but in its rational and philosophical sense. A critique is, to put it simply, an evaluation. It involves not only 'criticisms' in the sense usually understood but just appreciation both of the virtues and limitations of its object founded on appropriate contextualization of its aims.[84] In this sense it is closer to what we mean by 'literary' criticism. Other things about critique will emerge below but for now I simply note that polemic is only part of critique and not even the largest part at that.

Let me begin though with what a critique of religion is not. Religions contain things like symbols, narratives, images, schemes of representation and so on. One can take any of these in isolation and, robotically applying the law of non-contradiction, find incoherences in them. Finding a contradiction in something is generally the lowest form of criticism and this is especially true of images. Having noted that snakes do not talk many succumb to the temptation to trumpet this as a great achievement, perhaps the greatest achievement, of reflective consciousness. I'm afraid I do not agree. I think there are limits to standard binary logic and in this I stand with Marx, Hegel and Heraclitus. While there are vicious contradictions that are the result of sloppy thinking or bad writing there are, much more importantly, deep contradictions founded in the fundamental tensions of life. Contradiction in the second sense is what life is about which is why no one complains if *War and Peace* or *The Idiot* fail to display 100% rational consistency. All good books have these contradictions and it is no criticism of the Bible (or anything else) to say that it contradicts itself or that its images contain discursive contradictions. In fact, as Paul Feyerabend argues, anomalies, aporia and theoretical contradictions are an essential part of 'scientific' theories as every theory that lacks these is a dead theory incapable of development or further discovery. This is why he says that every good theory is falsified by the facts. This is evident in textual studies, which too many of you seem to disdain, where tensions and difficulties in a text are precisely what get the conversation going. This insight, which Blake gave such forceful expression to, seems to me the demarcation point between mature criticism and one that is merely boyish. I use the latter phrase quite deliberately as there are many aspects of your discourse that are in fact gendered and this over reliance on discursive rationality used in a purely agonistic sense is surely one of them. The notion that, at this late date in 2018, puncturing Bill Smith's third reformulation of the modal proof or Joe Barnes' latest twist on the free will theodicy will make an existential difference on the question of God is surely ludicrous. Philosophy

---

[84] It is a mistake in philosophy to think one has 'criticized' something when one has found a 'mistake' in some formalization of an author's argument that is yours and not the author's. There is a whole scholarly industry devoted to this empty procedure but a true 'critique' is dialectical: does a position deconstruct itself when its own principles are applied with due rigor? In other words, true critique is immanent critique. I say this in contradistinction to those who tout it as the task of philosophy to catch Marx or Plato affirming the consequent.

is about seeking truth in dialogue while winning arguments is, alas, the province merely of lawyers.

Let's however try to state the positive side of this. I will begin with Marx's poorly understood statement that religion is the opium of the people. Marx did not mean by this that it is stupid to believe in a talking snake. Under certain forms of oppression, it might be quite rational to believe in one! What he meant was that religion was a form of alienated discourse. Religion is displaced discourse meaning that it talks about A by talking about B. This takes a bit of unpacking. Hegel had pointed out in his philosophy of religion that religion is concerned with what he calls a 'vorstellung' or representation.[85] This means that there is the content A on the one hand and a schema of representation B on the other. In religion, as opposed to philosophy, the form of the representation is not the form of the content represented. Like our orbital model of the atom the divine life as we picture it (in three persons say) is one thing and the divine life in itself another (this particular symbol, the Trinity, comes very close to transcending 'religion' for Hegel but that is for another discussion). Marx takes this insight up and attempts to say what 'religion' is about. On his view it is alienated discourse about the human condition. We embody our desire for a better world in 'pictures' like a blissful after life.[86] We do this because we do not have true life now. If we are oppressed, we will project our consciousness of this oppression in images. Now, here is the crucial thing. While these images express our alienation they also occlude our alienation. The content we are trying to grasp (freedom) is hidden behind the forms in which we have pictured it to ourselves. To get at that content is impossible while we are simply held by the externality of the image. This is why religion is so useful for oppressors. To overcome religion means to reveal its true content to consciousness by overcoming the gap between

---

[85] In this religion does not differ at all from science. Hegel points out that science's 'representation' of the world is not its actual content. Science depicts the world as a set of material entities existing in a realm of determinate facts and laws exterior to the mind. This depiction though is false; it is a mere 'vorstellung' like the images of religion which place a God 'above us' at the apex of a ladder of beings. What science actually does is dissolve all the immediate content of sensation into a series of abstract relationships like positive and negative electricity or acid and base: at bottom science is idealistic not materialistic. On the above see the chapter "On the Observation of Organic Nature" in The Phenomenology of Mind.

[86] For Marx it is the underlying social and economic conditions that form the 'latent content' of religious traditions and symbols. For others, like Carl Jung, this content is psychological. For the broader theological tradition, the 'symbolic veils' encode metaphysical, moral and mystical knowledge. I simply note these differences here though it would be worth questioning whether these approaches are mutually exclusive as all three propose some purgation of the externality of the image. I suppose this would not please Marxist orthodoxy but I actually see no reason why a post capitalist society would not enable new and deeper explorations of the self and spirituality: for perhaps the first time we might have un-alienated religion as an option to explore along with 'Homer and fishing'. Indeed, removing (or at least diminishing) economic alienation might well have the effect of making basic human alienation all the plainer (contrary to the assumption of utopianism) to which religious solutions will always suggest themselves (assuming you think some moment of alienation like original sin or dhukka to be essential to a religious standpoint).

content and representation. Thus, if we simply take the image and use the categories of reflective consciousness to disintegrate it we have accomplished nothing and, in fact, the alienated and unfulfilled consciousness will simply go back to its representations and cling to them all the more fiercely. This is why the sum total of the achievement of secular hectoring in the United States is the creation museum in Kentucky.

A related question concerns the criticism of the Bible as a text. As I adverted to above criticism of the Bible does not consist in pointing out external contradictions in the narrative. Nor does it consist in pointing out aspects of bronze age morality that seem rebarbative to a contemporary reader. Atheists often read the Bible as a purported handbook of morality and through this moralistic lens miss much of its significance. In this again they agree with fundamentalists. When I have taught the Hebrew Bible I have always had trouble conveying the complexity of characters like Abraham or Joseph to students who only wanted to read them as moral exemplars. This is in fact as narrow and rationalistic an approach to text as your own. Let me then sum up for you what I typically find from very conservative evangelicals. Ask your selves what in their depiction of the Bible you actually disagree with. For the hard core fundamentalist, the Biblical text is hermeneutically 'flat'. I mean by this that they regard every part of that text as standing in the same relation to the whole. For this reason, they will not even admit factual errors into what is after all a human document. Every bit of the text utters a true proposition with truth here being primarily 'facticity'. What is more, this flatness is diachronic as well as synchronic. The earliest strata of the text utter the same propositional truths as the later ones and there is thus in the Bible no development or dialectical unfolding of truth over time. This means that slaughter of the Canaanites and the sermon on the mount are equivalent acts of revelation. This turns scriptural interpretation into mechanical proof-texting that is the diametric opposite of actual reading. Of course the Bible is not actually like this and that is because it is, at very minimum, a literary text and literary texts are simply not like that. If the Bible is more than literature (and I am open to that claim) it is not so by being less than literature and that distinguishes it from such pedestrian productions as the *Book of Mormon*.

How then do we read the Bible critically? There are of course many tendencies and theories that fall under the umbrella of the so called 'Higher Criticism' so I will only give my view here.[87] Firstly, any critical approach

---

[87]Higher criticism is through and through a theological project. A critic who says that the aim of reading Shakespeare is to find out only what his plays meant to their author and their original audiences is violating every sound principle of criticism. Yet the presupposition of much modern Biblical scholarship is that the first century sense of the Gospel text, say, is the real sense. This is only comprehensible on the presupposition that the text as originally, historically understood is somehow authoritative. This, of course, reflects the liberal Protestant project that wants to 'rescue' the text from the subsequent dogmatic tradition. To do so it must locate its authority elsewhere, i.e. in the scholar's empirical reconstruction of its 'original' meaning. This is, in its own way, as naïve as the popular notion that there existed a 'pure' 'original' text that the church

to the Bible has to begin with the question of genre. The Bible contains myths, chronicles, prophetic writings, lyric poems, collections of proverbs, dramas and so on. Each of these has its own rules of interpretation. Of course fundamentalists deny this. For them the Bible is all chronicle all the time. This is another example of a 'flat' hermeneutic. Bafflingly, it seems to be your hermeneutic as well. Genesis 1-13, for instance, is a kind of compendium of world mythology. The Psalms are lyric poetry. Job can be read as a tragic drama. When I make these kind of determinations about a text I limit the kinds of meaning I can find and set the interpretive problems I am going to face. So, in a lyric poem certain lines have the purpose of expressing or relieving strong emotion. In a myth I am looking for archetypal patterns of truth rather than factual statements. In a drama I take account of how character may develop through interaction and dialogue (possibly even the 'divine' character!). From each of these I am going to take a 'truth' uncovered by a different process of inquiry. Further, as a member of a faith community, I may read the text as part of a canon. Then I have to compare one text with another text and note the tensions and agreements between them. Finally, and I have to bite the bullet on this even though you will take me for a post-modernist whacko, texts *do not* have a fixed meaning.[88] They mean different things in different historical epochs. The interpreter has to take account not just of what a text might have meant in its original context but what it means for a reader today. Thus, no one can really read the Bible today as if the encounter of the Hebrews with Greek philosophy never took place. Even if they hate Greek philosophy and want to 'rescue' the Bible from it the resulting book will

---

'tampered' with. You cannot tamper with a text before there is even a fixed text to tamper with and if, say, a marginal note slipped into the 'official text' (whatever that phrase means) I have no problem with saying that that NOW is the text if it makes for an interesting reading. This is not to deny, however, that going back to the 'primitive truth' of any text can be an interesting move in a current discussion. I hope, though, we are past the notion that deconstructing the empirical author as an authority leads to an infinite subjectivity of interpretation as this is not the only way the intentionality of a text can be constructed. An important discovery for me was that in Augustine and the other church fathers there was a notion of 'deep intentionality' that was articulated in the practice of reading scripture according to a hierarchy of multiple senses. Indeed, I found that the 'corrupt' allegorical readings of the fathers were often better than the 'correct' modern ones for this very reason. This allegorical stance accommodated the genuine insights of post-structural critics without the cost of fragmenting meaning altogether (although allowing for a rich 'plurality' of contrasting readings).

[88]Let me explain. There IS a text in the empirical sense that sets limits on what we can and cannot say. No reading of The Song of Roland can make Charlemagne the emperor into Charlemagne the God. However, this given empirical structure is NOT the meaning of the text. How we read the Song of Roland will depend heavily on our response to the moral situations it describes. We need to bring a moral, spiritual or intellectual attitude to the text in order for it to mean something. Our mental furniture PLUS the empirical structure of the text produces the reading. This is why readings of a text can change radically over time while the text as an empirical object changes not at all. To put it bluntly, the empirical text underdetermines the reading. On this understanding a 'good' reading is one which synthesizes and renders consistent the broadest range of reactions to the text, particularly the most contrary and opposed reactions.

not be the original text restored to its pristine innocence (which is now gone). It will be a new text that is a move in a modern theological discussion. Thus, even if it were the case (highly doubtful) that the *Genesis* author literally believed in talking snakes that would only be that writer's interpretation of his text. It would have no necessary authority for us for the simple reason that everyone is a reader even the putative author and not every author stands in the relation of critic to his own work. Indeed, one is often struck by the fact that an author may have a take on his own novel that is quite unconvincing as our own creations are something we are often too close to to evaluate objectively.[89]

Let's tote up what we have uncovered. The fundamentalist employs a flat hermeneutic for which statements in the Bible are propositions that correspond to states of affairs. For many of them even ethical statements are simple statements of fact about what God's commands. None of you seem to question this hermeneutic and even philosophers of religion assume this 'divine command' theory to be normative for all Christians even though Catholic, Orthodox and Anglican divines almost universally reject it. Why is this so? Well the answer would take us all the way back to school of medieval philosophy known nominalism which essentially views power as the only real attribute of god and denies any inherent rational structure or 'logos' to the world, which simply consists of atomized facts that are the subjects of sense knowledge. Modern scientific positivism and Fundamentalist theology are both expressions of this world view. In fact, fundamentalism in theology, hyper-positivism in science, capitalist economics, technocracy and atomistic individualism all together form a seamless web. The externality of atomic facts in society and nature and their inherently manipulatable nature form the basis of all these positions. Secularism as you practice it, fundamentalism, and libertarianism are all from the same hothouse and proceed from a common metaphysic. Your wars are expressions of the narcissism of minor differences and that is why they are so nasty.

So, and here let me be frank, we come to the deepest problem which is that your critique of religion is anti-progressive. It is the instrumental rationality of the managerial class that represents all things in terms of what Hegel calls the 'understanding' or Buber the "I-it' relationship: the externalization of the world as 'fact' or 'matter' or 'object' to be manipulated

---

[89]Here one might consider Hegel's discussion of faith and enlightenment in the Phenomenology of Mind. (1967; 561-589) Hegel points out that the standpoint of 'faith' where I place my own good and my own reality in an absolute being rests on the same principle of inward freedom as the 'reason' which would reduce all 'belief' to folly, superstition and priest-craft. Atheism is thus correct that God is a product of human consciousness only it does not know what this means. Faith however grasps that the religious object, God, is for consciousness from the inward standpoint of the believer. What is more, faith knows (though it often forgets) that external sensuous representation is not the absolute. In this it contrasts with the positivism of 'enlightenment' which takes the external sensible thing as pure being. Of course, in this, enlightenment does not even rise to the level of a cow for whom grass, far from being a 'fact', is simply food.

and dominated by technocrats who understand knowledge as power not reflection, introspection or solidarity. This class uses 'science' and 'reason' and 'fact' entirely for its own purposes as part of the public rhetoric of its institutions. A 'fact' is a dead external thing to be used, manipulated and monetized. The nemesis of this stance is in fact the destruction of 'facts' (in the sense of truth) about which so many of you complain yet contribute to so mightily. It is also the central feature of the fundamentalism you profess to despise but whose assumptions you stubbornly refuse to question. This is why the supposed 'critique' of religion in the culture of instrumental rationality is at the same time a critique of the humanities and indeed of any humane model of economics. This is why many of you are in fact shifting rightwards in politics in a development as unhappy as it is inevitable. Marx for many of you is a hangover from idealism (which by the way he is) and it is Nietzsche who reigns.[90] Not the subtle ironist Nietzsche either but the right wing caricature of him who trumpets pseudo-Darwinian notions of competition and bogus (male) hero worship. As there are still many of you who cling to progressive egalitarian sentiments (and God bless you for doing so) this will be a hard pill to swallow. I think it is true nonetheless that the hyper-positivism and aggressive scientism you employ against religion does not now and has never fit your politics and that this is becoming increasingly clear.

There is a price we pay for lacking a culture of critique. Of course the primary locus of such a culture is the university, specifically the faculties of Humanities. Chemistry and Physics do not, by and large, utter critiques of themselves. Meta questions about science are handled by sociology of knowledge and philosophy of science. Discourses in the humanities are reflexive in a way that discourses in the sciences are not: they include themselves as possible objects. One can, for instance, write a history of historiography. There is, however, no science of science. This is not a problem with science in any way, it just happens to be how things are. Different practices make different demands on practitioners. This fact does reveal, however, that the scientistic biases of 'atheists' do their own cause a profound disservice. The critique of religion cannot be founded on a crude category mistake if it is to have any reach and influence beyond a sectarian clique. It is such a mistake to take a symbol, strip it of all its

---

[90]It is interesting to note in retrospect how optimistic Marx was. The crisis of Capitalism is far deeper and graver than even he foresaw, now engulfing the planet itself. It now seems the glossiest optimism to think that a simple crisis of overproduction would bring about revolution in short order. Partly this is because two global wars and the brief window afforded by the Depression for state intervention have served to buoy the system and save it from self-annihilation. Still, as fire consumes fuel so Capitalism must inexorably consume its social and natural ecology. Indeed, if neo-liberals are correct and market systems are simply too complex to allow for effective state intervention we are going down a cliff with no brakes at all. In the 20th century we pulled two rabbits out of the hat: a brief period of Keynesian intervention and a world war that sparked an economic boom. We may not have a third rabbit. Of course, Capitalism's last stand is to cannibalize public services and loot state treasuries but when everything profitable has been privatized and there are no more trillions for bailouts there will be literally nothing else.

valence, and translate it into the language of determinate fact as if one had thereby gotten at its content. The cultural malaise into which we fall by taking such a procedure as 'objective' and 'rational' is well described by the Swiss psychologist Carl Jung. Jung's claim, correct as far as I can see, is that we do not inoculate ourselves against the irrational by such a move but render ourselves much more readily prey to it. Even Christians of a more liberal perspective (who mostly share in this overly 'rationalistic' outlook) muddy the water by opposing the 'literal' sense of scripture to the 'metaphorical'. As S.T. Coleridge pointed out long ago the opposite of the literal meaning of the text is the symbolic meaning and symbolic meanings are not reducible to the mechanical associations of figure (metaphor and simile) and allegory (though they may include them as means). (1972; 30) An appropriate culture of criticism however allows us to see beyond these distortions that mask the real nature of phenomena and leave us helpless to deal with them all the while congratulating ourselves on the cleverness of our shallow and spurious 'critiques'.

14 Science: "It Works Bitches!"

So said the t –shirt in the ad I just saw. It came from a face book page called "Science doesn't care what you believe" . This is probably true but of course *scientists* care passionately about what you believe. They want you to believe the things they typically say. Individual scientists also want you to believe what they *in particular* say as opposed to their rivals in other labs. For this they have one all- purpose argument: you must believe science because it works. Planes, after all, do fly which, without science, they would not do.[91] Thus, there is aerodynamics. Because engineers have aerodynamics they can work out how to build airplanes by applying that theory. Historically I suspect this claim is unsound: I suspect a good deal of aerodynamics was worked out after the fact when scientists reflected on what engineers and inventors *actually did*. But leave that aside for now. Let's assume the standard hierarchy that has scientists working out a theory followed by lowly engineers *applying* that theory to make things.

When the things the engineers make work that proves the soundness of the underlying theory. In fact, engineers make so many things that work that it must be the case that the totality of our science is (give or take a few small issues) correct. By correct we reflexively (and often uncritically) mean "corresponds to the actual nature of the world" . I think many people intuitively accept this argument as sound. However, I think it is open to question. Indeed, in spite of its popularity I don't think it's a good ar-

---

[91]This is a favorite point of Mr. Richard Dawkins. There are, he tells us, no relativists at 30,000 feet. (237) I have no doubt this is true though, as we shall see, it is far from clear that our confidence in the airplane we are flying is a simple result of 'science'. This one of those (many) places where Dawkins kicks a stone and declares "Thus I refute Popper" . Paul Thagard seems to share this view: "Moreover, the impressive technological successes of science are utterly mysterious unless the scientific theories that made them possible are at least approximately true. For example, my computer would not be processing this chapter unless there really are electrons moving through its silicon chips." (ttp://cogsci.uwaterloo.ca/Articles/rationality.html). However, if I said "I navigated from point a to point b successfully therefore Ptolemaic astronomy must be true" the inference would be false. I might do just as well or better using a different theory such as the heliocentric one. In other words, multiple 'approximately true' theories might, in fact, do the same basic work. (see Putnam; 1981, 73-74) There are many reasons to prefer one theoretical entity over another but this is not (or not solely) a matter of simple instrumental success.

gument at all. In fact, it is very strange to think that the inventors of the airplane are, in fact, physicists of whom aeronautical engineers are mere servants. What is more, people who are hardcore proponents of science sense a difficulty with the claim that science is true (in the sense given above) because it is successful. Epistemological realism is a philosophical inference based on science. It is not itself a testable scientific claim. Claiming that science actually describes the 'real world' because it works would mean there are valid inferences outside of science! (see Mizrahi: 2017; 359 for a discussion) Such people tell us, for instance, that the 'realist' theory of science is no more instrumentally successful than the brain-in-a-vat hypothesis (or, to use a historical example, Berkeley's idealism). It may be the case that the implications of science, contrary to popular belief, are anti-realist and instrumentalist (it is not often recognized by the general public that instrumentalism and realism are often *opposed* positions). Also, it is open to question what we mean when we say something called 'Science' 'works'. We might mean scientific method (narrowly conceived) works or we might mean science as an institutional structure embedded in society works. If we mean the latter, then we must recognize that one of the things that makes science work is non-scientific know how such as the ability to read a bus schedule or use citation effectively. 'Works' also invites the question 'works at what?" and perhaps more importantly 'fails at what?" .

I have slightly different concerns though and I will proceed to outline them. There are at least three problems with this claim which I will label W. The first and most glaring problem with W is that it is an expression of massive confirmation bias. The public thinks science 'works' because the science that 'works' is the science they see. They do not see the many experiments with null results or the failed research programs. Most of this is tidied up *before* science reaches public consciousness. Waxing lyrical about the efficacy of the scientific method is like regarding movies as a real time process of miraculous continuity. We of course do not see the hours and hours of footage left on the cutting room floor. We do not see the failed experiments and theoretical breakdowns that litter the empirical history of science. We see spectacular successes like quantum mechanics and relativity but do not see the failure of anyone to make them consistent with each other. We have science that works, science that more or less works, science that works not well at all though better than its competitors and finally a great deal of science that has failed utterly.[92]

---

[92]Another problem is that science can work all too well. Consider a Neanderthal 'scientist' who theorizes that his arrow finds the target because (given the right initial conditions) it actively wills itself to do so. Of course, every time his arrow finds the target his theory will be confirmed by a true prediction. If a theory predicts an event that reliably happens anyway then that theory will be massively confirmed. How then do we distinguish a true prediction that confirms a theory from one that is merely consistent with a theory? Whatever science is about it is not simply about predictive success a form of which can be obtained by any awful theory. There is an art of designing significant tests of novel predictions and this seems to be an acquired skill. Science seeks not predictive success but a certain kind of predictive success. This means, of course,

The second problem is that W gives scientists far too much credit. Part of our story about why a plane flies includes the Bernoulli effect and other scientific concepts. However, engineering things like aircraft is not a straight application of theory. It also involves jury rigging, rules of thumb and seat of the pants stuff by engineers (all of which seem to have been employed at various points by the Wright brothers!). In fact, it involves at least one other kind of knowledge (experiential) supplemented by things like creativity and intuition. This I suspect is why cultures like Ancient Greece and China had many engineering successes while operating with different theories than the ones we use. So, while science (more or less) may work it only works in the context of a number of other things that are not science. Science is part of a web that functions as a totality. Theory is brought into relation to fact by persons possessing a range of skills many of which are not the skills of a theoretical scientist. Nor do engineers need to wait for science to do what they do and indeed scientists are often playing catch up to what inventors have *done*. What 'works' is in fact not just science but the entire set of skills, institutions and cultural attitudes that support it. Engineers and inventors are not servants but midwives! In other words, they play a significant role in *making* science work. *They* make scientific concepts real by using *their* abilities to *translate* those concepts into functioning machines. So in fact do workers, designers, craftsmen and machinists: all the people left out of the heroic progress of science without whom all kinds of science would never have become 'true' by 'working' at all. Thus, the notion that something called 'Science' 'works' is one that needs serious qualification. Science works in part because all kinds of people who get no credit make it work. This also leaves us with the question of the 'science industrial complex': the fact that the processes and institutions that make science are braided with political, corporate and military interests that determine who benefits from science, what scientific questions are pursued, and to a shocking degree can veto the results. Much of the good science that happens today happens in spite of this complex not because of it.

And this leads me to my third problem. It is not only westerners under the tutelage of science who make things that work. Even very basic societies have an array of tools that have functioned well for millennia. Anyone who doubts the significance of this achievement should attempt to make a flint axe-head. The Romans, Greeks, Indians and Chinese have monumental achievements in architecture, engineering and navigation yet their scientific concepts cannot always be easily assimilated to ours. Here I must declare a certain bias. The universal necessity of scientific concepts has been a central concern of Western Philosophy since the early modern period at least. I am quite open to the thought that, as Kant would have it, science cannot take just any form. There may be concepts, forms of

---

that, in part, the scientist gets to pick which tests a theory has to pass and which it does not. At any rate the notion that science is about predictive success founders on the fact that many sciences concern events in the past many of which happened exactly once.

intuition, like time or space or substance that apply to any possible science. Yet an enumeration of these categories does not commit us as far as I can see to any given historical construction of science. The achievement of Kant is not simply, as is sometimes asserted, that he gave a philosophical grounding to Newtonian physics. This seems to entail that there is no intrinsic necessity to scientific concepts having the shape they do. This is determined from the side of history with all that this entails in terms of contingency. For this reason, it does not seem to me likely (though I suppose it is not impossible) that, aliens, say, would have physics and chemistry identical to our own.[93] This would involve repeating all the historical accidents and cultural trends that produced *our* science. Even something so basic as the particularity of their *language* may predetermine the form and content of their scientific conceptions. Yet it is hard to imagine these putative aliens starving or freezing in the dark: I imagine (and it would be interesting to put this to the test) that within their scientific paradigms (whatever these are) there will be solutions to technical problems. Some of these solutions might well be better than ours! Consider this the response of the unsung heroes of science (many of whom were women!) who turn out to have had rather more to say about what science is than the science apologists have traditionally allowed.

---

[93]Imagine the following: An Earth ship visits a people known as the Zenon. Now we have a theory of four fundamental forces that we don't know how to unify. The Zenon however believe in a single fundamental force they call Q but differ on what elements to break it down into. How do you judge such a dispute? Each will point to the basic flaw of the other's theory in defense of their own. Further, the Zenon will almost certainly have their own property language which will not simply or directly translate into ours. This is a good bet because on Earth people like the !Kung have concepts like 'Num' (heat? passion? fire?) that have no clear translation equivalents (and remember these are people on our OWN planet who share our physiology!) Now what would surely happen is that the Zenon will talk to us and we to them. We will slowly learn their concepts and they ours. We would, in fact, have a debate about the one and the many such as the fathers of the church had about the persons of the Trinity. Reality would then be that on which the Zenon and Humanity converged in the course of the conversation. If the Zenon and us were the only intelligent beings, then we could call that the truth. However, if we went to another planet and found the people there had the same scientific concepts that would be spooky: it would strongly imply (if not exactly prove) some pre-ordained harmony between minds and the world. Only a bit spookier would be finding they had comparable religious concepts.

15 WHERE IS THE SCIENTISM DEBATE?[94]

Not where I work. I work in a university and in a university certain things are assumed. It is assumed that there are well established bodies of theory that have earned their keep. Here are some of them: literary theory, historiography, music theory, legal theory, mathematics, geometry, logic, philology, and (in some universities) theology. To this we can add philosophy which poses 'meta-questions' about knowledge, reality, the good and so on. We can also add the social and indeed the natural sciences. Practitioners of these disciplines generally know well enough to stay within their boundaries. Physicists are not attacking the historian across the hall over her understanding of Bismark's diplomacy. If she is being attacked, it is by other historians. Nor are they questioning her methodology or suggesting that the methods of physics would be better at answering questions about 19th century Prussia than those of historians. Now, cross disciplinary conflicts over method do exist. Some of what social scientists say about science impinges on the self-understanding of scientists. The same is true about philosophy of science. Mostly, however, people go about their business making claims and counter claims in terms of methods and standards internal to their discipline. Gone are the days when an unreconstructed Cartesian could propose a single universal method for making discoveries in all subject areas. This is not to say that there aren't useful analogies between explanation in science and explanation in other inquiries. It is just that these are only analogies: there is no pre-set form of explanation that all disciplines recognize as universally valid. This is borne out by actual practice where physicists dispute about physics and classicists dispute about classics but do not interfere in each other's domains.

On the face of it then there seems no reason at all why a debate about scientism should exist. Who seriously proposes replacing the deductive methods of mathematicians with the inductive and experimental methods of natural science? That there is one, however, I think has to do not with issues internal to the academy but with the public discourse about knowledge. Scientists who would never dream of lecturing the Regius

[94]This essay is adapted from material first presented in the Social Epistemology Review and Reply Collective.

Professor of Greek on the fine points of Ionic dialect speak differently when they present themselves as public proponents of the sciences. Or rather I should say *others* speak differently when they appoint *themselves* to speak on *behalf* of those scientists. In other words, there is science as a practice and 'Science' as a public ideology.[95] It is only in the latter context that 'scientists' make hegemonic claims they would never bother to put in actual practice. There are a couple of reasons for this. The first and obvious one is the quest for scarce resources. Every discipline has its weak moments when it dreams of colonizing all the others and setting itself up as the master science. The obvious advantage to pressing this claim is that the master science gets more prestige and thus more money. "Invest in us" it says "for then you will be investing in REAL knowledge." Thus, *public* proponents of 'science', who want more money and more attention for scientists, will press the case that the sciences are special and have an objectivity and rigor absent in all other disciplines. They will press this case loudly and publically even though privately they could never make these claims good by successful colonization of their rivals. There is a good reason why, say, Evolutionary Psychology's discourse on religion is an ahistorical and impressionistic shambles. It is because its proponents are generally biologists (or philosophers of biology) who have not mastered and have no realistic hope of mastering the relevant data on the history of religion.[96] Hubristic overreach that meets its nemesis and comes crashing to earth is the usual fate of humanities scholars who impinge too much on science and of scientists who set themselves up as philosophers or religionists.

It occurs to me though that humans are motivated not only by desire but by fear. The sciences have tremendous prestige and authority in our society but of course with great power comes great anxiety. Power is always aware of its inherent fragility, hence the notorious paranoia of tyrants. For

---

[95] By scientists I mean the chemists, biologists, astrophysicists and climatologists I work with on a daily basis. I have no beef with such people and as far as I can tell they have no beef with me. By 'scientists' I mean the public apologists for science whose claims often have little or nothing to do with the activities of ordinary working scientists.

[96] See Wills and Hynes "Biologizing Religion:Dennett's Breaking the Spell. Toronto Journal of Theology Spring 2008 24/1 (Co-authored with Darren Hynes) 7-20. See also "Biologizing Religion Part II" Toronto Journal of Theology vol.27. no.2 2011. 235-248. Dennett's efforts at an 'evolutionary' science of religion illustrate this problem. On the one hand he cannot waste time reading the 'non-knowledge' produced by comparative religionists, sociologists and historians because they are not 'scientific'. On the other hand, Dennett knows almost nothing about religion and can't learn anything about it without granting at least some cognitive legitimacy to people he does not regard as genuine researchers. His solution is to erect a theory on the basis of no data whatsoever imagining helmeted gods or whatever he pleases to create his account of pre-historic religion. He studiously avoids actual history in favor of an imagined pre-history where Darwinian 'just-so' explanations can have free reign. Had Dennett bothered to read up on his chosen subject he would have discovered that 'religion' is only a vague family resemblance concept anyway and as such does not have a single explanation of any kind let alone a Darwinian one. This is why all specific 'religions' (the only kind that exist) have historical explanations not biological ones.

all its power 'science' worries it does not have enough power. It worries there are other discourses that may challenge its hegemony in some critical area. There is something to this worry. Anti-vaxxers and creationists have some influence and clout. At some junctures they DO succeed in breaking up the assumed power relations and thwarting 'Science'. With fear comes defensiveness. When this happens people resort to rhetoric more extreme than they otherwise would. The discussion is no longer concerned with a nuanced understanding of the place of the sciences in the domains of knowledge but with a slash and burn policy that protects the status of 'science' at the cost of everything else. Here 'science' joins up with ideologies like 'naturalism' and 'secular humanism' and becomes part of their rhetorical arsenal. The threat to 'science' is then constructed as 'religion' and emptying the humanities of all cognitive legitimacy is a small price to pay for slaying the religious dragon. 'Science' is constructed as the only form of knowledge in order to nullify the claims of 'religion' with other bodies of theory being the collateral damage. This is why 'scientists' (in the sense of proponents of scientism) don't really care if no science can solve minute problems of attic grammar or explain Beethoven's use of the sonata form.[97] This is why they don't care if these other pursuits falsify their hegemonic claims (which they do) on a daily basis. The real enemy is not literary theory or historiography but new agers and televangelists.

As a philosopher one can do little but watch this process and hope it ends in a stalemate so reasonable people can just go about their work again. This is because the issues are really psychological, political and social and there is no refined argument about method and its limits that will allay these concerns or counteract these motivations. Still, it is at least half the battle won if we can show people the manner in which they may be massively overcompensating. It is something at least not so much to *show* people that scientism can't be true as to *remind* people of the glaringly obvious reasons why it is not true. First we might remind ourselves of why scientism is a temptation in the first place. Since Descartes at least we have been fascinated by the idea of the great epistemic purge. There is so much 'stuff' out there claiming to be knowledge that we need to light a great bonfire and burn all of it. This bonfire might be Cartesian doubt. It might be 'scientific method'. Either way all the 'pretend' knowledge is burned off leaving the useful core. This may well be a worthwhile endeavor and in the time of Descartes it surely was. However, I suspect this tradition has created a misleading impression. The real problem is not that we have too little knowledge but too much: as a phenomenologist might say it is a saturated phenomenon. Knowledge is all around us so that like bats our eyes are blinded by the sun. This is why I find the idea that only scientists produce knowledge the very definition of an ivory tower notion that has no basis in experience. There are so many perfectly credible claims to

---

[97]Paul Bloom writing in the Atlantic (Nov.24. 2015) defends 'science' without mentioning discourse in the humanities even once. The only perceived 'other' to science is religion! For my comments on this see Believing Weird Things Chap.6 47-59. (Minkowski Institute Press, 2018)

knowledge from outside the sciences that our initial presumption at least must be that scientism is untenable.[98]

This is easily shown with the typical statement of scientism (we shall consider a more nuanced version below) which holds that the sciences produce knowledge and that other disciplines and inquiries do not. Let me begin by pointing out though that people who defend scientism often claim that this term is simply pejorative. This is not the case. In this paper I am addressing people who defend scientism as a position AND label the position they defend as 'scientism'. Some defend a 'strong' version of scientism. Alex Rosenberg is one of these people: "When it comes to real understanding, the humanities are nothing we have to take seriously, except as symptoms. But they are everything we need to take seriously when it comes to entertainment, enjoyment, and psychological satisfaction. Just don't treat them as knowledge or wisdom." (2011; 6-8) This is interesting for it indicates an anxiety that runs through scientism. The 'scientist' IS NOT a philistine! He is eager for all to know that he understands and appreciates the humanities and arts in their proper place: aesthetic satisfaction and private reverie. None of these pleasant dreams have any cognitive content however. Positions like Rosenberg's have been echoed by people like Hawking, Crick, Wilson and Dennett with others like Steven Pinker being among the (slightly) more cautious 'attitudinal scientists'. Pinker seems to be happy to allow the humanities to exist though they should 'science up' and use things like evolutionary psych or behavioral genetics to explain Shakespeare. (2018; 406-408) Now I have read a fair bit in classics, philosophy, religion and literature. Reflecting back on this I naturally assume that I have learned a great deal about the world from doing so. The figures mentioned above assert that I have not. They are appealing to a sense of 'know' that excludes much of what I think of as knowledge. Prima facie this strikes me as utterly unconvincing: 'know' cannot possibly have the narrow restricted meaning these authors assert it does. I believe this both in a factual sense and in a structural sense for their narrow sense of 'know' cannot possibly be constituted without implicit or explicit reference to my broader one.

To show this let me make a list of the kinds of non-scientific knowledge people (like me) *seem* to have. As we shall see the problem is not making this list long but keeping it short. I offer this list to create an overwhelming presumption that strong scientism at very least is not true. This procedure may not be decisive in itself but I do think it puts the ball in the court of the 'scientist' who must show that all the things I (and most everybody else) call knowledge are in fact something else. What is more, the 'scientist' must do this without violating the criterion of scientism itself: he cannot

---

[98] So familiar are many of these that we tend, in fact, not to even notice them and this is the primary reason scientism can ever seem plausible in the first place. This is the ultimate nemesis of the Lockean identification of knowledge with self-consciousness. Science cannot exist without a myriad of informal inferences and tacit conceptions which are too basic to be consciously apperceived except when purposely made an object of direct reflection: something the scientist does not do qua scientist.

avail himself of any but scientific arguments. Moreover, he must show that science itself meets the criterion of knowledge he sets out which is not an easy task given such well known difficulties as the problem of induction. At any rate, *prima facie*, there seems overwhelming *empirical* evidence that scientism is incorrect: a claim so extraordinary should have an unusually strong justification, to paraphrase Hume. Let's see if the 'scientist' can produce one.

To begin, I should point out is that there are bodies of knowledge that produce 'results' not through scientific method but through analysis and application to cases. Two prominent examples would be Law and Music Theory, practitioners of which use an established body of theory to solve problems like whether Trinity Western should have a law school or how Scriabin invented the 'Prometheus chord'. What sense of 'know' can we appeal to in order to show that my daughter, who is a music student, does not 'know' that the Prometheus chord was derived from the over-tone series? Secondly, there is knowledge about the past that historians uncover through the interpretation of primary documents and other evidence. In what sense do we not 'know' that the Weimar Republic fell? This claim is even more remarkable given there are sciences that deal with the past, like Paleontology, which 'interpret' signs such as fossils or tools in a manner much more like historians (there is hermeneutic judgment in science which functions no differently than hermeneutic judgment elsewhere). Thirdly, there is first person knowledge which is direct. "Did that hurt?" asks the doctor because without accepting first-person reportage he cannot proceed with treatment. This is a kind of knowledge without which we could not even do science so that if scientism wants to deny this is knowledge science itself will be the primary victim.[99] Again science can go nowhere without direct factual knowledge (the strip turned green when I put it in water) that is not produced by science but which science itself rests upon. What about know how? Craftsmen and engineers know all kinds of things by accumulated experience. They know how a shoe is made or what makes for good beer. They also built the Great Wall of China and the Pyramids. What are we to make of disciplines like mathematics, geometry or logic? What about ethical or aesthetic or critical judgments? In what sense does a translator not 'know' Japanese? Does anyone really think literature scholars don't 'know' anything about the texts they discuss even on a factual level? What scientific justification does the claim "Marlowe did not write *King Lear*' have or even require? And while we are at it may well be that poor philosophers do not know much but they do know things like

---

[99] Rik Peels makes this point effectively "... it seems natural science cannot even get started without making use of evidence provided by the senses: science is based on the evidence of the senses. If the senses were among the belief sources that adherents of scientism reject, they could not rationally embrace scientific results and they would, thus, have to reject science itself. The main reason for this is that it seems that one cannot do science without, at least at some points, trusting the deliverances of the senses, such as beliefs based on visual perception. If the senses were considered unreliable and the beliefs they give rise to as irrational, science could not get off the ground. Science itself could, therefore, not deliver rational beliefs either. (2017; 3)

'logical positivism fails its own criterion of meaning' or 'Berkeley cannot be refuted by kicking a stone'. [100]

It could well be that in regarding all the above as instances of knowledge I am missing something fundamental. If so I wish someone would point it out to me. Let's take a hypothetical knower, Jill: Jill knows she is feeling cold, knows how to repair watches, knows why the Weimar Republic fell, knows how to speak Portuguese, knows there are 114 Surahs in the Quran, knows how Beethoven transformed the sonata form, has extensive topographical knowledge of places she has travelled, prefers the plays of Shakespeare to those of Thomas Preston, can identify Barbara as valid syllogism, considers racial prejudice indefensible, understands how attorney client privilege applies to the Stormy Daniels affair, can tell an stone age arrowhead from a rock, can comment on the philology of Hebrew, can understand Euclid's proofs, is engaged in correcting the received text of *Finnigan's Wake* , can explain the Quine/Duhem thesis and its relevance to the question of falsification, has written a commentary on Kant's third critique and on top of all this is performing experiments in chemistry. Scientism may be correct that only the last endeavor constitutes Jill's 'knowledge' but on what grounds can it defeat what to me looks like the overwhelming presumption that Jill is not just a Chemist who wastes her time at hobbies but a genuine polymath who knows many things in many fields along with all the ordinary knowledge all humans possess?

The 'scientist' seems, *prima facie*, to have surprisingly few options here. Will he point out that science makes true predictions? So have craftsmen for millennia. Further, many of these forms of knowledge do not *need* to make true predictions: I don't need to test the hypothesis that there 114 Surahs in the Quran because I know already having checked. Is science more certain of its conclusions? According to the post-Popper consensus at least, scientific statements are always tentative and revisable and in any case first person knowledge so surpasses it in certainty that some of it is arguably infallible. Is science more instrumentally successful? Craftsmen and hunters kept the species alive for millennia before science even existed in difficult circumstances under which no science would have been possible. What is more some craft knowledge remains instrumentally superior to science to this day: no baseball player chooses a physicist over a

---

[100]The underlying question here is one of Platonism (of a sort) vs. Aristotelianism. Scientism argues that there is one paradigmatic form of 'knowledge in itself'. I argue the Aristotelian position that just as 'being' is said in many senses (Metaphysics;9, 992b 15) so there are many analogical forms of knowledge. What all the things I have listed have in common is that each in its own peculiar way supports beliefs by appeals to evidence or other forms of justification. Everyday discourse may be wrong to use the word knowledge for these other forms of justified belief but I think the onus is on the 'strong scientist' to show this. Another thing I should point out is that I do not confine the word knowledge to beliefs that are indefeasible: a knower might say "to the best of my knowledge" and still be a knower. I say this to head off the problem of skepticism which asks whether the criterion of indefeasible knowledge (whatever it is said to be) is ever actually fulfilled. There are valid responses to this problem but consideration of them would take us far afield.

batting coach.[101] At any rate success is relative to one's aims and lawyers successfully produce legal arguments just as philologists successfully solve problems of Homeric grammar. Now as Aristotle would say science does have the advantage over craft of being explanatory but is explanation unique to science? No because hermeneutic practices in history, literature, classics and so on also produce explanations of the meaning of things like documents and if the 'scientist' wants to say that these explanations are tentative and changing (abductions as it were not inductions) then the same is true of a great deal of science. In short, none of the features that supposedly make for the superiority of science are unique to science and some are not even especially exemplified by it. Worse, there are inquiries where science is not only not superior but cannot produce explanations of any kind and these are all the studies we might label hermeneutic or interpretive. In such domains science may, of course, produce ancillary knowledge by, say, helping to date a manuscript. It cannot, however, answer fundamental questions of interpretation. It seems then that there is no criterion by which scientific claims can be shown to be knowledge in a unique and exclusive sense. Until such a criterion is identified it seems to me that my initial presupposition about Jill being a polymath rather than a chemist with distractions stands. Perhaps this is why Scientism is more often an assumed attitude than an explicit position: on its face there seems no defense of it unless one undertakes the hopeless task of trying (as some of the positivists did) to show that disciplines like history formulate testable general laws!

Rik Peels addresses this problem in his article "Ten Reasons to Embrace Scientism" (2017). In this pieces he makes some modest suggestions towards a *possible* scientism though he is skeptical of scientism on the whole. Scientism he takes to be the view that science and science alone produces "rational belief and knowledge" (2) His contrasting term for science is 'common sense': there may be some respects in which science is better than common sense though these are not easy to identify.[102] In contrast with science, common sense delivers false beliefs in the preponderance of cases. Actually I think 'common sense' is far too vague a term here.

---

[101]Here in fact we get to the nub of the problem. The ultimate problem with scientism is that in the real world different knowledge forms interact with each other constantly. Science advances with the help of craftsmen as with the invention of the telescope. Craftsmen make use of science as when a running coach consults a physician. Archeologists and paleontologists employ abduction or hermeneutic reasoning. Art historians call on chemists while biologists call on the local knowledge of indigenous peoples. In a sense there is no such thing as 'science' pure and simple as other knowledge forms are inherent to its own structure (even deductive reasoning, the proper province of logicians, is essential to standard accounts of scientific method). This is one reason why, in fact, there is no one superior knowledge form but rather systematic interdependence of ALL knowledge forms.

[102]"Examples of common sense beliefs as I have just defined the term are moral beliefs, memorial beliefs, beliefs about one's reasons for doing something, some religious beliefs, basic mathematical beliefs, basic logical beliefs, beliefs about whether or not one performed an action freely or not, beliefs regarding the truth of falsehood of certain metaphysical principles, and beliefs issuing from introspection." (3)

What contrasts with 'science' is A. hermeneutic or interpretive knowledge B. craft knowledge or know how C. philosophical knowledge (say, that a certain position embodies a performative contradiction) D. pure deduction as in mathematics or geometry E. informal or tacit knowledge F. direct knowledge and G. intuition (intellectual or moral-in the sense of our direct knowledge of first principles which are, as the Scholastics would say, *per se nota*). [103] What is more most of us, scientists included, are using most or all of these at once in some combination. So, can we justify the claim that science produces 'rational beliefs' whereas these other forms do not (assuming, that is, that we could even separate science from these other functions)?[104]

Science, some might think, is highly successful and is broad in application. (4-5) Others might suggest that science is self-correcting (6) and can test and corroborate its assertions. (5) Perhaps the counter-intuitive nature of science *vis a vis* 'common sense beliefs' shows that they are a higher order of knowledge. (5-6) One might also hold 'common sense' beliefs contradict each other whereas scientific beliefs are broadly consistent. (7) One might argue (in what seems to me a nakedly circular procedure) that evolution provides a basis for believing in the rationality of scientific beliefs over others: "The point is rather that one can rationally believe, let alone know, that p, only if there is a plausible story to be told about how one knows that p." (7) This 'plausible story' would, of course, be an evolutionary account that showed accurate scientific beliefs to be favored by natural selection. (7) One might argue that science can produce debunking accounts of common sense beliefs. (8) One might argue that common sense beliefs are permeated with cognitive bias. (8-9) Finally, one might argue that science shows common sense beliefs to be illusory. (9)

Peels is not bullish about any of these possibilities and with good reason. Simply pointing out that science is successful and broad in application tells us nothing about whether or not other things are successful and broad in application. (4) I can test and corroborate 'memorial' knowledge AND

---

[103]Peels recognizes that journalism and the humanities produce close and elaborate chains of reasoning that might be called 'scientific' at least in the sense of resulting in 'rational beliefs'. (3) A classicist can produce a pretty strong argument for dating a text and a journalist can just as rigorously get to the root of a scandal. Thus he already concedes most of the case to the opponents of scientism. His 'common sense' seems to contain what I have placed in categories D, E and G. It is these that he considers as possible (though unlikely) objects of scientistic critique.

[104]Which Peels admits we cannot: "Second, science is also based on certain common sense beliefs, such as memorial beliefs. We use beliefs based on memory: we believe it was us who gathered the data on, say, the genetic profile of a particular sample of twins, and on that basis we believe that data have been gatheredin a reliable way. We rely on basic logical intuitions, such as the intuition that modus tollens is valid, whereas an ex consequentia is not. We trust our basic mathematical intuitions, such as that $2 + 3 = 5$ and that $1x2 = 2$. And so forth. If we had to discard all common sense beliefs, then the project of science itself would have to be abandoned." (7) Dr. Rosenberg, he informs us, is working on the problem of explaining mathematical beliefs or eliminating them from science altogether which seems a long way to go simply to maintain a thesis of little practical relevance anyway: journalists will still do journalism and people will still use modus ponens to cross the street whatever Rosenberg comes up with.

direct sensation: "I can check a belief based on memory by revisiting my memory. Doing so sometimes leads to belief revision. I can also check the belief by asking other people about how they remember the things I think I remember, look things up online, or consult another source that does not rely primarily on my own memory." (5) Lots of non-scientific beliefs are counter-intuitive such as the ontological argument. (6) Common sense knowledge is easily corrigible such as when I revise my maxim that cheaters never prosper in light of experience of prosperous cheaters. (6) Many scientific beliefs contradict other scientific beliefs: "First, it is not clear that there is more disagreement in common sense than in science. On the one hand, there is much disagreement in science, such as on why there is far more matter than antimatter in the observable universe or how it can be proven that there are Bose Einstein condensates for general interacting systems. On the other hand, there is much agreement when it comes to common sense beliefs." (7-8) One would have to not live in the real world to think that scientific beliefs are not permeated with the kinds of bias feminists, for instance, have pointed out. Thus "The history of science, and this also applies to each of its sub-disciplines, displays enormous amounts of false beliefs, misguided experiments, and deficient control mechanisms, but it does not follow from that that science is an unreliable enterprise." (9) At any rate the mere fact of a bias does not invalidate *per se* any particular belief nor does the mere fact that that belief has a potentially debunking evolutionary explanation.[105] If one were into that sort of thing one could devise evolutionary explanations for moral beliefs as easily as scientific ones: just-so stories can be devised to account for just about anything.

One should keep in mind that these claims, in Peels' account, only apply to things in the 'common sense' grab bag and leave the vast terrain of research in the humanities and journalism untouched. In every case the proposed distinctions between science and common sense turn out to apply equally to both. At best Peels thinks science *may* at some point prove common sense beliefs to be illusory though remember it may have to do this without *counting* such beliefs or adding and subtracting them from the list of rational beliefs! As he says: "... I argue that only three of these reasons are potentially good reasons to embrace scientism. It will turn out that whether or not scientism is tenable depends on (evolutionary) debunking explanations of religious and moral beliefs, empirical research allegedly showing that there is widespread and reliability undermining bias in our

---

[105]Of course without biases no process of inquiry could ever get started. The process of interpretation involves establishing critical controls over negative or debilitating biases but some bias or other always structures our approach such as the basic assumptions we make about the genre of a text or the belief in the validity of induction. Of course even these 'biases' can be tested (am I sure that is a poem?) though for most ordinary operations they are not. I tend to the view that even the most fundamental biases can be tested by processes like retorsion: I cannot for instance state that 'nothing is' without immediately contradicting my assertion. This indicates that if I have a bias towards thinking that 'something is' that bias may be inexpungable as it is a fundamental condition of stating anything at all.

120

logical and statistical reasoning, and scientific research that shows that our metaphysical views about such things as acting for reasons and free will are illusory." (4) Peels thinks that the jury is still out on this but that these three reasons *may* at some point provide reasons to support scientism. It is remarkable to think that science will have to prove its superiority to common sense without the aid of reliable logical and statistical reasoning. It is even more remarkable to thinks that 'scientists' will do so without acting for reasons or making choices. It is also sobering to think that evolution has no biases in the matter and may have equipped us with cognitive biases that render science as subjective and unreliable as morality and religion. This latter depends, as Peels admits, on the questionable assumption that 'true factual beliefs' (which by the way are pre-scientific) confer an evolutionary benefit that false religious and moral beliefs do not. (7)[106]

It seems, then, that no matter where we look 'common sense' beliefs can be as rational (or irrational) as scientific ones. Perhaps it is the awareness of such difficulties that leads some to attempt a more nuanced statement of the 'scientistic' position. In this spirit Moti Mizrahi has attempted to defend something he labels 'Weak Scientism'. I have had an extensive exchange with Dr. Mizrahi on the *Social Epistemology Review and Reply Collective*. The following comments are a digest of my three replies to Mizrahi. As I say, Mizrahi tells us he defends a position called 'weak' scientism. It is not a stance he himself entirely sticks to. Some of his statements seem to imply the strong version of scientism as when he tells us the knowledge is "... the scholarly work or research produced in scientific fields of study, such as the natural sciences, as opposed to non-scientific fields, such as the humanities... " (22) Still, when pushed, he seems content with the position that all the things I mentioned above might count as knowledge in a weaker sense but that scientific knowledge is still better both quantitatively and qualitatively. Thus, he tells us: "Scientific knowledge can be said to be qualitatively better than non-scientific knowledge insofar as such knowledge is explanatorily, instrumentally and predictively more successful than non-scientific knowledge." (Mizrahi; 7). Furthermore: "Scientific knowledge can be said to be quantitatively better than non-scientific knowledge insofar as scientific disciplines produce more impactful knowledge- in the form of scholarly publications-than non-scientific

---

[106] The problem here is the problem of the criterion as the Ancient Skeptics understood. Say natural selection equipped us with beliefs which are 90% accurate and 10% inaccurate. By what mark or criterion would we know that any given belief was in the first category rather than the second? The fact that some of our beliefs are false renders all our beliefs doubtful unless true and false beliefs have some mark that distinguishes them as such. A naturalist would have to say that natural selection has solved the epistemological problem by providing us the 'criterion' but I have difficulty conceiving how this could be so especially as evolutionary theory is one of the things that depends on the soundness of our cognitive faculties and thus can't provide a justification for it. Sometimes there is just no escaping Descartes' first meditation. In this case, it may well turn out that the beneficent non deceiving god of natural selection is actually the evil demon.

disciplines (as measured by research output and research impact)" (7) He further claims that:" ... if distinct fields of study have the same aim (i.e., to explain), then their products (i.e., explanations) can be evaluated with respect to similar criteria, such as unification, coherence, simplicity, and testability (Mizrahi 2017a, 360-362; Mizrahi 2017b, 19-20; Mizrahi 2018a, 17). This is important to his argument as claims that science adds the 'good making' property of testability over and above other disciplines and is thus qualitatively superior by simple arithmetic. One further point: Mizrahi insists that he is considering only 'academic' knowledge and not extra –academic knowledge such as "sensation, introspection and the like" . (2017;356) If it could be shown that science is superior to all other knowledge in general that would be a powerful argument for saying it is superior to non-scientific academic knowledge but this is not an argument Mizrahi avails himself of I suppose to avoid some of the problems Peels describes above.

He is wise to do so for a consideration of non-academic-non-scientific knowledge shows no particular inferiority to science even if we could agree on the relevant standards of comparison. Just take the example of quantity so favored by Mizrahi. Does science produce more knowledge that anything else? Hardly. As Augustine pointed out I can produce a potential infinity of knowledge simply by reflecting recursively on the fact of my own existence. (*City of God*; XI, 26) Indeed, I can do this by reflecting recursively on my knowledge of ANY fact and this recursion is not a scientific process even if it is performed on scientific propositions. Similar recursive processes can extend our knowledge indefinitely in the field of mathematics. Does science have (taken in bulk) more instrumental success than other knowledge forms? How would you even count given that craft knowledge and experience have a roughly 3 million-year head start? This does not even count the successful record of problem solving in law, politics, or art.[107] Is science more successful at explanation? Hardly, if science could solve problems in literature or history then these fields would not even exist. Science only explains the things it is good at explaining which is no more and no less than one can say of any other discipline. This is why many proponents of scientism tacitly assume that the explanations produced in other disciplines only concern frilly, trivial things that science needn't bother about anyway.[108] Does science make more true predictions?

---

[107]Again the problem is that the instrumental success of science rests on the instrumental success of a multitude of other things like the knowledge of bus schedules that gets us to the lab or the social knowledge that allows us to navigate modern institutions. No science tells us how to write a winning grant proposal or informs us that for as longs as Dr. Smith is chief editor of Widgetology the truth about widgets is whatever he says it is. Thus even if we confined the question to the last 20 years (as Mizrahi does) it is clear that science cannot claim instrumental superiority over the myriad other anonymous, unmarked processes that make science possible in the first place.

[108]My son, when he was a toddler, ran about the playground proclaiming himself 'the greatest'. When he failed at any task or challenge he would casually turn to his mother and say "well, the greatest doesn't do that" ! This seems to be the position of many

Again how would you even count given that for millions of years, human beings survived by making hundreds of true predictions daily on the basis of accumulated observation and experience? What is more, the inductive procedures of science seem relatively useless in the many endeavors that do not involve true prediction but some other method of justification like deduction or direct observation.

Thus, weak scientism seems in no better a case than strong scientism for the same reasons: there is no clearly applicable, context-independent, criterion that shows the superiority the 'weak scientist' claims: certainty, instrumental success, utilitarian value, predictive power and explanation all exist elsewhere in ways that are often not directly commensurable with the way they exist in science. This is as true of non-scientific-academic knowledge as it is of non-scientific-non-academic knowledge. As I told someone once (who asserted the superiority of the French language over all others) French is indeed the best language for speaking French in.[109] Science is the best way to do science. This is even true if, as Mizrahi insists, his thesis only concerns *academic* knowledge and he, unlike Peels, is not contrasting science with 'common sense' but only with other disciplines in the university. Many non-scientific disciplines show, exactly as 'common sense' does, the same 'good-making' properties as science does and where they do not it is because they don't require them. The scientistic assault on 'non-scientific –academic- knowledge' seems to fail exactly as much as the scientisitc assault on 'common sense' and for the same fundamental reasons. Weak scientism fails exactly as much as strong scientism does.

Mizrahi is still bedeviled by the same problem as the 'strong scientists'. How is science supposed to show its superiority in domains where its explanatory procedures are simply not necessary and would add no value to existing explanations? I do not think Mizrahi has established the point that:" ... if distinct fields of study have the same aim (i.e., to explain), then their products (i.e., explanations) can be evaluated with respect to similar criteria, such as unification, coherence, simplicity, and testability (Mizrahi 2017a, 360-362; Mizrahi 2017b, 19-20; Mizrahi 2018a, 17). Mizrahi says

proponents of scientism. If scientists cannot produce good explanations in a field like literature or classics, then it must be that those fields are not really knowledge or if they are, knowledge of a frilly, unimportant kind.

[109] Aristotle made this point ages ago. No inquiry into ethics he tells us can have the rigor of geometry any more than the mathematician need employ the art of rhetoric. (Nichomachean Ethics; 3, 20,25) Ethics employs phronesis or prudential judgment not logical deduction. Each discipline is answerable to its own internal standards which do not apply outside that discipline. There is, then, no overall 'super-science' (like the Platonic dialectic) that embodies a universal method for dealing with all subjects. Aristotle's world is pluralist, discontinuous and analogical. For this reason, scientists have tended to be Platonists and modern science might be viewed as the revenge of the Platonic/Pythagorean tradition against its wayward pupil. Contemporary philosophy of science, if this author understands it correctly, seems to have restored Aristotelian praxis to the center of the scientific enterprise. Students of Wittgenstein will no doubt appreciate the point that knowledge comes in as many varieties as games do and there is no more a single account of the first than there is of the second. A good criticism of 'method fetishism' and an explanation of how informal judgement underlies any application of 'scientific method' is given by Putnam (1981; 188-200)

'similar' but his argument actually depends on these criteria being 'identical' such that we can judge all explanations by one pre-set standard: in this case, I suppose, hypothetico-deductive method. But this is nonsense. All disciplines use abduction, true, but they do not all arrive at the 'best explanation' by the same procedures. Their procedures are analogical not univocal. Failure to see this distinction seems to be at the root of Mizrahi's errors. Differing explanatory processes can be compared but not identified as can be seen if we imagine a classicist taking his copy of the *Iliad* down to the chemistry lab to be analyzed for its meaning. The Chemistry lab here is the classicist's brain! To use a less flippant example though there are sciences such as paleontology that make liberal use of narrative reconstruction (i.e. how those hominid bones got in that tiny cave) which is a form of abduction that does not correspond simply to the standard H/D model. Still, the story the paleontologist reconstructs, if it is a good one, has unity, simplicity and coherence regardless of the fact that it has achieved this by another, less formalized, form of inference.

Let's consider a couple of examples here. I take it as a given that a masterful exposition of *Portrait of the Artist as Young Man* will show the unity, coherence and simplicity of the work's design to the extent that these are artistically desired features. What about testability? How does a Joyce scholar test what he says? As I said he tests it against the text. He does this in two ways. First on the level of direct observation he establishes what Stephen Daedalus, say, does on page 46. This is, as far as I can see, a perfectly reputable kind of knowledge and if we can answer the question about page 46 directly we do not need to resort to any more complex explanatory processes. The fact that such a procedure is perfectly adequate to establish the truth means that scientific procedures of a more complex kind are unnecessary. The use of scientific method, while it may mean better knowledge in many cases, does not mean better knowledge here so Mizrahi's complaint on this score is beside the point. (47)

Of course the Joyce scholar will also have an interpretation of *Portrait of the Artist as a Young Man*. This is where he answers broader questions about the work's meaning, structure, unity and so on. This also entails the test of looking at the text not at any particular point but as a whole. What in this hermeneutic process would be improved by 'scientific method' ? Where does the Joyce scholar need to draw testable consequences from a novel hypothesis and test it with an experiment? What would that even mean in this context? His test is close reading as this is practiced in the discipline of English literature and he has peers who judge if he has done this well or badly. What is amiss with this process that it could be improved by procedures that have nothing to do with determining the meaning and significance of books? How on this question could science even begin to show its supposed 'superiority'?

I think, however, that I see where Mizrahi's confusion lies. He seems to think I am saying the following: Joyce scholars look at a book to determine a fact just as scientists look at the world to determine a fact ergo

Joyce scholars are scientists. (47) Let me reassure him I am not so je-
june. Of course, field notes and other forms of direct observation are part
of the arsenal of science. Plus, scientific statements are, at the end of the
day, brought into relationship with observation either directly or indirectly.
Still, Joyce scholars do not just look at page numbers or what characters
are wearing in Chapter 2. They formulate interpretations of Joyce. In this
way too scientists not only observe things but formulate and test hypotheses, construct theories and so on. In some ways these may be comparable
processes but they are not identical. Hermeneutics is not just an application of hyothetico-deductive method to a book. Conclusions about Joyce
are not products of experimental testing and I can conceive of no way in
which they could be strengthened by them except in a purely ancillary
sense (ie. we might learn something indirect about *Ulysses* by exhum-
ing Joyce's bones). Thus, Mizrahi's argument that scientific explanations
have more 'good-making properties' overall (47) is, whether true or not,
irrelevant to the myriad of cases in which scientific explanations are either
A. unnecessary or B. inapplicable. Once again we teeter on the brink of
strong scientism (which Mizrahi rejects) for we are now forced to say that
if a scientific explanation of a phenomenon is not to be had then there can
be no other form of explanation.

Let me go back to my daughter who was not out in a field or cave
somewhere but in a university classroom when she presented her analysis
of Scriabin's Prometheus chord. This, I hope, satisfies Mizrahi's demand
that I confine myself to an 'academic' context. Both her instructor and
her classmates agreed that her analysis was sound. Why? Because it
was the clearest, simplest explanation that answered the question of how
Scriabin created this chord. It was an abduction that the community of
knowers of which she was a part found adequate and that was the end of
the story. The reason, let me emphasize again, is that this was all the
question required. Kristin did not deduce a "... consequence that follows
from a hypothesis plus auxiliary hypothesis" (47) to be made subject of a
testable prediction. Why? Because that is not how knowledge is produced
in her domain and such a procedure would add no value to her conclusion
which concerned not facts about the natural world but Scriabin's thought
processes and aesthetic intentions. Again it seems that either Mizrahi must
concede this point OR adopt the strong scientist position that Kristin only
seems to know something about Scriabin while actually there is nothing to
be known about Scriabin outside the experimental sciences. So, to make
his case he must still explain why science can produce better results in
music theory, which IS an academic subject, than explanatory procedures
currently used in that domain. Otherwise the superiority of science is only
contextual which is a trivial thesis denied by no one.

I think the best description of what my daughter did with the Prometheus
chord is that she *reverse engineered* it. She worked backward from it to tell
a story about how it came to be. Obviously this did not require any novel
prediction about future Prometheus chords by future Scriabins. There

is one Prometheus chord and it already exists. Further, the process by which it was created occurred once in the past. Thus we are constructing an explanatory story about the past concerning a singular object not formulating a general law or making a testable prediction. This kind of story is used in all kinds of contexts. It is used here in music theory. It is even used in those sciences concerned with past events. It is used by law enforcement to reconstruct a crime. Now, even if by some feat of prestidigitation one could contort such explanatory stories into the form of testable predictions this would be an after the fact rationalization not description of how actual people reason. Thus, let me emphasize ONCE AGAIN that testability does not make science superior to on non-science for the simple reason that non-science does not typically NEED tests such as Mizrahi describes. Or, to put it another way testing is not employed in the same way in science and non-science so that if one says that, in some sense, the Joyce scholar 'tests' his ideas against the text one is speaking ANALOGICALLY not UNIVOCALLY as I attempted to point out in my second reply. (Wills, 2018b, 38)

This speaks to a certain triviality lurking in Mizrahi's thesis. He tells us that the best explanation is one "explains the most, leaves out the least, is consistent with background knowledge, is the least complicated, and yields independently testable predictions." (Mizrahi, 28) He then adds "Wills seems to grant that "unity, simplicity and coherence are good making properties of explanations, but not testability. But why not testability?" . (Mizrahi, 28) Well I have said why not. Testability as Mizrahi defines it is not relevant to all inquiries. It is not even relevant to all scientific inquiries. 'Testing' can take different forms that resemble each other *analogically* not *univocally*: the test of a thesis on metaphysics is *elenchic*. The test of a thesis about Joyce is a close examination of his texts. The test of an archeological claim is the examination of artefacts. Mizrahi's entire argument boils down to the claim that science beats non-science 4 to 3! Yet clearly Mizrahi has tilted the field by asking non-science to conform to a standard external to it and applied arbitrarily. Unity, coherence, testability and so on are resemblance terms that cash out differently in different inquiries and this is to say nothing of how they cash out in different time periods and other cultures. Mizrahi insists that "... if IBE is ubiquitous in scientific and non-scientific reasoning and good explanations are those that are comprehensive, coherent, simple and testable, then it follows that, in both scientific and non-scientific contexts, the best explanations are those that are comprehensive, coherent, simple and testable explanations." (2017; 362) However, this is an utterly misleading statement if we assume that all these terms have univocal meanings in both domains. As Aristotle said long ago (and as I noted above) it is absurd to judge rhetoric by the standard of geometry and vice versa: standards are particular to particular domains of knowledge when their subject matters formally differ as they do in those investigations that concern singulars as opposed to testable general laws.

If the comparatively mild versions of scientism analyzed above fail resoundingly there seems to me little hope for the stronger versions. Of course as I began by saying 'scientism' is an ideological position that has little to do with science, reason or logic. In part it is an aggressive ideology underlying the political and cultural dominance of western technocrats. In part though it is defensive: proponents may well be reacting to a real and threatening decline in the public authority of the sciences. To this extent one can sympathize with them though just saying 'science' in a louder voice is no solution. As I explained above the problem is one of authority and accountability of public institutions. Political and social reform is fundamental for the future health of science and for the public acceptance of science. In this 'scientism' in whatever iteration, strong or weak, has to take a back seat to politics. Under different social and political relations, we might well have better science that the general public trusts more: we might have, for the first time, democratized science.

16 Strangeness

It was once a part of any educated treatment of the world to leave room for marvels. If one picks up Pliny's *Natural History*, Augustine's *City of God*, Burton's *Anatomy of Melancholy*, Browne's *Religio Medici* or any of a number of works by such figures as Agrippa or Paracelsus one finds a world where apparently impossible things are asserted as facts. One finds out that people with the heads of dogs live in the antipodes, that little green children live among us, that writing can be projected on the face of the moon and that a human/pig hybrid lives just down the road. One finds out that humans can generate children with mer-folk and that gnomes can pass through solid rock. One also finds these things asserted as facts well attested and reliably witnessed. There are several possible explanations for this. The first is thinkable from a philosophical perspective but immediately dismissed from a human one: that is that the world altered profoundly around the 17th Century and that it now operates under different laws.[110] We could also regard the authors above as liars or gullible fools. A simpler thought occurs to me however: humans have a fundamental need for marvels and for this reason Pliny and the rest included them as part of their account of the world. If I were to articulate the nature of

---

[110]It is commonly assumed that the world remains the same while our conceptions of it change. Some assert, however, that as sour conceptions change so does the world because conceptions of some sort are a constitutive principle of any 'world'. Blake is one of these people: "The eye altering alters all" . (1978; 501) Nature certainly can change from the standpoint of the subject and may be, as the Buddhists tells us, constantly doing so. It may also, and simultaneously, be changing in its 'objective' pole. For the sake of convenience though, we will assume some stability in the principles and laws under which the world operates though from a purely empirical point of view nothing guarantees it (which is why on this problem I tend to agree with Kant- though that's another matter). For an interesting discussion of how things can be as historical as our opinions about them see the chapter "The Historicity of Things" in Bruno Latour's Pandora's Hope. His claim is that we create the conceptual and institutional spaces in which beings can (and perhaps must?) appear as microbial. This skepticism (if it is that) has the result of returning us to the immediacy of the world for if beings are such as our activity constitutes them there is no epistemological problem: knowledge of things is at the same time knowledge of our own productive social and institutional powers. Thus, the bugbear of epistemology, the subject-object distinction, is removed at a stroke for, as Latour tells us, the stability of objects, once the function of an out there 'substance' is now performed by the 'institution' which gathers an assemblage of agents into a whole. (1999; 151)

this need I would say that humans like and need regularity and order and that they need and like surprises as well. Each is predicated on the other. Without order and regularity there are no surprises and surprises are the exception that proves the rule. We like to have scripts and gaps in our script that reinforce the script. All known scripts in fact have gaps as, for instance, all the 'uncanny' things that fall outside our current script called naturalism.[111] Just as the magician always has an explanation for why his magic fails every culture has a set of stock answers for when its scripts fail. Depending on how basic the script is we invoke ad hoc explanations to close the gaps. Some scripts, though, we are willing to be looser about than others; ordinary people (though not intellectuals) are happy and indeed eager to admit gaps in the script of naturalism no matter how much they are hectored or ridiculed.

Anyone interested in our contemporary sense of weirdness can find a rich field of investigation simply by turning on the television. One thing I have noticed about the endless parade of paranormal shows on television is how careful they are NOT to offer certainty. The first rule of searching for Bigfoot or Nessie (at least on TV) is that Bigfoot and Nessie are never found. Nor do shows like *Ghost Adventures* or *Paranormal Survivor* ever quite show you a ghost.[112] This may reflect the fact that there are no ghosts or monsters to show. Still, no one goes away from these shows frustrated or unhappy (or they would quickly go off the air). That the monster is never found or the ghost never clearly appears seems to be a structural feature. The consumers of such programs want clues as to what *might* be there but don't particularly want to know. The product being sold is teasing uncertainty and this mood is more pleasurable then discovering, say, that Nessie is a hitherto unknown species of shark (whatever Nessie ACTUALLY turned out to be would be disappointing!). I suppose this means that a. we take some relief from the thought that monstrous things are not, after all, real but that b. we derive some frisson from the *possibility* that they are. In other words, monsters and ghosts appeal to

---

[111]A simple example would be the phenomenon (well known to parents of twins) of sympathetic pains and other 'action at a distance' events. I am told that this is not considered a 'scientific' phenomenon as the evidence for it is anecdotal. To be fair, such an intuitive phenomenon might be very difficult to replicate in the artificial setting of a lab. Not being a scientist, however, I am free NOT to think that the twins and parents of twins I know are liars or too incompetent to report their own experiences accurately (some of them are academics after all!). As a human I have to take them at their word. Of course, if such phenomenon exist I have no doubt that they are 'natural' in some sense though we might require a broader concept of 'nature' to accommodate them: one that involves systematic interconnections between things not contiguous in space. Quantum mechanics already makes this thinkable in certain ways but here (on the question of the interpretation of this phenomenon) I must defer to the authority of psychologists and other researchers in the relevant fields.

[112]I must single out Ghost Adventures for the tact with which it walks this very fine line. The 'ghosts' are largely a product of breathless narration. The 'adventurers' describe things viewers can barely discern themselves or appeal to purported 'scientific instruments' which only they can read. Thus clicks and pops and other sorts of ambient noise become supernatural communications. They also, for no reason I can discern, only conduct their adventures at night though ghosts seem just as active in the day!

a complex mood composed of contrary elements. Though we need not commit to any particular monster we do want to believe in monstrosity itself. We want a safe, comfortable, predictable world with just a hint of the dangerous or uncanny lest we settle too easily into the "same dull round" (as William Blake puts it). (76)

This thought is worth teasing out with Blake as our guide. Blake was a great enemy of what he took to be the emphasis of Locke and other empiricists on knowledge inferred from experience. This is because he took a radical stance to the world both politically and religiously. Though the ears of empiricists might burn at this Blake thought the empirically given to be inadequate to human potential and the flowering of human freedom which for him involved *rejecting* 'what is there' for what we can make the world to be. The danger he saw in Locke and Bacon was that the repetition in nature which makes induction possible might be applied to human society. This would imply some kind of necessity to the given structures of society that would make creativity and genuine change impossible. It is interesting to note that politically Blake has won this argument at least among the heirs of Marx. At the same time many of the same people accept philosophies such as naturalism which are very much in the tradition of Locke's empiricism. These are deeper waters than we need to swim in at present though. People drowning in lives of repetition and ennui crave novelty because novelty offers the hope that something might change. (as we shall see below). This change might appear on its surface disruptive and even dangerous.[113] Yet, to quote a Canadian poet Margaret Avison we struggle against a 'congealing it' (2005; 15): the ghosts which toss objects across rooms or make unnerving noises are introducing chaos into unfulfilled lives that the persons involved *want to change*. Chaos is dangerous but with danger comes opportunity.

This mood is a perhaps a bit different from what has come to be known as Forteana after the American writer Charles Fort. Fort devoted his life to collecting stories of odd or inexplicable events generally of the raining frogs variety. The key to Forteana however is that it is random and uncorrelated. Fort sought evidence that contrary to what we assume the world is not law governed or patterned or regular but a random heap of events: to quote another television show "Just a bunch of stuff that happens!" .[114]

---

[113]'Monster' (from Latin monstrum) is, it is interesting to note, etymologically related to words like 'monstrance' (i.e. a container made for displaying the host) or 'demonstration'. A monster is a 'showing' or 'manifestation' of something unfamiliar and possibly sacred or dangerous. Comets, for instance, used to be 'showings' because of the rarity of their occurrence. A monster is also, because it is portentous, a warning as in our word 'remonstrate'. All these words boil down to 'moneo' to advise or warn I suppose because a warning reveals or shows a future consequence.

[114]Another feature differentiates Fort from his predecessors and that is that figures like Pliny, Augustine or Burton lived in a world of text. Things were true because they were in books and the symbolic world of text was its own higher reality. The Anatomy of Melancholy is, thus, a web of intertextuality and allusion culled from a lifelong habit of reading. I suppose the Christian concept of the Bible as the book of God had some influence over this but even the 'book of nature' as a man like Burton understood it was a textual artifact. It was Bacon who, in early modernity, decisively replaces 'reading'

Ghosts however exist in the context of stories and do not exist outside of them. A narrative about the past (and no doubt a potential future) always frames the activity of the ghost. I do not quite mean by this that ghosts are imaginary but that they are 'narrative objects' in which they do not, perhaps, differ from things like atoms or black holes.[115] Perhaps one could call them 'poetic fictions' if one can think of these without surreptitiously introducing the notion of unpoetic 'facts'. There may be 'un-poetic facts' of a kind but no 'world' is just a collection of these because all 'worlds' have a narrative structure that turn dead 'facts' into 'objects' or things with which I interact. As Heidegger might say things are objects with which we dwell on the earth.

Another popular show, *Dead Files* offers a good example of what I mean. The show is not in fact about ghosts at all but about the living subjects who suffer from them. It is concerned with the miseries of life: illnesses both physical and mental, marital or family tensions and all round fatigue or malaise. I am tempted to say that the spirits tormenting these unfortunates are largely their own (or at least that is how they present on the show). If I were a psychologist, I would be tempted to interpret the events depicted in this show in psychoanalytic terms though I can offer no opinion on the relative merits of seeing a registered therapist versus processing your issues through the medium of a ghost story. I simply note that the ghost is an apt metaphor for all the events and traumas of the past that burden the present and this is why writers like Shakespeare to Ibsen have resorted to this image. Indeed, the ghost itself is (according to some occultists) a kind of 'residue' (semi-physical perhaps) of unresolved trauma and probably not in itself a conscious entity. I suspect that as long as such traumas exist people will see and hear ghosts whatever 'status' one decides to grant them (and I have no particular bias on that question).

In ancient times though ghosts and monsters were rather more serious business, indeed too serious business. By this I mean that people attempted to order and rationalize our experiences of the 'supernatural'. It is often asserted that works like the notorious *Maleus Mallificarum* are products of a superstitious mentality but nothing could be further from the truth. If they are monsters, they are monsters of reason as they attempt to categorize and explain the uncanny (particularly its evil, threatening aspects) and this almost certainly a mistake. Some things are better left uninvestigated and it is with good reason that demonology is no longer a

---

with 'looking'. Today we are told yet again, in a somewhat different sense, that 'there is nothing outside the text': my rather more cautious assertion is that there is nothing apart from the text.

[115]Perhaps one might use the word 'posit' here to designate an unseen object which connects two or more seen ones. I borrow the term from Quine though I am using it to ends he would firmly reject. At any rate different peoples have different posits. I once spoke to a lady with experience in the mental health system. She told me of a certain patient who, in state of distress and extreme agitation, performed physical contortions on their face impossible. Her 'place holder' word for this kind of thing was possession. I could re-describe the same thing as 'mental illness' but I'm not sure that is any less of a 'place holder' word for something neither I nor her understand in the least.

science as it was in the early modern period. He who concerns himself too closely with monsters becomes one. Evil has an obsessive hold on the psyche that is neither healthy nor safe. Still, this is the wisdom of hindsight. To people in antiquity and the middle ages it seemed natural to apply the light of reason to 'paranormal' things as much as to 'normal' things.[116] If a set of phenomena existed, it was natural to correlate and categorize them as much as any other.

As good example let's consider the "learned Constanipolitan" Michael Psellus and his *On the Operation of Demons*. People who are students of literature may recall that Psellus is mentioned in the notes to the *Rime of the Ancient Mariner* and seems one of Coleridge's sources for the idea of 'elemental spirits' who inhabit distant regions of the world. The book is interesting in itself however. Psellus was a Byzantine Platonist who, both as a Christian and a philosopher, accepted the basic proposition of late Platonism that along with human beings and other animals there was a vast network (hierarchically ordered) of intelligences and spirits (what we would now label angels and demons). Along with these was a range of accepted phenomena that revealed their operations. Psellus tends to focus on their malign operations and we may take this as a regrettable Christian bias. Late Platonists tended to assimilate the intellectual creation to the traditional Greek gods. This lead Christian critics of polytheism to attribute the miracles and wonders worked by the ancient gods to demons where they could not dismiss such tales outright. Thus the Greek *daimon,* a name denoting a mediating spirit and having no particular moral connotation, became our 'demon'.

On all hands though it was agreed that some spirits (at least) were shady characters it would be better not to know. How do we know about such beings, their natures and characteristic operations? Psellus indicates

---

[116]This entire discussion is bedeviled by a conceptually imprecise vocabulary. Nature, where older writers more apt in such matters were concerned, was whatever happened by a cause or principle. Thus words like 'super-natural' were used only in very restricted contexts as when one said that the capacity of the waters of baptism to cleanse sin did not belong to them by nature (i.e. by essence or inner principle) but 'supernaturally' by the grace of god. The 'supernatural' was a relation of the natural to what is higher. Accordingly, all angelic or demonic activity is 'natural' because the actions involved flow from the essential nature or 'form' of those beings. As such they are also 'normal' because they conform to the norms which govern such beings so that they do nothing miraculous. Thus, 'paranormal' is scarcely an apt word either for things that, if they happen, happen by law and are to that extent 'normal'. Paranormal, here, can only mean 'things we rarely if ever observe' and this includes many normal things like Halley's comet. One can perhaps clarify this by saying that 'paranormal' things are things that happen contrary to currently understood physical laws but I suspect the extension of the term is narrower than this. If an asteroid had an erratic orbit that could not be explained by current celestial dynamics I'm not sure anyone would call this 'paranormal' though we might suspect the asteroid was an alien vessel (another perfectly 'natural' explanation!). Alternatively, we might call paranormal things 'non-natural' or 'non-physical' but this too is to assume more about them than we know. Perhaps 'paranormal' means nothing more than 'weird to 21st century people educated in the sciences'. No more helpful is the attempt to distinguish 'naturalistic' explanation from 'magical' explanation as anyone familiar with the history of magic knows that magical operations involved principles thought eminently 'natural'.

a range of phenomena that the posit of 'demons' correlates and connects. Some of these overlap with our 'ontology' and some do not. The first is the power of suggestion. Negative and unproductive thoughts arise in our minds unbidden often when they are least wanted. (2016; 19) They are 'as if' they were suggested or insinuated to us by persons not solicitous of our welfare. Demons offer a way to explain this very basic and ordinary experience. This is the very reason it is, for Psellus, a phenomenon in the first place. *We* tend to think the spontaneity of certain thoughts to be random and fortuitous but that of course is because we don't have an explanatory scheme for them. If we have a ready explanatory scheme for something we are far more likely to regard it as a real 'phenomenon' as opposed to an uninteresting anomaly. This is why we ignore things like hunches or sympathetic pains between twins. The second range of phenomenon is of course possession: the sense that someone has crossed the line from being 'themselves' to being 'someone else'. This manifests itself especially in the phenomenon of tongues: people who in extreme states of derangement speak languages they cannot in their normal state.[117] (25-26) The third range of phenomena involve uncanny knowledge of the future such as an ordinary human would not possess but a demon might. This need not involve actual knowledge of the future. (32-33) Demons might be simply shrewd guessers (like phone psychics!) or able to discern causes operative in the present that we cannot. What we should note though is that the posit 'demon' allows us to understand these three ranges of phenomenon as unified. Conversely, our lack of such a posit causes us to leave these phenomena uncorrelated. For this reason, we fall back on *ad hoc* explanations for such things (like fraud) or ignore or dismiss them altogether.

This is to say that one aspect of weirdness is simply relative to our available explanatory schemes.[118] This does not exhaust our subject however. St. Augustine, for instance, holds that 'weirdness' is in fact good for us and that God has providently provided for it. Why, he wonders, has God created the dog-headed men of the antipodes, humans with faces on their

---

[117]Whatever one thinks of demons this is a fascinating phenomenon. To Burton (428) it suggests the possibility that the human mind actually contains all languages and that speakers of tongues are, in Platonic fashion, recollecting something they cannot access in their ordinary waking consciousness. Coleridge, in his Biographia Literaria, mentions a fascinating case which he traced to the fact that a barely educated girl had spent part of her youth in the care of a classicist and Hebraist. (58-61) If true, this at least reveals a striking, and unsuspected, power of human memory.

[118]'Demons' as an explanatory mechanism were given not only by our experience of them (which might after all be dismissed) but a. by the Christian scriptures which mention them and b. by the Neo-Platonic conception of a hierarchy of intelligences and souls which identified, a priori, a structural need for incorporeal intelligences. This is why in the middle ages Aquinas will argue that angels exist because otherwise there would be a surd and irrational gap in the structure of creation. Given this availability it was natural to put them to explanatory use. I should also note that for Psellus intelligences and spirits operated alongside ordinary natural causes and did not replace them. He accepted the view that there were two parallel streams of events in nature linked metaphysically by causal hierarchy but not directly correlated.

chests or the other monstrosities described by Pliny? (1971; 662) Surely these things represent disorder and ugliness unworthy of the creator! His answer might interest those concerned with issues surrounding disabilities or alternative sexualities (as these strange beings include hermaphrodites). Augustine does not fetishize the external human form. While considering the descent of living human beings from the sons of Noah he pauses to consider whether the monsters of classical legend are to be counted among them: a quaint question for us certainly but one with an unexpected answer. God cannot, Augustine tells us, make a mistake and if there are dog-headed men, hermaphrodites or men who hop speedily on one foot it is because god has determined by a wisdom we cannot fathom that they contribute to the perfection of the whole. (662) In other words, their monstrosity is fully 'natural' and if they are rational creatures they are descendants of the sons of Noah and indeed of Adam. This is so in spite of any external differences of physical form (which suggests the possibility of the human form evolving?). Monsters are thus an object lesson: human hubris cannot dictate to providence on the basis of what it considers normal or expected. Monsters disrupt our presumption concerning what is beautiful or fitting.

They have a further function. Augustine informs us that monstrosity of a milder form exists among humans ranging from people born with extra fingers to a reported case of a child with two heads. Again, certain 'ordinary' humans are born with the genitals of both sexes. These are no more mistakes than races with backwards feet. Augustine says: "... it may be suggested that God decided to create some races in this way, so that we should not suppose that the wisdom with which he fashions the physical being of men has gone astray in the case of the monsters which are bound to be born among us of human parents... " . (663-64) This strikes me as a remarkable passage; one that even our contemporary world has barely caught up with. Augustine is saying that the purpose of monsters is to remind us that really there are no monsters but divinely willed variations in human form. There are no 'tragic mistakes' only persons capable of reason. This is very far from the ancient attitude of mind which saw monstrous births as omens of evil and ill fortune to be shunned and even exposed as infants. In Augustine's view everyone has the form intended for them by God. This is so whatever is the case about Antipodeans.[119]

---

[119] Interestingly Augustine is skeptical of what will later become the medieval 'principle of plenitude'; the notion that nature abhors a vacuum and that all media and all spaces are inhabited. (664) Antipodeans are posited on the basis of the principle that the southern zones must be inhabited just as the northern ones are. Augustine seems to think it just as likely that they are empty. Interestingly, contemporary belief in aliens also appeals to the principle of plenitude: a universe so vast as ours could not all be empty of life! At any rate Augustine has his doubts about the antipodeans (if they are to be thought of as children of Adam) on the grounds that it is hard to imagine life diffusing itself across the (to the ancients uninhabitable) equatorial zone. This may remind us that in some ways the image of 'Adam's family' is inadequate to express the notion of the community of all rational beings as Augustine himself would have admitted (i.e. the City of God includes the intellectual creation).

Augustine reserves judgment on the existence of such beings; however, it is, again, the possibility that they exist that is of central importance. Our aesthetic criteria and our other norms are important but only up to a point for there is always a greater intelligence which can manifest itself contrary to them. The ultimate expression of this is, of course, the miraculous but there are many smaller scale events that demonstrate it as well.

The *Book on Nymphs, Sylphs, Pygmies and Salamanders* by the early modern physician Paracelsus gives us another perspective on the strange. Paracelsus regards the titular creatures of his short book as ecological guardians and stewards of nature, husbanding resources till they are needed or can be used responsibly: "Thus gnomes, pygmies and *mani* guard the treasures of the earth, the metals and similar treasures... They are guarded by such people, are kept hidden and secret so that they may not be found till the time for it has come." (251) Their status as non-human persons is essential for this for this means they, and the resources they guard are not a 'standing reserve' for human exploitation and greed. Ovid used the image of mining to invoke the passing of the golden age and it is interesting to note that as a physician Paracelsus was deeply concerned with the health of miners. To be brief, mining seems on its face a violation of the sanctity of the earth and an idle and destructive prying into her secrets. In fact, though, not only the earth but the medium of each of the elements, fire air and water has its living spirit. These spirits are at home in these elements the way a fish is at home in water with gnomes (earth beings) being able to pass through rock as a fluid medium as we pass through air. These guardians, of course, shepherd the elements they inhabit but they are not exactly hostile either; they are giving to humans when and where providence determines this is appropriate and this is why we can mine the earth or fish the seas at all. In sum, they are that in the natural realm which withdraws from the human into its own sphere, into their own 'inwardness' as it were.

Unlike Augustine or Psellus, Paracelsus does not rush to demonize the nymphs and salamanders. He lets them be as they are outside the cosmos of Christianity. Like the righteous Pagans in Dante their life and destiny is entirely within the context of nature. They are not, like humans, caught up in the cosmic drama of sin and redemption. Though rational they are not immortal. They live natural lives solely and have no supernatural destiny or afterlife to concern themselves with. They are neither with god nor with the devil. Whoever wrote the ballad *Thomas the Rhymer* understood this as well:

"'O see ye not yon narrow road,
So thick beset with thorns and briers?
That is the path of righteousness,
Tho after it but few enquires.

'And see ye not that braid braid road,
That lies across that lily leven?

That is the path of wickedness,
Tho some call it the road to heaven.

'And see not ye that bonny road,
That winds about the fernie brae?
That is the road to fair Elfland,
Where thou and I this night maun gae."

Thus, while Paracelsus is a devout Christian he is not radically anthro-pocentric. The drama of human sin and Christ's redemption is central to *him* as human but oblique to other beings. The central drama of OUR creation is a sideshow to theirs. As any reflective Christian would no doubt admit, with C.S. Lewis, there may be no gospel for Saturnians (if they exist) as they may not require one.[120] I mention Saturnians here because it seems to me that aliens currently fill the role of gnomes and fairies: beings that may not fit with any of our ordinary categories and to whom our concerns are (potentially) oblique. This can be illustrated by the quirky and I assume co-incidental fact that Paracelsus' gnomes who pass through rock and guard the depths of mines show up on the *Star Trek* Episode *The Devil in the Dark* as the Horta! Why is it that our imagination populates alien planets with forgotten beings from our own folklore?

I confess I'm not sure I know. What I can conclude however is even the supposed absolutists of our classical and Christian pasts saw a place for weirdness even when it created tensions with their stated beliefs. The behavior of elephants caused even Augustine to wonder if the line between humans and animals was really so absolute and gaps and fissures (such as the distinction between celestial and terrestrial matter) existed and were accepted even in the rigorous systematizing of the high middle ages. The monster seems to be one of these gaps. This is true in the Aristotelian sense that a natural cause can fail in its effect (at least in the sublunary realm) producing, say, a three toed cat[121]. It also seems to be true in the sense that there are things which violate our sense of order and sense of

---

[120]See "Religion and Rocketry" in The World's Last Night. Lewis' comments seem very much in line with Paracelsus as he makes no assumption that any putative aliens would be embedded in our salvation stories whether those be sacred or (I would add) secular. Indeed, the following words, concerning meeting aliens, might be taken as a motto for this book: "What I do know is that here and now, as our only possible practical preparation for such a meeting, you and I should resolve to stand firm against all exploitation and all theological imperialism. It will not be fun. We shall be called traitors to our own species. We shall be hated of almost all men; even of some religious men. And we must not give back one single inch." (90-91) As an amusing sidebar I note that the very first science fiction film, A Trip to the Moon has our heroic astronauts slaughtering the 'Selenians' within minutes of landing.

[121] Augustine is in radical dissent from Aristotelian cosmology, a cosmology followed later by medieval scholastics. Aristotle and his successors accepted the traditional cosmology for which the recalcitrance of matter limited the perfection of things beneath the circle of the moon. Augustine seems to have little such conception and in this he anticipates the modern scientific revolution for which all phenomena celestial or terrestrial were subject to the same mathematical principles laid down by God. For

aesthetic form that nonetheless have their rationale and place in the total order. From this perspective the monster seems to be part and parcel of the broader question of theodicy. It also gives us some purchase on the question with which this book began: the question of the oblique. Do we want the real systematically ordered with all phenomena correlated and unified under the smallest possible number of principles? Do we want to leave room for things that aren't quite right and don't quite fit lest the world become closed and oppressive to the spirit? Is it better to have one account of the world or move between two or three or more as need be? Can we partner systematicity and unity with the maximum possible richness and diversity? The most order with the most interesting surprises? Of course, as I have adverted to above, politics and culture are areas where are trying to answer this very question. Metaphysics and theology might be another area though that is beyond the scope of the present book. I will go out on a limb however: I think a criterion of completeness governs out thinking and if some ideal system existed (whether religious, philosophical or scientific) which balanced the demands of order and diversity, predictability and novelty, monstrous surprises with the familiar and sane then that system would be the truth. It would be the truth because it would be the whole though I offer no speculation here on whether such a system exists in the world or out of it.

---

this position a monster is not an anomaly or a failure of law to operate but a necessary expression of it. Thus we today have 'mutations' which are 'random' in the sense of uncorrelated but still necessary expressions of the laws of chemistry and physics.

17 / BATTLES BETWEEN PARADIGMS

As some people might consider me a relativist about paradigms or conceptual schemes let me lay out why I think I am not. I say these things by way of hypothesis but it is the hypothesis I work with daily and what I say here seems implied by the attitude I take towards the many texts and other things that cross my desk. I am not given to fabricating novel theories and I have never had much time for theories of interpretation, argument or evidence that go beyond the interpreting and arguing and appealing to evidence that I do in classrooms, academic papers and in trying to make my children see sense about something. To that extent I am quite without sophistication: I do not read theory, say, and think about how I can apply it but advert to it only when it helps me understand something otherwise troubling. From this rough pragmatic standpoint, it seems to me paradigms or conceptual schemes exist: animists and mechanists disagree not about what they see but about *how* to see it, not seeing *that* but seeing *as*. [122]Seeing *as* and seeing *in relation to*, moreover, is essential to seeing *that*. At the same time there seem to me, as to Davidson, some basic limits to the independence of paradigms: "Different points of view make sense, but only if there is a common coordinate system on which to plot them." (1973; 6) Let me try and indicate what I think of these are. I will do so in a way that does not depend solely on the unmediated realism of statements like 'my skin is warm is true if and only if my skin is warm' (16) and in that respect I differ from Davidson. Part of what

---

[122]This is not a quaint or idle example: one faculty member in my program is a Miq'maw person of traditional views and that means she is very much an animist. Part of the problem I am trying to address here is that it makes no sense to me at all to claim that she is simply mistaken about a 'fact' even though I do not share her belief. In particular, it seems to me silly to argue that there is no spirit animating a lake because a chemical analysis of water has not revealed one (nor does it help if, as Davison would have it, we both share the sentence 'my skin is wet'). If my colleague is mistaken it is not because there is something about lakes she has simply failed to see. The situation is parallel to the famous Tower of Pisa experiment where, as Heidegger points out, Galileo and his Aristotelian opponents saw a different event: "Both Galileo and his opponents saw the same "fact" . But they interpreted the same fact differently and made the same happening different to themselves. (266) As we all do, the Aristotelians saw what they were trained to see (different bodies falling at different rates) whereas Galileo demanded they see something different (different bodies falling at the same rate with air resistance factored in).

needs to be related are conceptual systems *and* such common referents as they may happen to share or indeed must share as there seems to me no way back to the simple innocence of warm skin.

Let me work out what is now my rough working hypothesis and see where it takes us. Part of what a word or concept means concerns its function within a system of other words or concepts. I can take a series of sounds like *forsuch, blator* and *tungle* and create from them a system of determinate linguistic contrasts using categories like sameness, difference, opposition and so on. *Forsuch* may, for instance, be the opposite of *blator* and *tungle* the genus to which it belongs. These placeholders, however, mark only the logical skeleton of a language and this is because none of them perform the function of picking out the content of some 'world' that is directly given. Also, there are the many other combinatory rules of grammar and syntax that differ from language to language though they fall into broad groupings like SOV or SVO. The data organized in any language or scheme (for now we will follow Davidson in taking these as mutually overlapping) must be (in part) independent from that language and therefore from any other. If there is no observation without theory, there is no theory without observation. As Kant would say there is a receptive, empirical, moment to knowledge; what we would call data or 'things given'.[123] As well as internal systematic function of the logical or grammatical type there is 'aboutness' and this 'aboutness' or function of reference will be *in principle* translatable for all linguistic or conceptual systems that share the same world (however challenging this may sometimes be in practice). A Papuan and an Englishman will, say, agree roughly (if not exactly) about what is a dog. Even if another speaker refers to foxes as dogs and we don't there is no intrinsic bar to learning his usage for as longs as furry, canine mammals are running around somewhere.[124] This might be a problem for dead languages (what is 'white'

---

[123] For our present purposes I will define this minimally (and only minimally) as the flow of ordered sensation whether or not these sensations correspond to an 'external world' and whether or not this order is constituted apriori by such categories as space, time, substance and causality. Berkeley for instance went no further in speaking of our passive knowledge with the rarely noted result that he restored a radical realism to epistemology and returned to humans the immediacy of the life world (against the specter of epistemology). He does so with an elegant nod to Homer's Odyssey: "And although it may, perhaps, seem an uneasy reflection to some, that when they have taken a circuit through so many refined and unvulgar notions, they should at last come to think like other men; yet, methinks, this return to the simple dictates of nature, after having wandered through the wild mazes of philosophy, is not unpleasant. It is like coming home from a long voyage: a man reflects with pleasure on the many difficulties and perplexities he has passed through, sets his heart at ease, and enjoys himself with more satisfaction for the future." (Three Disalogues Between Hylas and Philonous :1984, 4) Berkeley's idealism, I should note, developed (in his later writings) beyond his early and notorious 'esse est percipe' towards a more Platonic (or perhaps Parmenidean) 'to be is to be thought' or, as Aquinas might put it, there is the potentially intelligible and the actually intelligized.

[124] Of course some schemes of categorization will puzzle us as when sisters are put in the same class as cassowary birds. However, if we share the incest taboo and a fear of ferocious animals we can readily draw the connection: "dangerous objects" . I owe this

for an ancient Greek? We don't have one to ask though the sky seems to have been white) but not living ones. We overrate drastically the limits of translation because we tend to notice only the frustrations and failures; it is actually remarkable that so much English will go into Italian and vice versa. Any two languages that are languages *at all* will have a high degree of translatability.

Part of this is the fact that linguistic acts *qua* linguistic acts share the same basic functions such as the articulation of judgments, beliefs, attitudes and so on. Speakers, if they are speakers at all, seem to be doing the same kinds of things and this gives one language a basic purchase on what is going on in any other. Part of this is grounded in common physiology including the physiology of perception (the senses deliver to all of us sights sounds and smells.) Thus, conversation between paradigms does not require a 'neutral' stance outside all frameworks which will always share content and standards of some kind. It is certainly wise and appropriate to remember that medieval astrologers, say, organize the world differently very from modern physicists (see *Believing Weird Things*) but each can recognize, minimally, that the other is talking about lights in the sky. Each can see minimally that the other is doing such things as describing and explaining and if one paradigm cannot identify such acts in the other it seems it could not recognize it as a paradigm or a language at all. To revert to the example of reading, we all agree there are marks on a page and that these are artificial signs not natural ones and that convention attaches certain physical sounds to particular marks and sans this we could not recognize something as a text at all. In short any two paradigms must share a subset of values, observations, terms and concepts along with the new ones introduced by the new paradigm and the ones unique to the old and this is what allows for 'friction' between any two paradigms.

What all paradigms must have in common to be paradigms at all (if we could identify it) would be the condition of the possibility of friction itself. This would be the unity of any given act of differentiation; the one of any dyad and here Davidson would agree would agree with Plato

---

example of Bruno Latour. (1987; 199) As far as 'data' go I think they are inexpungable. I might argue that the word dog is defined not by its function of reference to dogs but by its use in language games played in a zoology department or on a family vacation where 'dog' is what you say when a certain yapping noise is heard outside the tent. On the other hand, it seems the use of some words within linguistic systems to directly refer to something given (I can have a direct experience of red though red is not an atomic fact i.e. it involves the rest of the color scale). To what you might ask? Davidson tells us, in a manner that oddly echoes Berkeley, that truth functional sentences bring us into unmediated touch with "familiar objects whose antics make our sentences and opinions true or false." (20) If one replaced 'objects' with 'social and institutional processes that constitute objects as objects' this overcoming of epistemology would be comparable to Latour's though the deceptively simple word 'object' has now taken on a more sophisticated meaning. If one replaced both 'objects' and 'social processes that constitute objects' with 'categorical ultimates such as motion, rest, identity, difference and being that constitute the basic conditions for the appearance of any object whatsoever in whatever conceptual scheme' one would have Plato's position and most likely my own.

and indeed with ontology in general: "The method is not designed to eliminate disagreement, nor can it; its purpose is to make meaningful disagreement possible, and this depends entirely on a foundation- *some* foundation- in agreement." (19) Plus, there may be mean terms between opposed paradigms as Buridan's impetus theory may connect Galileo and Aristotle. Thus gestalt shifts (which happen all the time in ordinary experience) may be progressively and retroactively shown to have been more and more rational even though their initial form may have been an imperfectly rationalized 'leap'. The challenge of course is that there is no clear line to be drawn between form and content such that we can say absolutely what belongs to one side and what belongs to the other: all data is preshaped in some way for our consumption by categories cultural, linguistic and perhaps even a-priori. As Putnam says: "Internalism does not deny that there are experiential inputs to knowledge; knowledge is not a story with no constraints except internal coherence; but it does deny that there are inputs *which are not themselves to some extent shaped by our concepts,* by the vocabulary we use to report and describe them or any inputs *which admit of one description, independent of all conceptual choices.*" (1997; 54)

Data abstracted from the conceptual scheme in which it occurs, then, seems no longer data in any meaningful sense and that is why the world cannot be the list of sensations and acts that all speakers share in common; these, as much as logical relations, are bare scaffolding, a basic potential for constructing a world. This is why I am not content with Davidson's 'warm skin' (though it is fine as far as it goes) for this simple proposition relates not just warmth to skin but dermatology to astronomy to pick just one among a long list of holistic relations that constitute the possibility of this sentence meaning anything at all.[125] Words do refer but only do so in the context of webs of meaning and belief: neither language nor the world resolve into simple atomic propositions. It seems to be Davidson's view (15-16) that conceptual schemes are resolvable into the truth value of individual sentences (at least he seems to be saying this) and this (if it is Davidson's view) seems to me incorrect (see my essay "The Zeus Delusion" in *Why Believe*). If this is the case I suppose there ARE no conceptual schemes except in a loose manner of speaking though Davidson, frustratingly, sometimes speaks of them as real. To advert to the issue mooted above, however, the sentence "a spirit inhabits the lake" is not equivalent to "my skin is warm" and not subject to the same truth conditions. To ask about animism is to ask about its value as a way of perceiving and

---

[125]Here Davidson contrasts with Latour who rejects the view that scientific practices can be understood on the model of statements with individual truth values such as 'my skin is warm' or 'microbes exist'. (148) He tells us that: "A lactic acid grown in a culture in Pasteur's laboratory is not the same thing as the residue of an alcoholic fermentation in Liebig's laboratory in Munich in 1852. Why not? Because it is not made out of the same articles, the same members, the same actors, the same implements, the same propositions." (150) Here he seems to taking what I would term a holistic view of reference. If reference is what "circulates through the whole series" then "every change in even one element will make for a change in the reference." (150)

organizing and relating to things not about whether a chemical analysis of water will ever reveal spirit nor is it to ask about the truth functionality of individual sentences uttered by animists. It is to ask about a foundational metaphor which is one form a conceptual scheme can take. It is to accept that conceptual schemes contain content that is pre-empirical and not subject to ordinary propositional logic: there are foundational metaphors and metaphysical, moral or epistemic principles whose nature is not really captured by being stated in truth functional sentences (as they are not contingent facts about the world but state the boundary conditions of it). Metaphors are a pertinent example; "All the world's a stage" is not a truth functional proposition; it may well be 'good or bad' but is it not, in its direct form 'true or false' though considering it as a metaphor may dispose us to discover true or false things.

Of course, the reader may also want to know whether we can say modern physics is better than medieval astrology not just different. Many readers will want the quickest possible answer to this question so they can get on with their day.[126] Others will assume all such arguments are a waste of time and that astrology and physics are like windowless monads: conceptual schemes so different that their proponents cannot interface in any productive way. Can we judge between different conceptual articulations of the world even though we cannot get outside such systems to compare them directly to the world of things and objects? The answer it seems to me is neither easy nor unobtainable. No magic bullet (such as an isolated experiment or observation or appeal to some logical or methodological principle supposed obvious) allows one paradigm to slay another. Nor is discussion between paradigms futile or incapable of progress. It is hard to judge between paradigms but not impossible. This should become evident the moment we give up on the magic bullet theory and try to understand how contrasting paradigms might actually interact.

To advert to the example above, astrology and physics do share one aim (conceptually unifying celestial and terrestrial phenomena) and at present it seems Newtonian physics has done this more fully and adequately and

---

[126]In what sense might modern physics or modern science as a whole not be 'true'? Well, one might comprehensively re-describe phenomena in the world from some other viewpoint but this would (for us) require such a deep and comprehensive re-description that simple economy dictates that for us science (as part of our way of life and our total web of beliefs) should be regarded as 'true'. We (European descendants that is) have imposed such basic re-descriptions on others so I suppose there is no reason why others might not impose the like on us. At some point in the no doubt distant future, then, 'science' might no longer be true. Of more immediate interest however is that fact that we may, at some point, encounter the scientific conceptions of aliens. We would then be faced with the task of finding translation equivalents for their scientific concepts among ours. At the end of such a drawn out (and difficult) process what would we find? They (the aliens) may believe that something called xorg causes a stone to fall but would we then translate xorg as gravity without further ado? Not if we understood the perils of translation. It is far more likely (to me at any rate) that we will have two bodies of science to deal with between which we will be able to draw many interesting analogies but not always exact translations. In this we will be like a person translating English into Italian; many things will cross over easily but some will not and these might be the most significant things.

Relativistic physics more fully and adequately still. The Newtonian, for instance, can point out that rather than having two types of matter, celestial and terrestrial, unified by symbolic and analogical bonds we now have one sort of matter unified by the same set of quantifiable universal laws and this is the very simplification of things the astrologers sought in vain. It is Kepler and Newton (never mind for now that the first was an astrologer and the second an alchemist- we assume a history here neater than actual empirical history) who can explain how reason, divine reason, uses the language of mathematics to unite heaven and earth in a way that astrologers and magicians of the renaissance had barely gestured towards.[127] The two paradigms share a standard or aim that one fulfills better than the other. If you like: one paradigm can subsume the values embodied in the other and can add value of its own making for a better overall theory. Newtonian physics can unify new phenomena and still provide same (or better) unification as the old.

The other paradigm can always hit back though (by shifting the ground of the debate say) even when it seems to have been well and truly routed and it is this capacity no doubt that creates worries over relativism. A defender of the old view can still say that this has happened only at the unacceptable cost of reducing the world to dead mechanism (an unacceptable moral or spiritual consequence). He might argue that one function of a theory is to serve human (and perhaps even animal) flourishing and that Newtonian mechanism has been a cultural disaster that has separated humans from nature and underwritten such as evils as vivisection and hideous cruelty to animals. In short, he might become a 'new ager' or 'romantic' (of some sort) and if he does not look to revive Astrology (say) he may wish to revive *something about it*; the vitalism or animism or holism that was conveyed by it or the spiritual consolation it sought to provide.[128]

Of course here a third voice may intervene (that of William Blake!) and he will assert that far from being opposed Astrology and Newtonian physics are both iterations of the fundamental error of determinism and

---

[127] It is well to remember that the 'enlightenment' as an actual historical movement (as opposed to an ideological construct) was deeply entangled with what we would now consider 'irrational' 'occult' philosophies. Newton and Kepler are far from the only examples. The animism and panpsychism of Leibniz or Lady Anne Conway are also notable in this regard. What is more so called romantic 'critics' of the enlightenment, like William Blake, fully accepted its radical politics. At what point in time the 'enlightenment' became the thing we now construct it as is perhaps a good question. It is the total lack of any such historical consideration that vitiates such popular defenses of the 'enlightenment' as Steven Pinker's Enlightenment Now (see my essay "Pinker's Enlightenment" in Why Believe). Of course it is just this mutual entanglement of supposedly opposed paradigms that makes discussion a possibility!

[128] Here the Kabbalah played a certain historic role. Early Modern thinkers were careful not to over-advertise their dependence on despised Jewish sources but in at least one instance, the brilliant Anne Conway, Lurianic doctrines became the explicit foundation for an anti-mechanist philosophy. (1999; xviii-xxii) Conway subsequently took the scandalous step of converting to Quakerism which reminds us that dissenting religious groups like the Quakers, Shakers, Ranters, and so on became an important vehicle for both radical political and social thought and esoteric philosophies.

that their conflict expresses only the narcissism of minor differences (and here he is performing the 'weird' function of pointing out how much positions assumed opposed actually share). Both will object that modern physics has produced a regional unification only at the cost of a deeper dualism which is, for various reasons political, cultural or moral, unacceptable. They might agree with E. E. Harris who tells us that: "Thus the advance of technology facilitated by Newtonian science is threatening the very survival of the civilization it has helped create, and is destroying the conditions on which all life on earth depends." (2000; xiii) If it is objected that this has nothing to do with the truth or falsity of Newtonian physics he might answer with Putnam that rationality is just one part of our overall conception of the good (xi) and indeed that the two are not separable: after all, if I justify rationality by, say, prudential principles I have admitted it is not *self*- justifying but depends on the good (which is prior). He will also, no doubt, point out that if modern science (which has in fact evolved beyond Newton) has unified celestial and terrestrial phenomena it *has not* unified the great and the small. Our account of very small things, quantum dynamics, is not consistent with our science of very big things, relativity. The old dualism has in fact returned in a new form!

The physicist will at first be very puzzled by this. It is unlikely to have even occurred to him that science or theory could be anything but Baconian science or theory. Science tortures nature for its secrets in order to subject it to prediction and control.[129] Since Newtonian physics has clearly done this with great success then that is all that needs to be said in its favor. The function of eccentric people however is to question assumptions it would never occur to other people to question. If questioned on this (and assuming he has not left in a huff) he could then argue that science, technology and civilization have made more progress under the Baconian paradigm than under any of its potential rivals. In spite of problems here and there (like the atom bomb) he could claim that the Baconian paradigm has overall been an enormous boon to humanity. Science is now pragmatic and instrumental instead of contemplative as in antiquity: it *changes* the world as it studies it and studies it *by* changing it. The debate would then become a debate about what ends humans should pursue and not pursue. Are good theories ones which subject nature to control and make human life more commodious or do good theories also serve other aesthetic, social, political or even spiritual aims? The physicist could then argue that historically everyone has preferred health to disease and plenty to famine

---

[129]Bacon applies to science the Gospel principle 'by their fruits ye shall know them'. The test of a principle or axiom is direct experience which confirms or refutes it: "Of all signs there is none more certain or more noble than that taken from fruits. For fruits and works are as it were sponsors and sureties for the truth of philosophies." (73) Thus, experimenta fructifera are the gold standard of the 'interpretation' of nature. (99) This 'interventionist' account of knowledge (where knowledge is a product of action) certainly differs from the active receptivity (it is active productivity) of the Ancient contemplation of nature though Bacon is far from denying all value to the latter (124). For this reason, the Platonist/Romantic Coleridge tends to view Bacon more favorably than our ecologically minded contemporaries. (150)

and that science under the Baconian paradigm has alleviated these evils for great masses of people (though only, alas, in privileged sections of the globe and indeed for certain classes within those sections).

The argument will go on then till some kind of consensus is reached which satisfies both conceptual rigor and the other basic goods at play in the dispute (including agreement on what a theory should do). In the course of a broad ranging discussion one of the positions will supplant the rest OR they will all merge in some synthesis OR the speakers will agree to disagree; the truth (if it emerges) is the result of the total discussion and as we are always in the discussion truth may be an eschatological end towards which we aspire rather than something we can immediately and directly obtain by means of a 5 minute *You Tube* video. This is disappointing I suppose but the problem is that in any discussion of fundamental principles there are many factors or angles to consider and many of these will only emerge over time and in unforeseen ways (as when a principle assumed self-justifying is suddenly put in question). Here of course is where philosophy comes in for when paradigms encounter other paradigms the questions in play are fundamental limit questions. What is knowledge? What does a good theory do? Is there one model for good theories or different models for different things? Is goodness opposed to truth or both to freedom? Can any of these values be pursued separately from the others? This is not an easy discussion but it is not an impossible one for we are discussing basic goods that all humans have some stake in and some rough (if not perfect) common understanding. This debate over the meaning and implementation of basic goods is not simply a debate over untranslatable terms. It is a debate too in which the participants share a common history in which all three are mutually implicated.

Which is not to say decidability between differing schemes isn't a problem only that it is a different problem than incommensurability. If, for example, there were rational, linguistic creatures with the perceptual apparatus of sharks there might well be untranslatable (to us) phrases in their language not because they have different conceptual schemes but because they have sensations we do not. It is not the case that the three standpoints mentioned here have no means of coming to grips with each other and are conducting a dialogue of the deaf. The problem is rather that it is so rare for an answer to preclude the emergence of another question. One of the positive things that is happening however is that each disputant is coming to understand the grounds of his own position better. Plus, historically there are debates which have more or less resolved themselves when the greater part of the participants settled on a formulation. The Ancient debates about the trinity and the dual nature of Christ are a perfect example of this for the consensus they created lasted over a millennium.[130]

---

[130]The Council of Chalcedon, for instance, decided that Christ was one substance subsisting in two natures. Of course Monophysites and Nestorians rejected this consensus. They may have done so however for adventitious reasons such as a language barrier between Syriac and Greek or a long history of ethnic resentment. Of course, authority (arm twisting) also underwrites any consensus whether that authority be the Emperor

If aspects of the ancient position are in play again after so many centuries that may be lamentable, as is the fact that debates thought settled by natural science are suddenly live questions again. This, though, may reflect nothing more than the human condition itself. The challenge of course is that the farther away one goes in time and culture the harder it is to get traction in a discussion for with distance the common assumptions (or opposed assumptions which for that very reason are related) and shared history correspondingly diminish. Getting a discussion going between a contemporary biologist and an ancient Hittite would seem monumentally difficult however much Davidson assures us that it MUST in principle be possible if the Hittite inhabits a 'world' or is speaker of a language at all. This is the same sort of conversation we would have with a putative 'alien'. It is obvious why most of us want to have discussions *within* the parameters of a tradition rather than between them.

To conclude though let me point out one interesting result of this brief discussion. There are indeed relativist implications IF it turns out that ancient, medieval and modern iterations of science are radically incommensurate. This would raise the possibility of further revolutions which will over throw our science as we did that of the ancients. We would have to say ancient science or medieval science is not radically wrong but radically different. A look back at the history of science might lead us to think otherwise at least in the cautious sense I have proposed here. It might even lead us to think that modern scientists have it right and that by standards common to all cultures (or at least all cultures currently in play) they are the demonstrable victors. The result of this though is that the demonstration of the universal necessity and validity of OUR science is not demonstrated in science itself but by history and that the master science is not chemistry or physics but hermeneutics and the reading of ancient, medieval and modern events and texts. If Kuhn (on some interpretations of him at least) argues that paradigms are incommensurate one cannot as a scientist prove him wrong. One must tackle the question as a scientifically informed *reader* of primary events and historical texts. Having done this one must then become a philosopher; identifying the different goods at play (should a good theory 'save the appearances'?) and either making a determination or suspending judgment. If it were the case that 'science' never encounters an 'other' then it might well be the case that science is all we need. Unfortunately, historians have described past cultures in ways that can make them appear as systemic and rational as ours and anthropologists have done the same thing with current cultures. If mediation between these perspectives MUST occur, it is only as *readers* and *thinkers* that we can undertake it. Of course, we must also think about

---

of Byzantium or a granting agency or research council. That too is just the human condition. A fine introduction to the rational process by which the Ancient Church developed its dogmatic formulation of the Trinity is The Road to Nicea by Bernard Lonergan. I mention this because of the persistent tendency to assume the doctrine of the trinity to be the height of irrationalism and surd mystery than which nothing could be farther from the historical fact as we can uncover it in the actual texts.

the context in which we are working. If I wrote a book entitled *Navajo Ontology: A Refutation* that book could serve no innocent purpose in our current environment. Creating a social environment in which paradigms can *freely* undertake to discuss fundamental values without implied threat is the presupposition of any honest exchange or mutual dialogue or critique.

18 Waiting for the End: A Palinode

Perhaps I have been too optimistic and bland. My concerns are braided with my own personal history. I suppose too much of my education has been ad hoc and personal in this way but at my age a man is stuck with who he is more or less. I have a certain ideal in mind when I think of philosophers and, somewhat gallingly, that is not the philosopher I am. These are thinkers of the 19th century, perhaps the last one in which philosophy in a comprehensive sense of thinking the whole was possible. It was an age in which it was possible, say, to think about the heritage of the middle ages and antiquity in relation to the demands of modern thought and science. The exemplar of this is of course G.W.F Hegel who directly or indirectly wads the tutelary spirit behind my early education. One might think too of the later Schelling or the great Catholic philosopher Antonio Rosmini (condemned by Leo XIII and un-condemned by Benedict XIV!). One might also mention the American 'pragmaticist' C.S. Pierce. What all these thinkers shared (in varying degrees) was a historically informed approach. They did not pretend to philosophize as if no one had ever philosophized before them or that they had personally discovered the profound and simple truths occluded by the history of universal error. Like Aristotle in *metaphysics alpha* they brought forth philosophy out of its history. That Hegel was the most comprehensive and successful of these thinkers does not diminish the fact that this kind of synthetic approach was part of the general spirit of that century (at its best and that fascinating century was often not at its best). It is not so in ours and not only because the 19th was the last century in which anyone could realistically hope to master and synthesize knowledge from a broad cross-section of domains. The thinkers mentioned above were giants before the flood. They lived before the fragmentation of knowledge and before collapse of philosophy into warring and mutually excommunicating 'continental' and 'analytic' camps. They lived in the final age of absolutes before 'acute historical self-consciousness' raised the question of whether absolute beginnings in philosophy (or science for that matter) were historically, linguistically and (ultimately) contingently given. They lived in the age before it came to seem that "Every sort of thought, however, is always only the execution and consequence of a mode of historical Dasein, of the fundamental position taken towards Being and toward the way in which beings are manifest as such i.e., toward truth." (271)

I don't have an answer (positive or negative) to the question of 'acute historical self-consciousness' and if I did I would be peddling that rather the rather limited and skeptical reflections contained in this and my previous two books. Quite apart from whether any possible statement of relativism or historicism is self-contradictory (a point I was once fixated on) historicity is a genuine challenge.[131] I do note though that my colleagues in Anglo-American philosophy do not seem to have acute historical self-consciousness (at least to the degree I do) which of course raises the question of how I contracted the disease.[132] I contracted the disease as I suppose many do, by studying the past (another gateway into historicity is studying theology but that discussion is for another day!). The thing I studied was the construction of subjectivity in the late Roman world mostly in St. Augustine but with reference as well to Plotinus and the Hellenistic Stoics and Skeptics. Now there is a view of mind that goes as follows: there is an 'out there' thing called mind. Philosophers like Descartes or Ryle or the Churchlands have theories on mind and those differ from mind itself. When we look at mind itself we can see which theory corresponds to this thing better than the others. If I am a 'philosopher of mind' (which I am not) I am likely to think that Descartes did not see what mind was but that Ryle, say, was at least on the right track though some more sophisticated iteration of 'mind' may have developed and vastly improved his account. Mind is a thing in this world and we now can see this thing more clearly and correctly than we could in the past. We see this

---

[131]This retorsive anti-skeptical argument is one people like Putnam, Davidson and Nagel employ though the first person to work it out in (exhausting) detail was Augustine in his Contra Academicos. 20th Century mind and late Roman mind seem to agree that reason constitutes itself reflexively.

[132]It was with some eagerness that I picked up Putnam's paper "Reason and History" . Alas my first impression was that it was all reason and no history. All the history in it consists of an arbitrarily chosen example "The Divine Right of Kings" considered without context and misplaced in time (it is not a 'medieval' notion: the fullest development of the idea is early modern though its roots are indeed medieval). Reason, we learn, tells us there is no divine right of kings. That reason, immanent in the evolution of the modern state, might have said something different to the 17th Century is something Putnam freely admits, however, in a nod to Hegel. (158) A responsible person of good intellectual character might have arrived at this doctrine by the application of reason within a certain set of historically contingent assumptions. For Putnam this is a debased account of reason (158) though, alas, almost ALL of our reasoning is so debased almost ALL the time. Putnam seems to want some sense of a belief that is rational in itself apart from historical context as radically historicized reason, in his mind, ceases to be normative. I by no means deny the possibility of such beliefs: there may be transcendental conditions for any possible thinking whatsoever and a sufficiently deep inquiry might identify them. As Putnam argues there may be no coherent way of stating the negative of certain propositions (it takes time to say 'time does not exist'). (162) Plus there are surely intellectual virtues we all recognize as part of good character. (163) This latter point is all the more important in that Putnam, elsewhere, asserts that canons of reason and method do evolve over time (x). In this he claims to follow Quine though with reservations about the self-refuting character of some propositions. (83)

when we see that mind is not a 'sui generis' sort of thing but is a natural phenomenon like hearts, livers or flowers. Mind is mind naturalized. It is a thing we can objectify (by getting outside it?) and place in the world of things or publicly observable events. Having placed it in the world of things we can look at this thing and see who has given the best account of it.

It is not at all easy to explain why I don't think this is a necessary or inescapable assumption. To be brief though, I don't think there is a readily accessible thing in the world called mind against which we can compare the historical iterations of mind. I think all the iterations of mind are historical (even textual) and there isn't a 'mind' against which we can measure 'Late Roman' 'Early Modern' or '20th Century' mind and determine which is the best picture of what mind is in itself. I think this is surprisingly easy to show once one has taken the step of admitting the possibility (admittedly a large step). As a student I was very caught up in the drama of Late Roman subjectivity because it seemed to me very like my own drama in a way that in retrospect was not entirely healthy. I had leapt, it seemed, across a historical divide and found myself in a sense that had nothing to do as far as I could see with neurons and synapses. The thing to note about Late Roman mind is that Late Roman Mind is mind 'de-naturalized'. It occurred to few important thinkers to ask where among the objects in the world was mind (except by way of getting a discussion going). The point was to distinguish mind from objects in the world and the point of this was to establish mind as self-constituting: as a reflexive sphere of freedom and inwardness from which wisdom could be pursued. Thus mind was found not in the sensible world as an object but in abstraction from objects and as a condition of the appearance of objects. Mind was a transcendental object of self-reflection whose nature was given immediately in self- knowledge and as such it was to be distinguished from the externality of sensible extension. Mind withdrew from things into itself and discovered its own freedom there. Ontology and the quest for the good life met in mind's discovery of itself as a non-natural fact.[133] Now here is the thing: if the above assumption is true then it would have to be that Late Roman Mind was a 'mistake' of some kind. However, my examination of those texts did not then and does not now reveal a simple and identifiable logical or empirical error that led to a particular iteration of historical mind that was different than true mind. Mind is not the kind of thing on which a sufficiently informed Neanderthal and a modern analytic philosopher could meet and agree because mind is a historical construct we inhabit as much as it is a thing in the world (as Schelling

---

[133]Schelling puts this remarkably well "If the self is not a thing or affair, it is likewise in vain to enquire about any predicate thereof, for it has none, save only this, that it is not a thing. The character of the self consists in this very fact: that it has no other than that of self-consciousness." (1997; 26) Here Schelling reproduces the reasoning of St. Augustine in On the Trinity (Book X, 3-10). Proclus gives us the same basic idea (i.e. that the self-reverting is not extended and hence not material) in proposition 186 of the Elements of Theology.

says it is a free self-production). It may well be, as I suggested above, that for the Neanderthal to have a world at all he must share some categories with the philosopher though this might be cold comfort when faced with an actual discussion underdetermined by such categories which, if they could be identified, might prove too bare and abstract to form a basis for discussion: having agreed on the principle of contradiction the Neanderthal and the philosopher might not get much farther. Such basic differences are part of the reason why, as I have emphasized throughout this book, public or *exoteric* reason is, in our day, inescapably plural (whatever might be the case in the privacy of our own meditations).

For make no mistake 20th mind is a historical construct too. It was constructed as Late Roman mind was as part of a historical project and that is the mathematization of all things under the reign of quantity. Mind must be subject to the same kind of account as electrons and rabbits. It must be folded into the natural sciences, weighed, measured and quantified exactly as any other physical object (or if not this resolved into patterns of observable behavior). The ghost in the machine must be exorcized rather than liberated. Mind in whatever iteration is given in the historical projects we undertake and is as sound or as unsound as those projects are. Undertake fundamentally different projects and mind will alter. This is the case regardless of how 'successful' one is. No doubt many useful and interesting things have been discovered under the reign of naturalized mind. Many mental phenomena have been correlated and illuminated in novel ways. The problem is not one of success however for of course Augustine and Plotinus discovered fascinating things too under an entirely different paradigm. Moreover, a comparison of their successes and failures with ours would not reveal any obvious superiority of one or the other for both succeed and fail at different things. The question comes down to whether you think one project is better than the other; whether you think the self-liberation of the soul is more important than universal quantification or the reverse.

Oddly there is a sort of answer to this question at least where the contemporary world is concerned for we now have another operative sense of mind. Naturalized mind is an obsession of philosophers and neurologists not people in general. People in general are concerned with 'deep selves' in a manner far more Late Roman than modern for this deep self is not constructed by them as a natural fact though it is not constructed as an 'immaterial immortal substance' (as in Augustine or Descartes) either. The deep self is not taken to be an expression of biological and physical necessity, of universal quantity, but as something that supervenes on it and indeed opposes it. Gender is far more interesting to the students I teach than sex. One thing the deep self can say about itself is that its 'real gender' is something not expressed in its physical sex. I very much doubt there is a physical state of affairs that corresponds to the proposition "I am a woman trapped in a man's body" for protein strings and synapses know nothing of how we construct gender behavior or view ourselves in relation to those constructions. Gender dysphoria does not seem to refer to some physical, naturalized fact about someone: even if it *did* correspond (or fail to correspond) to identifiable brain states that would be irrelevant to the introspective claims of transgendered persons. No one gets a CAT scan to see *if* they are a trans person *or* to justify their claim to be one: their claim is not based on publicly observable behavioral or natural criteria. In fact, the relation is the other way round. The 'deep-self' seeks to alter the 'natural fact' by, for instance, pursuing gender reassignment surgery. An obscure perhaps occluded dictate of the self seeks to constitute itself in different external signs. It seeks a different *interpretation* of what it is both in opposition to yet at the same time in relation to cultural codes and signals of which DNA knows not a thing. The deep self seems to me, frankly, another emerging form of mind that is not Augustinian/Cartesian *Mens* nor the neural net of the brain but a third thing. I could be wrong about this of course but mind has flipped from a duck to a rabbit before and if I am correct about that is likely to do so again.[134] In this instance we may be seeing something akin to the ancient religious stance of Gnosticism which offered people in classical antiquity a powerful metaphor for naming their alienation: the deep self is *trapped* by the conditions of its instantiation which it has not chosen for itself. At any rate, as a colleague once put it, no one who asks "who am I?" at four in the morning pulls out their driver's license. Few if any people discover they are transgendered by drawing a neutral, disengaged inference from their publically observable patterns of behavior. Trans people, it seems, have put introspective claims about the self at the center of our culture.

This explains my heresy about mind. Some might think I am doing a reverse Ryle and accusing philosophers of mind of making a mistake like a category error or a false inference. That is not my game however and books with titles like *Descartes' Big Mistake* or *Hegel's Fundamental Error* do not make my reading list. I don't actually believe in mistakes. It was out of deep historical necessity that European thinkers undertook the quantification of nature and it was inevitable that mind would try and include itself in that quantification: that it would attempt the construction of itself as a scientific 'object'. However, I think there are other minds as I think there are other natures and my heresy amounts to this: 20th century

---

[134]I think Judith Butler gives a good description of this 'deep self' though she might not like the term. Speaking of the psyche (as opposed to the self-conscious 'subject' constructed by modern philosophy) she says the following: "This psychic excess is precisely what is being systematically denied by the notion of a 'volitional subject' who elects at will which gender and /or sexuality to be at any given time or place. It is this excess which erupts within the intervals of those repeated gestures and acts that construct the apparent uniformity of heterosexual positionalities, indeed which compels the repetition itself, and which guarantees its perpetual failure." (725) This disruptive excess that surpasses every repetition of gender is sexuality or, as we might once have said, eros. (725) Whatever this 'excess' is it resembles the subjectivity of Augustine more than the 'mind-brain' and I do not know if Butler ever considers giving it a physio-chemical description. This seems not to be an accident for in Lacan, Lyotard and others there has been a certain post-modern appropriation of Augustinian subjectivity minus, of course, the metaphysics behind it.

mind cannot from within the circle of its own assumptions eliminate other iterations of mind in other historical dispensations however much we might think with Davidson that x, y or z must hold if something is to be called a dispensation at all. Nor will it do to point out that we all feel warmth on our skin though to be fair Davidson's point seems to concern the mutual intelligibility of competing schemes NOT their decidability (19). I think though, as readers of this book have no doubt discerned, that this is not a cause for wailing and lamenting but an appropriate correction to out tendency to triumphalism and hubris.

To soften the blow one might think of the history of aesthetic styles. Aesthetic movements like Bauhaus or twelve tone music developed by a deep underlying necessity. They were then elevated to international styles, universally 'correct' answers as to how write music or build buildings. Of course these are now just stylistic options. This does not render them invalid for any particular artist: it only means they have no assumed hegemony. They are valid for individual artists but not universally prescriptive. Naturalized mind and the mechanistic science that underwrites it are also styles and may be in the future (if they are not already) subject to a similar adjustment. This is no big deal really: the medieval Aristotelian tradition underwent such an adjustment and Aquinas has as many readers now as he ever did. All this indicates to me is that, if I may borrow a phrase from Kuhn, we are not in a period of 'normal philosophy'. In North America the post war years to the present were a period of normal philosophy where people discussed the analytic/synthetic distinction or the nature of qualia within the parameters of a tradition that had entrenched itself institutionally (i.e. in universities). Analytic philosophy set curricula, controlled hiring, journals and grant money and reproduced itself as a living tradition. Scholastic philosophy had done the exact same thing in the middle ages by analogous means. This book exists however because we are not in a normal period and it is inadequate to simply do normal philosophy (at least collectively, people *do* also have to follow their personal inclinations). Accordingly, I have attempted to philosophize at the margins between traditions because I think that is the sort of conversation we now need to be having at this point in history.

I suppose this makes me a mind-skeptic: I don't know what mind is though I know what matter is even less though I have my private predilections. Interestingly Putnam seems to agree at least to the extent that naturalizing mind is something he only *recommends*: it is not in itself an absolute demand of reason. (79) Indeed, a perfectly naturalized account of mind would simply be a preference or an option if one could, with equal success, mentalize nature. One might well have equal and opposed presentations as in Pyrrhonism. Of course this could also suggest that we have to deal with subjective and objective poles that cannot be resolved one into the other: as the entire notion of necessity presupposes the corresponding idea of freedom so might mind exist on a kind of continuum with matter which of courses brings us around to a kind of mind I haven't mentioned which is hylomorphic mind (as in Aristotle's notion that the soul is the first actuality of a body potentially having life).[135] Still, if I had an answer about mind I would, as I said above, be writing about that so I will call myself a skeptic for now though in a sense some of my readers might find odd.

One thing that is rarely mentioned about skepticism is what I call the piety of skepticism. This might shock people whose knowledge of the skeptical tradition is limited to the idea that skepticism is skepticism of religious doctrine or the reality of the supersensible. This understanding of the term is a-historical. Skepticism is not a malign will to destroy all determinate mental content or at least it is not simply that. Skepticism is also an attitude of waiting. It is a confession of the futility of the human in which, paradoxically, the human realizes its greatness. We are still waiting for mind, freedom, nature and the rest of the cast of characters to fully manifest. Our task is to clear away the detritus, the finite, historicized determinations that occlude in the act of revealing. I admit this is a 4 A.M mood and for most of the day I go about as everyone does cheerfully dogmatizing. Still, it is hard to think in our world without the awareness that we may well be among the last of thinkers. That the play is ended and the actors about to exit the stage. What is worse is that I am writing from the heart of the very historical tradition which is ending the show for everyone else without asking anyone's permission. Our tragic fate is everyone else's external disaster. What we choose to fill the void yawning at our feet with is of course a very personal choice. There are various species of hope of course one of which is that there are beings in the universe wiser and better than us and that humanity may not be such a great loss. Perhaps there are other universes or perhaps we are simply one phase in an infinitely repeating cycle. I decline though to think past the end in this rather external manner. I prefer an image from the old Hermetic philosophers which also occurs in the *Gospels*. There is in us all a seed or germ of love whose potential is too great for confines of this world of cramped sensation and external necessity. What is more we have all, in

---

[135]See De Anima II, 412b.Putnam's 'functionalist' account of mind seems to have some affinities with this view though Aristotle insists that there are some functions of mind (i.e. the highest ones) which do not depend on a material substrate for their realization. (III,5) This bequeathed to the European middle ages (and indeed the Muslim world) the thorny question of how this 'pure mind' or 'agent intellect' was related to individual minds as well as to those lower functions of soul only realized in matter. Such thinkers were acutely aware that mind is a problem to itself as the only object we are directly involved with at the same time as we try to step outside of it and study it as a 'datum'. The holy grail of such objectification is the reduction of mind to a determinate thing and everyone's favorite candidate for this thing is the brain. I respect the humble, useful brain as much as anyone but there are oddities about this procedure that are little commented on. The chief one is that the brain as an object of study is a simple object of sensation and as such subject to the same skeptical deconstruction as any other sense object. Yet I have no doubt that somewhere a philosopher of mind is arguing, with no sense of irony, that metaphysical realism is false because reality is a construct of the brain! Clearly the brain is more than a physical object for philosophers of mind but a metaphysical posit, an ultimate that survives the historicization or deconstruction of any other content whatsoever: so much so that they can exist happily in vats!

our blindness and folly, failed to nurture this seed to anything like its true potential even in terms of this world and this one finite existence. If the universe or its creator cares (and it or he or she need not) I humbly ask both for myself and the human race as a whole that in whatever manner and in whatever place that seed be permitted to complete the development it has slowly and painfully begun here. If not there is, I suppose, no real (i.e. positive) harm in being forgotten.

References

Anonymous, "The Ballad of Thomas the Rhymer" (https://www.poemhunter.com/poem/thomas-the-rhymer-3/)

Arendt, Hannah. *On Violence* (Harcourt Inc., New York, 1970)

Aristotle. *Nichomachean Ethics* in *Basic Works* trans. R. McKeon (Random House, New York, 1941)

Augustine. *City of God* trans. H. Bettenson (Penguin Classics, London, 1971)

Augustine. *On the Trinity* trans. E. Hill (New York City Press, New York, 1991)

Avison, Margaret. "Old Woman at a Winter Window" in *Always Now* (Porcupine's Quill, Erin, 2005)

Bacon, Francis. *The New Organon* (Cambridge University Press, Cambridge, 2000)

Berkeley, George. *Three Dialogues of Hylas and Philonous* (Hackett Publishing, Indiana, 1984)

Blake, William. *The Complete Poems* (Penguin Classics, London, 1978)

Blake, William. *The Complete Poetry and Prose* ed. D. Erdmann (Anchor Books, Toronto 1988)

Borovoy, Allen. *When Freedoms Collide: The Case for our Civil Liberties* (Lester & Orpen Dennys, Toronto 1988)

Burke, Edmund. *Reflections on the Late Revolution in France* (J.M. Dent and Sons, London, 1916)

Burton, Robert. *The Anatomy of Melancholy* (J.M. Dent & Sons Ltd., London, 1972)

Butler, Judith. "Imitation and Gender Insubordination" in *Literary Theory: An Anthology* (Wiley-Blackwell, Hoboken, 2017)

Blondel, Maurice. *L'Action* (Presses Universitaire de France, Paris, 1950)

Bloom, Paul "Scientific Faith is Different from Religious Faith" (Atlantic Monthly, November 24, 2015)

Bray, Mark. *The Antifa Handbook* (Melville House, Brooklyn, 2017)

Cochrane, Charles Norris. *Christianity and Classical Culture* (Oxford University Press, New York 1957)

Coleridge, S.T. *Biographia Literaria* (J.M. Dent, New York, 1908)

Coleridge, S.T. *Lay Sermons* (Routledge and Keegan Paul, London, 1972)

Collier, Arthur *Clavis Universalis* (https://archive.org/details/metaphysicaltra01collgoog/page/n9)

Compton, James. "Remembering Labor Rights and Academic Freedom" (Nov. 2017 CAUT Bulletin)

Comway, Anne. *The Principles of the Most Ancient and Modern Philosophy* (Cambridge University Press, Cambridge, 1999)

Cook, Jonathan (https://mronline.org/2018/11/14/long-read-the-neoliberal-order-is-dying-time-to-wake-up/?)

Curlew, Abigail. (https://www.vice.com/en_ca/article/pa3jzg/for-trans-folks-free-speech-can-be-silencing)

Davidson, Donald. "On the Very Idea of a Conceptual Scheme" (https://www2.southeastern.edu/Academics/Faculty/jbell/conceptualscheme.pdf)

Dawkins, Richard. "What is True." in *The Devil's Chaplain* (Boston: Houghton Mifflin Harcourt, 2004)

Dennet, Daniel. *Breaking the Spell* (Humanities Press, New York, 2006)

Descartes, Rene. *The Philosophical Writings of Descartes vol. III* trans. Cottingham, Stoothoff, Murdoch, Kenny (Cambridge University Press, Cambridge, 1991)

Dussan, Maria. "A Critical Reflection on the Humanities Program at Grenfell Campus: The Importance of Including Voices from the Margins." Independent Project for Humanities 4950.

Feyerabend, Paul. *Against Method* (Verso, New York, 1988)

Flim and Fluss. (https://jacobinmag.com/2018/10/steven-pinker-enlightenme.nt-now-review).

Fludd, Robert. *Essential Readings* (North Atlantic Books, Berkeley, 2001)

Frost, Robert. "The Black Cottage" (https://www.poemhunter.com/poem/the-black-cottage/)

Gadamer, H.G. "Authority and Critical Freedom" in *The Enigma of Health* (Stanford University Press, Stanford, 1996)

Guenon, Rene *The Crisis of the Modern World* (Sophia Perennis, Hillsdale, 2004)

Harris, E.E. *The Restitution of Metaphysics* (Prometheus Books, Amherst, 2000)

Hegel, GWF. *Phenomenology of Mind* trans. J.B. Baillie (Harper Torchbooks, New York, 1967)

Heidegger, Martin. *Basic Writings* (Harper and Row Publishing, New York, 1977)

Hippocrates. "The Sacred Disease" in *Hippocratic Writings* (Penguin Classics ,London ,1978; 240

Kochan, Gary (https://social-epistemology.com/2018/11/20/decolonising-science-in-canada-jeff-kochan/)

Latour, Bruno. *Pandora's Hope* (Harvard University Press, Cambridge Mass. 1999)

Latour, Bruno *Science in Action* (Harvard University Press, Cambridge, 1987)

Lewis, C.S. *The World's Last Night* (https://archive.org/stream/worldslastnighta012859mbp/worldslastnighta012859mbp_djvu.txt)

Lilburn, Tim. "The Ethical Significance of the Human Relationship to Place" in *The Larger Conversation* (University of Alberta Press, Edmonton, 2017)

Marx, Karl. *The German Ideology* (International Publishers, New York, 1970)

Mill. J.S. *On Liberty* in *The Utilitarians* (Anchor Books, New York, 1973)

Milton, John. *Selected Prose* (Penguin Classics, London, 1974)

Mizrahi, Moti. (https://social-epistemology.com/2017/10/05/in-defense-of-weak-scientism-a-reply-to-brown-moti-mizrahi/)

Mizrahi, Moti.(https://social-epistemology.com/2018/06/28/weak-scientism-defended-once-more-moti-mizrahi/)

Mizrahi, Moti. (https://social-epistemology.com/2018/09/11/why-scientific-knowledge-is-still-the-best-moti-mizrahi/)

Newman, J.H. *An Essay in Aid of a Grammar of Assent* (*Essay in Aid of a Grammar of Assent*, University of Notre Dame Press, 1992)

Ottman, Jaqueline "Indigenizing the Academy: Confronting "Contentious Ground" in *The Moring Watch*: *Indigenizing the Academy*: (Vol.40 (nos. 3-4, Winter 2013)

Owen, Wilfred. "Strange Meeting" (https://www.poemhunter.com/poem/strange-meeting/)

Ramos and McClay (https://policyoptions.irpp.org/magazines/june-2019/urban-rural-divide-atlantic-canada-myth/?fbclid=IwAR0UZirnTV5_kYOCERnsMyF2z3JBG0verMUrj1CckVi-6eN8yeBPOQJTClg)

Riggio, Adam(https://social-epistemology.com/2019/02/28/belief-in-a-weird-world-adam-riggio/# comments)

Rosenberg, Alex. *An Atheist's Guide to Reality* (W.W. Norton, New York, 2011)

Rousseau, J.J. *Discourse on the Origin of Inequality* (Washington Square Press, New York, 1967)

Paracelsus. *Four Treatises* (Johns Hopkins University Press, Baltimore, 1996)

Peels, Rik "Ten Reasons to Embrace Scientism" (Studies in History and Philosophy of Science, 2017, 1-11)

Pinker, Steven. *Enlightenment Now* (Viking, New York, 2018)

Plato. *Meno* in *Collected Dialogues* (Princeton University Press, Princeton, 1961)

Plato. *The Republic* in *Collected Dialogues* (Princeton University Press, Princeton, 1961)

Proclus, *The Elements of Theology* trans. E.R. Dodds (Clarendon Press, Oxford, 2004)

Proclus. *On the Hieratic Art* (https://www.google.ca/search?q=proclus+on+the+hieraticart)

Putnam, Hilary. *Reason, Truth and History* (Cambridge University Press, Cambridge, 1997)

Psellus, Michael. *On the Operation of Demons* (CreateSpace Independent Publishing Platform, 2016)

Thagard, Paul. "Rationality and Science" (http://cogsci.uwaterloo.ca/Articles/rationality.html)

Tillyard, J.M. *The Elizabethan World Picture* (Chatto and Windus, London, 1943)

Traherne, Thomas. *Selected Poems and Prose* (Penguin Classics, London, 1991)

Truscheit, Tori (https://slate.com/human-interest/2018/10/man-hating-lesbian-insult-reclaim-anger-metoo-activism.html)

Salee, Daniel "Indigenous Peoples and Settler Angst in Canada: A Review Essay" (https: //www.erudit.org/en/journals/ijcs/2010-n41-ijcs3881/044173ar/)

Savage, Luke (https://www.jacobinmag.com/2014/12/new-atheism-old-empire/)

Schelling, F.W.J. *System of Transcendental Idealism* trans. P. Heath (University of Virginia Press, Charlottesville, 1997)

Simmonds, Deborah (http://uppingtheanti.org/journal/article/11-residual-stalinism,252)

Sherrard, Phillip. *Greek East and Latin West* (Oxford University Press, Oxford, 1959)

Smith, Linda. Decolonizing Methodologies: Research and Indigenous Peoples (Zed Books, 2012)

Strauss, Leo. *Persecution and the Art of Writing* (https://www.jstor.org/stable/pdf/40981803.pdf)

Swift, Jonathan. *Gulliver's Travels* (Penguin Classics, London, 2003)

Wallis, R.W. *Neoplatonism* (Duckworth, London, 1972)

Weil, Simone. *The Need for Roots* (Beacon Press, Boston, 1952)

Wills, Bernard. *Believing Weird Things* (Minkowski Institute Press, Montreal 2018)

Wills and Hynes "Biologizing Religion:Dennett's *Breaking the Spell*" *Toronto Journal of Theology* (Spring 2008 24/1 7-20)

Wills and Hynes "Biologizing Religion Part II" *Toronto Journal of Theology* (vol.27. no.2 2011. 235-248)

Wills, Bernard. "Notes on the Rhetoric of Trolling" ((https://social-epistemology.com/2019/05/02/notes-on-the-rhetoric-of-trolling-part-1-bernard-wills/)

Wills, Bernard. *Why Believe* (Minkowski Institute Press, Montreal 2015)

About the author

Dr. Bernard Wills teaches Humanities and Philosophy at Grenfell Campus Memorial University. He has degrees in Classics and Religious Studies from Dalhousie and McMaster. He has published a number of articles on Ancient, Medieval and Early Modern thought as well as occasional essays and poetry. Dr. Wills was born in Toronto but was raised on Cape Breton Island. He currently resides in Corner Brook NL. He can be contacted at bwills@swgc.mun.ca.